Loving Jewish People

Loving Jewish People

Paul O. Bischoff

FOREWORD BY
Andrea Cosnowsky

RESOURCE *Publications* · Eugene, Oregon

LOVING JEWISH PEOPLE

Copyright © 2025 Paul O. Bischoff. All rights reserved. Except for brief quotations in critical publications or reviews, no part of this book may be reproduced in any manner without prior written permission from the publisher. Write: Permissions, Wipf and Stock Publishers, 199 W. 8th Ave., Suite 3, Eugene, OR 97401.

Resource Publications
An Imprint of Wipf and Stock Publishers
199 W. 8th Ave., Suite 3
Eugene, OR 97401

www.wipfandstock.com

PAPERBACK ISBN: 979-8-3852-4386-0
HARDCOVER ISBN: 979-8-3852-4387-7
EBOOK ISBN: 979-8-3852-4388-4

VERSION NUMBER 08/08/25

For Melissa Jayne,
In God's Care

Contents

Foreword by Andrea Cosnowsky | ix
Preface | xi
Introduction | xv

Part One: Thinking Hebraically

Chapter 1: Hebraic Thought | 3
Chapter 2: The Story of Israel | 23
Chapter 3: The Hebraic Parable | 44
Chapter 4: The Hebraic Kingdom of God | 58

Part Two: Thinking Christianly

Chapter 5: Christian Thought | 75
Chapter 6: The Story of Jesus | 98
Chapter 7: The Parables of Jesus | 120
Chapter 8: The Kingdom of God in Jesus' Parables | 137

Part Three: Distortion

Chapter 9: The Synagogue | 159
Chapter 10: The Church | 171
Chapter 11: A Parting of the Ways | 187

Part Four: Restitution

    Chapter 12: Rediscovering Christianity | 209

    Chapter 13: Loving Jewish People | 220

Conclusion | 237

Bibliography | 243

Foreword

I MET DR. BISCHOFF in the wake of tragedy. After the Tree of Life synagogue shooting in Pittsburg, our congregation held a Shabbat Service of Solidarity. Many came to stand with us. But when Paul spoke, we all sat up straighter. His words were not only thoughtful—they were brave, raw, and utterly unexpected. He stood before a grieving Jewish community and confessed the complicity of his own family and church in the atrocities of the Holocaust. Then he did something even rarer: he asked for forgiveness.

That moment marked the beginning of a friendship that has shaped me as a rabbi, a Jew, and a human being.

In the years since, Paul and I have continued a dialogue that's spanned countless lunches, theological debates, and shared community events. We've shared pulpits and stages, asked hard questions, and disagreed more often than we've agreed. But iron sharpens iron. And in the space between our theological differences, I've found clarity, humility, and an ever-deepening commitment to interfaith work.

What began in public solidarity became profoundly personal. When Paul's beloved daughter Melissa died during the pandemic, I donned a mask and stood in a church filled with mourners—rules or no rules. There was nowhere else I could have been. Paul and his wife Jayne with me too—at my children's B'nai Mitzvah celebrations, at my mother's funeral. We have shown up for one another, time and time again. That is what friendship means.

In over two decades of congregational leadership, I have rarely encountered a Christian thinker so deeply invested in understanding and honoring Judaism—not as a precursor to his own faith, but as a living, breathing covenant between a people and their God. Paul's insight, candor, and teaching have been gifts to me and to our community. His work challenges Christians to confront uncomfortable truths, to unlearn inherited prejudices, and to rediscover the Hebraic roots of their own story.

That's why I am proud to bless this book.

Loving Jewish People is not a call to convert, correct, or co-opt. It is a call to friendship—hard-earned, honest, and sacred. It is a challenge to love without agenda, to see the Jewish people not as theological problems but as neighbors, partners, and fellow seekers. I believe in my friend Paul. And I believe that this book will open hearts and minds—just as our friendship has opened mine.

Rabbi Andrea Cosnowsky
Congregation Etz Chaim
Lombard, Illinois
June, 2025

Preface

In his "After Ten Years" piece in *Letters and Papers from Prison*, Dietrich Bonhoeffer stated, "It remains an experience of incomparable value that we have for once learned to see the great events of world history from below, from the perspective of the outcasts, the suspects, the maltreated, the powerless, the oppressed and reviled, in short from the perspective of the suffering."[1] Dietrich Bonhoeffer, a 20th-Century martyr and advocate for the Jewish people, is qualified to view the world through the lens of the oppressed and powerless. Yet, in this essay, he's not concerned about himself, but with the Jewish people whom he loved.

The inspiration for this book derives from Bonhoeffer's advocacy for the Jewish people who suffered under the terror of Nazi oppression for twelve years in Germany. Just as Jesus Christ became sin for humanity's salvation, Bonhoeffer committed sin in a plot to murder Hitler as a vicarious representative for the Jewish people; that is, he exercised free responsibility on behalf of the marginalized. He substituted concrete action for principle on behalf of the other, the Jews. His identification with oppressed Jews redefined how he viewed the church. As a community of forgiven sinners, the church exists for others.

Just as he challenged the antisemitism of 19th-Century liberal German theology constructed upon the unnecessary "Jewish Question," Bonhoeffer was one of the first to speak out on behalf of the Jewish people. During his years in prison he read and reread the Old Testament which radically changed his Christian faith from inward piety to participating with the sufferings of Christ for the world.

1. Bonhoeffer, *Letters and Papers from Prison*, "After Ten Years," 52.

Loving Jewish People seeks to challenge today's weak Christianity which for centuries has existed with little to no mention of the Hebraic thought from which it is derived. It is as if the Christian faith hung in the air as the second story of a house without a first floor securely fastened to a foundation. For centuries the church forgot its status as a twig grafted into a branch of *Etz Chaim*, the Tree of Life. Arrogantly, the church reversed God's order replacing the covenanted Jewish People with itself as "the New Israel." It failed to grasp how its liturgy derived from the synagogue. The church chose to define its identity more by what it was not [Judaism] than by what it was—a community of forgiven sinners [both Jews and Gentiles] as one new humanity. It neglected the Jewishness of Jesus. The church failed to grasp its claim that the story of Israel is fulfilled in the story of Jesus and the story of Jesus is anticipated in the story of Israel, even though Jewish thought would disagree.

This book asserts that an authentic Christian community, the church, is one which retains its Hebraic roots while worshiping Jesus as Messiah, the Lord and Savior of all people. The Jewish community anticipates a unique human being [not divine] as Messiah who will return when global conditions are repaired. This book also asserts that theological disagreement cannot ever be a reason not to love one another. It's more than merely agreeing to disagree. It's loving one another as friends and people of faith in the one God of Abraham, Isaac, and Jacob.

While Dietrich Bonhoeffer's theology and life have provided inspiration from the past, I wholeheartedly acknowledge Rabbi Cosnowsky's motivation to think about the issues related to Jewish—Christian friendship. She models unfailing love for the other. It's my privilege to be one of those others. Worshiping God in her congregation impresses upon me how much Christians and Jews have in common liturgically. The *Jahrzeit* for our daughter, Melissa Jayne Bischoff, is remembered every October during worship in her synagogue. Rabbi Cosnowsky has invited me to her synagogue on several occasions to facilitate open discussions about Christian—Jewish relationships that must substitute understanding, acceptance, and love for misunderstanding, rejection, and hostility, among all people, and especially between Jews and Christians.

I'm a better Christian through my collegial friendship with Rabbi Cosnowsky which has opened the door to further discussions and friendships with members of her synagogue, Congregation Etz Chaim. The hope that I feel today for improved future Christian—Jewish loving relationships, despite the brokenness in today's global village, derives from my continued friendship with Rabbi Andrea Cosnowsky.

June 8, 2025
Pentecost Sunday
P.O.B.
Wheaton, Illinois

Introduction

LOVING JEWISH PEOPLE IS about *loving* Jewish people. It is about loving *Jewish* people. It is about loving Jews as *people*. The book intends to motivate and challenge Christians to take the lead in befriending Jewish people as human beings created in the image of God, not as objects of traditional church disdain. The book claims that basic human love and friendship of our Jewish sisters and brothers is a viable alternative to the global anti-semitism currently rising in degree to WWII proportions.

Loving Jewish People maintains that knowledge dispels fear. Knowing Judaic philosophy and the history of the Jewish people hold the potential to replace ignorance with a renewed awareness leading to love Jews. That said, the book seeks to replace historic attempts at ecumenical naivete with an intellectual treatment of Jewish-Christian dialogue which, while respecting doctrinal boundaries, builds on commonalities between the two ideologies.

Christians derived their existence from a man, Jesus of Nazareth, who claimed to be God's son. Judaism holds that the One Ineffable God cannot be represented by any image, human being, statue, icon, or picture. Christians claim that their Savior Jesus was the Messiah. Jewish people continue to look for that unique human being who will usher in the messianic age. Christianity asserts a Tri-unity of a Father, Son, and Holy Spirit, the Trinity. Jews quote the *Sh'ma*[1], the Lord our God is *One*. Historically, Christian apostles preferred to speak about the afterlife and spending eternity in Heaven since life on earth was temporary. Jewish people speak of their faith in terms of ethical monotheism

1. Deuteronomy 6: 4.

characterized by living justly and mercifully in this life. Belief in the afterlife does not make living justly, loving mercifully, and walking humbly with God on earth.[2]

What might possibly bridge such a gulf of separation between a mother and child? How might we treat one another as in very early days when The Way of Jesus followers was Jewish?

Loving Jewish People seeks an answer to the above question. I write as a professing Christian with no intention of altering my beliefs in the core tenets of the Christian faith succinctly stated in the Apostle's Creed. Nor is this book an attempt to convert Jewish people to Christianity. If any conversion [I use this term cautiously] is to take place, I'd rather hear that both Christian and Jewish readers discovered centripetal forces pushing them toward each other. That friendship might become possible in the same way all human friendships are made. A foundation of trust must evolve which at very least triggers mutual advocacy. Christians and Jews might just find that they really do care for and can love each other.

The book is organized into four parts with thirteen chapters presenting the theological and ethical basis for why and how we should love the first people of the one true living God.

"Part One: Thinking Hebraically" provides a Jewish worldview rooted in the oneness of God. On the other hand, Western thought is constructed upon a Greek way of thinking—that dualism represents reality. Because the Scriptures were written by Jewish authors, readers must realize the authors' Hebraic cultural and social location to interpret the Bible fairly. Reading the Bible through a Greek lens misleads and distorts the truth about Israel as an ethnicity, a nation, and most of all as people through whom God chose to reveal himself to all humanity.

Chapter One defines Hebraic thought derived from the Semitic culture to which the Jewish people belong. Beginning with the *Sh'ma*, the first prayer of Israel, the chapter discusses the Hebrew language from an oral and literate perspective. It describes the key characteristics of thinking Hebraically and concludes with an analysis of the main differences between the abstractions of Greek thought and concrete Hebraic thinking.

Chapter Two tells Israel's story located in the Torah employing three themes: the covenants, the desert, and the land. Thinking Hebraically is embedded in the *covenants* God made with the first Jew, Abraham,

---

2. Micah 6: 8b.

followed by Moses, David, and a new covenant mentioned by Jeremiah. God promised to make Abraham's name great, to make him and Israel a blessing to all the world's nations, to bless all nations who bless Israel, to curse all nations who curse Israel, and to give Israel its own land. God stated that His covenants to Israel were eternal. Despite historic and current conflicts, God continues to maintain His promises to Israel

After an account of Creation, the destruction of the world in a global flood [promised never to reoccur in a covenant with Noah], and the beginning of the nations, the Torah tells the story of Israel's meandering journey through the Sinai *desert*. Israel's biography written primarily by Moses, the nation's first of many priests, is an adventurous account of God's intervention in the nation's life. The monumental event in Israel's story is its release from slavery in Egypt called the Exodus, the title of the Torah's second book. While on its way to the land promised in the covenants, God gave Israel ten huge commandments followed by hundreds of specific rituals for the forgiveness of sin. The Torah concludes with Moses' farewell address which urges the nation to choose life.

Finally, the chapter analyzes the nation's life from the desert wanderings to settling into a new *land* as its home, establishing its own government, the tension between its kings and prophets, deportation, captivity, and then restoration leading to the first century's Second Temple Judaism.

The story of Israel, a Semitic Mid-Eastern nation, is, ironically to many, the basis for freedom and liberty at the core of Western thought. Culturally, Western Civilization is primarily Hebraic with the later influence of Hellenism; yet, Jerusalem has little to do with Athens. Theologically, thinking Hebraically provides the basis for Christian thinking.

Chapter Three gets into Israel's contribution of storytelling to world culture. While fables, allegories, and legends persisted among the nations, the parable as a story with a message is unique to Israel. This chapter discusses the parable as an expanded analogy, a fictitious saying picturing truth, or as Klyne Snodgrass suggests, an imaginary garden with toads in it. The Tanakh tells Israel's story with only a few parables, the classic of which is a conversation between a prophet and a king. This chapter also includes an analysis of parables from the Talmud which conveys the important Hebraic concept of an integration of body, mind, spirit, and soul.

Chapter Four defines and analyzes the kingdom of God conveyed through parables from the Tanakh and the Talmud. *Kingdom of God* never explicitly appears as a phrase in the Early [Old] Testament or the Talmud. It's implied in Creation where the Creator-God gives humanity sovereignty over His work. The kingdom of God is also implied in the Tanakh's repeated use of *king, sovereignty* and *dominion*. A special relationship between *yoke* and *the kingdom of God* exists within Hebraic thought conveying the rule of God in one's life. The chapter concludes with examples of parables of the kingdom of God from both the Tanakh and Talmud.

In sum, this segment discusses Hebraic thought, Israel's biography, and the Hebraic idea of God's kingdom expressed in parables.

"Part Two: Thinking Christianly" gets into the person and work of Jesus Christ as the King of the world whose life, death, and resurrection save humanity from sin. It addresses Jesus' biography authored primarily by Jewish eye witnesses followed by an analysis of Jesus' teaching method—parables which are derived from the oral Hebraic tradition and his original down-to-earth stories. Jesus used parables to teach about the kingdom of God. The Jewishness of Jesus is key to understanding the Gospels.

Chapter Five speaks of the Jesus of faith and the Christ of history as the basis for thinking from a Christian perspective. It establishes a foundation for Christian thought derived from the Lord's Prayer, Jesus' manifesto for ministry, the Sermon on the Mount and a thorough analysis of his radical claims. One eyewitness heard Jesus say that the time is fulfilled, the kingdom of God is near, repent, and believe the good news. The chapter concludes with how the above sentence defines the gospel which informs all Christian ideology.

Chapter Six analyzes Jesus' biography written in the Gospels of the Younger [New] Testament. The sayings and events of Jesus' life are a major contribution to thinking Christianly. Christianity asserts that the story of Jesus is the fulfillment of the story of Israel just as the story of Israel anticipates the story of Jesus. Respecting a doctrinal boundary with Judaism, no rabbi would ever teach that Judaism contains a deficiency which requires fulfillment in Jesus. This chapter gets into Jesus' supernatural birth, baptism, and the Transfiguration. Most of each Gospel pertains to the last week of Jesus' life which includes the Passion of his suffering, death, resurrection, and appearances to hundreds of people.

Chapter Seven discusses Jesus' teaching method using parables drawn primarily from the agriculture of his day. The chapter concerns itself with this key question: *What does this parable say about Jesus?* While many parables could be discussed, the book analyzes three stories with the following titles: *The Parable of the Hearers, The Parable of the Father of Two Lost Sons* and *The Parable of a Samaritan and an Innkeeper*. Jesus' parables are often edgy stories which dismantle any domestication of Jesus. His stories are not inherently religious. They do however recommend a specific intent/command located in the *nimshal*—a parable's takeaway drawn from the *mashal,* the story itself.

Chapter Eight analyzes Jesus' ten parables about the kingdom of God. Each parable displays Hebraic thought beginning with the familiar phrase, "The kingdom of God is like..." Key themes include the growth of the kingdom, how Jesus turns religious norms upside down, God's grace, His judgment, and the timing of the kingdom's appearance be it internal, present or in the future. A discussion of Jesus' parabolic stories of the kingdom includes extended similes, metaphors and mini-dramas drawn from the Jewish Oral Tradition. Jesus' parables of the kingdom often indicate their origins in the Talmud or conversely show how Jesus' stories may have influenced later Talmudic sayings.

To summarize, this part of the book describes how Christians know what they know put forth in the story of Jesus followed by a discussion of how he used parables to convey God's kingdom.

"Part Three: Distortion" shifts the book's theme from the foundational aspects of Hebraic and Christian thought to how a dysfunctional church forgot its origin in the synagogue, distorted the gospel, and marginalized the kingdom of God.

Chapter Nine analyzes the origin, history, purpose, and liturgy of the synagogue as a house of prayer, worship, and study. The chapter recalls the Tabernacle as the only meeting place that God ever requested. The two Temples are examined in Israel's history leading to the synagogue, begun during the Babylonian Captivity, which became the center of Jewish worship after the destruction of the second Temple in 70 C.E. The chapter concludes with a brief analysis of the synagogue's liturgy which includes the Sh'ma and other important prayers. Other significant elements of synagogue liturgy include readings and blessings followed by the *Kiddush* [Benediction] which commemorates the holiness of the Sabbath.

Chapter Ten discusses how the synagogue birthed the church. It restates the normative biblical church as a Jewish-Gentile community of persons who celebrate their Hebraic roots while following Jesus Christ as their Messiah, Savior, and Lord. Paralleling the method used to analyze the synagogue, this chapter gets into the origin, history, purpose, and liturgy of the church. The analysis traces the evolution of the original

Jewish community of Jesus followers called the Way into a normative Jewish-Gentile congregation.

Christian liturgy owes its exist to the candles, prayers of praise, confession, repentance, thanksgiving, and intercession, prose and poetic readings, choral singing, congregation recitation and singing, the homily taken from the Torah and the Prophets and the Benediction—the essential elements of the Shabbat worship service.

Chapter Eleven analyzes how the normative Jewish-Gentile church departed from its Hebraic roots to become a conduit of theological anti-Judaism and racial antisemitism. Within the limited timeframe of 33 C.E. to about 400 C.E., this chapter analyzes how Christianity gradually marginalized and ultimately departed from its Jewish roots. While no specific date earmarks a precise turning away, early signs of departure include theological disagreement within the Jewish community and the conflicts pertaining to ritual among Jewish and Gentile persons. This chapter highlights the details of the First Church Council in Jerusalem which defined the criteria for Gentile participation in the church. Included in the important aspects of conflict and rift between the synagogue and church are Gnosticism, supercessionism, patriarchal hierarchy, and the role of creeds devoid of Hebraic thought in the early church.

In sum, segment offers a transition from Hebraic and Christian philosophy to a discussion of how the separation church and synagogue resulted in a permanent fissure between Judaism and Christianity.

"Part Four: Restitution" proposes a Christianity incarnated in a biblically normative Jewish-Gentile church. It addresses how the church may love the Jewish people. Such love requires a restitution involving its return to a Jewish Jesus and Hebraic thinking while simultaneously worshiping Jesus as Messiah, the Lord and Savior of all humanity.

Chapter Twelve seeks to undo the dysfunction of a church which lost its way by neglecting its Hebraic origins. It urges Christianity to recover its gospel, restore its church, and reclaim the kingdom of God. The gospel is the good news that Christ's death has accomplished victory over sin and that Christ's resurrection has proclaimed victory over death. A restored church is a Jewish-Gentile community of redeemed sinners united as one new humanity using the Apostle Paul's ecclesial language.[3]

Chapter Thirteen provides a theological and spiritual basis for loving the Jewish people. Claiming to love God without loving the Jewish

---

3. Ephesians 2: 11—22.

people doesn't succeed. Loving Jewish people atones for the historic and cultural past which disallowed Jews to *live as Jews*, then disallowed them to *live as ordinary citizens*, and finally disallowed the Jewish people *to live at all*. This chapter includes an analysis of two leading Jewish scholars Franz Rosenzweig and Leo Baeck both of whom offer a thoroughly philosophical justification for loving the first people on earth who worshiped that One God who is the Lord of the universe.

The Conclusion of the book offers a distilled summary of all its chapters. It then offers a parable whose mashal includes a mutuality of both the story of Israel and the story of Jesus with this nimshal: Loving God with all one's heart, mind, soul, and spirit implies loving Jewish people as the other, your neighbor, your conversation partner, and your friend.

PART ONE
Thinking Hebraically

— Chapter 1 —

Hebraic Thought

ACCORDING TO RABBI ABRAHAM Heschel the Bible contains more than a sum of doctrines; it represents *a way of thinking*. He's as concerned about how to process knowledge as he is about knowing information. Heschel distances himself from conceptual Western thought patterns rooted in Greek philosophy. For him, Jerusalem has nothing to do with Athens. Christian theologian Marvin R. Wilson says this: "If today's church is to uncover more of the depth and breadth of the Christian faith, concern about the very foundational teachings of Christianity, our Hebraic heritage, is . . . . a necessity."[1] In his second edition of *Our Father Abraham*, Wilson comments: "Christianity could not exist without Judaism."[2] When Christianity parted ways with its Hebraic roots, it traded its Hebrew birthright for a Greek pot of lentils and "accepted the inheritance of ancient—Greek and oriental—romanticism . . . [with their] . . . traits of . . . emotion, flight from reality and the longing for an experience."[3] Today's church must adopt a Hebraic exegesis constructed upon "the reasoning and philosophy developed within the Hebrew Bible, continued into the New Testament . . . "[4]

---

1. Wilson, *Exploring Our Hebraic Heritage*, 21.

2. Wilson, *Our Father Abraham*, 19. Wilson quotes John Shelby Song's article, "The Continuing Christian Need for Judaism," *Christian Century*, September 26, 1979, 918-22.

3. Baeck, *Judaism and Christianity*, 196.

4. Dru Johnson, "Why Does Hebraic Thought Matter?"

Using a sibling metaphor for the relationship of Christians and Jews, A. Roy Eckhardt, pioneer in the interfaith dialogue between Jews and Christians in the late 1960's, urged the church to see itself as Israel's younger brother.

> "Through the freedom given to him in Jesus Christ, a freedom from the enslavement of 'tradition' as from all other bonds, the Christian no longer need behave as an upstart. He has learned to *live* the mystery of Israel. He has been met by the Lord's faithfulness to the sons of Abraham. He is persuaded that only the Second Abraham is able to make him joint heir with his elder brother. That Man is the Christian's risen Lord. Christianity is the religion of the upstart who is granted an odd chance to find out what faith is. That chance comes to him wherever he fills a lowly seat in his hidden Father's house, the only seat proper to a younger brother."[5] [author's italics].

In 1975 Franklin H. Littell, stated: "The built-in problem is this: while affirming the right of the Jewish people to self-definition, the Christian must deal with the truth that he cannot achieve his own identity and self-definition apart from the role of the Jewish people in meaningful history . . . a reconstructed and genuinely Christian theology will have to deal affirmatively with the contribution of the Jews in the last two millennia as well as with our fathers-in-God before the Christian era."[6] Today's church needs to once again hear the voice of those early-on theologians who saw how Christianity relies upon Hebraic thought not only for its very existence, but also to more accurately read the Old Testament.

The objective of this chapter is to define Hebraic thought as the foundation of the Jewish people. The task is epistemological; that is, it seeks to analyze how Judaism processes knowledge. Once Christians discover how the Jews have historically viewed the world, the church can read the Tanakh, as it must be read, through a Hebraic lens.

This chapter is organized into five segments: The Shema [Sh'ma], Orality and Literacy, Language, Key Characteristics of Hebraic Thinking, and Hebraic Thinking vs. Greek Thinking. We begin with the most important prayer of the Jewish people—the Shema.

---

5. Eckhardt, *Elder and Younger Brothers: The Encounter of Jews and Christians*, 162.
6. Littell, *The Crucifixion of the Jews*, 4-5.

The Shema

Shema Yisrael Adonai Eloheinu Adonai Echad . . .

"Hear, O Israel, the LORD is our God,
The LORD is One. Love the LORD,
your God with all your heart, and with all your
mind and, with all your soul, and with all your strength."[7]

"The Shema is an affirmation of Judaism and a declaration of faith in one God."[8] *Oneness* is embedded in its way of thinking. The Shema proclaims God's unity and sovereignty over the world. *Hear* in Jewish thinking is not passive listening. It is a call to action; that is, one is to *do* something, to obey a command . . . to love the LORD wholeheartedly.

LORD is the most sacred name for God, the unspeakable YHWH. R. Kendall Soulen states that the Tetragrammaton refers to God alone and so is the mark of God's unique identity par excellence. Not only does Soulen focus on the importance of God's name, but he also emphasizes that the Jewish people are God's elect. He chides the church for its historic heresy "that the Jews are no longer what they once were—God's elect people."[9] Sadly, the church has forgotten that its election is the result of being a twig grafted into the Jewish Tree of Life, the *Etz Chaim*. The concept of a divine being selecting one nation from all His universe and all nations is uniquely Hebraic.

The LORD is *one*. This second sentence of the Shema combines the Tetragrammaton with the unity of God. The unspeakable most sacred name of God is combined with the oneness of God's being. This four-word sentence [The LORD is one] alone has massive implications for Hebraic thought. Heschel suggests that the minimum meaning of God is "the idea of ultimacy. God is a Being beyond which no other exists or is possible. It means further, One, unique, eternal."[10] He derives his thinking from the Shema's explicit statement of oneness. He continues, "We proclaim God is One; it would be intellectual idolatry to say that One is God . . . ,"[11] which would say nothing about the essence of God. He concludes that God's oneness implies that God is alive. Hebraically speaking,

---

7. Deuteronomy 6: 4—5.
8. Schoenberg, "Jewish Prayers: The Shema."
9. Soulen, *Irrevocable*, 50.
10. Heschel, *God In Search of Man*, 125.
11. Ibid.

the LORD, who is Israel's possession [*our God*], is "a Being to whom we may confess our sins, of a God who loves, of a God who is not above concern with our inquiry . . . a father, not an absolute."¹² [author's italics].

In Martin Buber's thinking, God "was not an It but an I or a You."¹³ He supports Heschel's focus on the living God—for we are to love this God wholeheartedly with body, mind, soul, and spirit. No one loves a mere object in this way—only a person. Buber says, "The designation of God as a person is indispensable for all who, like myself, do not mean a principle when they say 'God.' "¹⁴ The Jewish people think about God as a person engaged with every detail of a worshiper's life—the Ineffable One about whom we cannot speak is the One who wants to speak with us.

In sum, the Shema gives birth to the essence of Judaism proclaiming One living God possessed by one nation, Israel. We now turn our attention to how the Hebrew language has influenced Hebraic thinking both orally and literally.

Orality and Literacy

Rabbi Elisha Friedman points out the importance of the Jewish Oral Tradition. "The Torah we have is composed of two distinct parts: The Written Torah—including the 24 books of the Tanakh (Bible), and the Oral Torah—which includes everything else, but primarily refers to the Mishnah, Talmud and the many collections of rabbinic traditions in the Tofsefta and Midrashim . . . percentage-wise most of the Torah is Oral, the Written Torah constitutes the smaller section. According to Jewish tradition, these two sections were given to Moshe at the Revelation at Mt. Sinai."¹⁵ Rashi¹⁶ believes that the Torah's texts were spoken, not written, to Moshe at Sinai and he passed them along orally. The importance of the Oral Tradition within Judaism is captured in Rabbi Hirsch's statement: "From the mouths of scholars, but not from the mouth of books."¹⁷ Historically, clear evidence exists for hearing the Torah, not

---

12. Ibid., 126.

13. Buber, *I and Thou*, 33.

14. Ibid., 180.

15. Rabbi Friedman, "An analysis of the Role of the Oral Torah," *Shavuot 5780: Self-Guided Torah Study Experience,* ou.org.

16. Rashi, a French rabbi (1040—1105) who wrote a comprehensive commentary on the Talmud and is considered "the Rabbi of Israel."

17. Friedman, *Kuzari* (2: 72) . . . which also states, "God did not want people to

reading it. Even in today's modern world of written words in all types of media, the best way to learn Torah is from a human encounter with a teacher. It involves making good use of the oral and aural word; that is, hearing a spoken word.

At the outset of her book, *Oral World and Written Word*, Susan Niditch advances the "idea that large, perhaps dominant, threads in Israelite culture were oral, and that literacy in ancient Israel must be understood in terms of its continuity and interaction with the oral world."[18] She chides the Documentary Hypothesis and form criticism for positioning Israel as "romantic . . . naive . . . rural . . . [which] . . . is misguided, devaluing the power of oral culture and misconstruing the characteristics of orally-composed and oral-style works . . . ."[19] The nineteenth-century Documentary Hypothesis falsely challenged the Moses-authored Torah's five books of the Jewish Bible. Historic Critical Thought negated all things Hebrew as the basis for liberal Protestant theology which continues to reduce Christianity to a romantic inner-only spirituality.

Niditch views the composition and transmission of the Hebrew Bible as "an interplay between orality and literacy . . . [which appreciates] . . . the nature, meaning, and context of a legacy of Israelite self-expression, preserved in written form."[20] Her thesis uplifts and dignifies Israel and its sacred tradition handed down through the generations. Recall the Shema. "And these words which I command you this day shall be upon your heart, and you shall teach them diligently to your children, and shall talk of them when you sit in your house, and when you walk by the way, and when you lie down, and when you rise."[21] Israel's story of the Exodus, for example, was told during a forty-year journey in a desert, sitting around campfires, among families gathered in their tents, or more formally during Passover. These stories were *written* much later. Susan Niditch insists that "the oral culture and the written culture fully interact and intertwine in the implicit attitudes of

---

study Torah through books but from a human being . . . to guard against self-study . . . seek out a rebbe (Torah teacher) in order to be initiated." Rav S.R. Hirsch Commentary on the Torah, *Shemot* 34:27, ou.org.

18. Niditch, *Oral World and Written Word*, 1.

19. Ibid., 2-3.

20. Ibid., 7.

21. Deuteronomy 6: 6-7.

Israelite authors. Evidence of orality exists such that there was no "conflict with what I mean by an essentially oral world."[22]

In his *The Babylonian Talmud: Tractate Berakot*, The Rev. A. Cohen says that the Talmud is difficult to translate because " . . . [it] . . . is not a literary composition, but a compilation of *precis* notes which were intended to be amplified and explained *by oral teaching*"[23] [author's italics]. Sympathetic with how Hebraic thought bears no resemblance to Greek thinking, he says " . . . the Talmud cannot and should not be judged by the canon of modern literature . . . [because] . . . it reflects a mode of life and thought . . . utterly foreign to the Western culture of this age."[24] Also supportive of Niditch's thesis, Jon D. Levenson talks about the one God who gave commandments orally to Moses from whose mouth the people heard: "You shall be to me a kingdom of priests and a holy nation."[25] Regarding the tradition of commandments handed to Moses, Levenson says, "There is . . . no voice more central to Judaism than the voice heard on Mount Sinai."[26] Finally, in his comprehensive treatment of how the Bible became a book, William M. Schniedewind notes that a "fierce ideology of orality would persist in Rabbinic Judaism even as the Torah and the written tablets were merged into one pre-existent Torah that was with God at the very creation of the world."[27]

Echoing Schniedewind, Rabbi Tzvi Freeman explains how Jacob could study the Torah in his tent years before God revealed Torah to Moses. "The Torah is G-d's wisdom, as He considers Himself, as He considers us, and as He considers His world. It contains the wisdom with which He creates the world and manages it . . . Abraham, Isaac and Jacob . . . knew the Torah . . . Moses was special . . . [he] was empowered to bring this Torah to all the people . . . at Sinai, Torah was no longer only wisdom, but a command."[28] Freeman implies that the wisdom to know Torah came with Creation and was available to anyone with insight into the hidden most secrets of the universe. God spoke wisdom into his universe on the first day of creation. That's why Jacob could "study" the Torah before it was written.

22. Niditch, *Oral Worldl and Written Word*, 7.
23. Cohen, *The Babylonian Talmud: Tractate Berakot*, vi.
24. Ibid., vii.
25. Exodus 19: 6
26. Levenson, *Sinai and Zion*, 86.
27. Schniedewind, *How the Bible Became a Book*, 213.
28. Freeman, "How Did the Torah Exist Before it Happened?"

Here we see a novel element of orality—the Torah implicit within Creation. Torah is not merely the first five books of Moses, but *instruction*. An eternal God knew what his instructions would be for his chosen people *before* he spoke or wrote them. For example, God in his eternal wisdom knew what the Ten Commandments would be prior to stating them to Moses or etching them with his finger onto two stone tablets. Torah is revealed by the LORD. It existed prior to the Creation. The Shema was in the heart and mind of God at Creation. An unspeakable YHWH spoke Creation into existence. The Psalmist reminds us that the heavens declare God's glory.

Language

Israel passed the nation's story down through generations using orality and literacy. What do we know about Israel's language and how does it impact Hebraic thought? Does Hebraic thought impact the Hebrew language? Detailed analysis of these two questions, while critical, lies outside the scope of this book. We'll answer them briefly by analyzing Hebrew.

Martin Luther said, "'The Hebrew language is the best language of all, with the richest vocabulary . . . the Hebrews drink from the spring, the Greeks from the stream that flows from it, and the Latins from a downstream pool.'"[29] To answer the above questions, we turn to Jeff A. Benner and his comprehensive lexicon of the Hebrew Language whose purpose "is to restore the original Hebrew to the Hebrew language of the Bible."[30] How is the Hebrew language like a spring of water—a never-ending source of orality and literacy?

Benner states that the Hebrew language informs an important aspect of Hebraic thought—knowing concretely. "The Ancient Hebrew language is a concrete-oriented language of Hebrew words rooted in the five senses such as the words *tree* which can be seen, *sweet* which can be tasted and *noise* which can be heard."[31] [my italics]. A context for the language may be summarized by one word—visceral. "The Hebrews have sometimes been described as a very visceral people."[32] Visceral describes organs of

---

29. Wilson, *Our Father Abraham*, 139. Note: This striking metaphor is from Luther's *Tischreden* (Table Talk).

30. Benner, *Ancient Hebrew Lexicon*, 8.

31. Ibid.

32. Wilson, *Our Father Abraham*, 141.

the human body—the heart, bowels, liver and kidneys. For example, the Hebrew language speaks of *bowels of mercy* to connote compassion. The Hebrew people viewed the normal functioning of the body's organs as an affirmation of being fully human with all the physical, mental, spiritual, and emotional components that make up one's personality. For example, David "*leaped* and *danced* before the Lord with all his *might*."³³ [my italics]. "The Song of Songs is an example of a passion-filled love poem that openly celebrates the sensual purity of marital love . . ."³⁴

Hebrew letters originated as pictographic symbols depicting the five senses. For example, *Hebrew* means *praise*. Praise as an abstract concept is foreign to how Hebrews think. *Praise* in Hebrew appears in three letters with the picture of someone with raised hands followed by the same two symbols of a staff used by a shepherd to direct his flock. Combined, these letters mean directing one's eyes toward a light in a distance in the stars. Praising then is associated with shining stars . . . to shine through one's actions by praising or giving thanks.³⁵ Here we have a detailed evolution behind *praise* in Hebrew. A person is *praising* with hands raised, *looking* up with one's eyes and *singing* with one's vocal cords and mouth. Eventually, a Hebrew word goes back to the visceral nature of the Jewish people expressed concretely in action involving the five senses.

Henk Rijstenberg speaks of Hebrew as a language of action. "In a typical Hebrew sentence, the verb comes first . . . Hebraic concepts are written to emphasize actions . . . Moshe writes, 'to look' is to 'lift up the eyes'. . 'to be angry' is equal to the 'nose is burning' . . . to 'reveal something' is to 'unstop the ears' . . . and to 'have no compassion' on someone is to 'have a hard heart' drawing a parallel with the hardness of Pharoah's heart."³⁶ Note how the above phrases associate the body parts with verbs.

George W. Benthien points out how Hebrew speaks of the heart [*levav*] as the seat of the mind and will, unlike non-Hebraic languages more inclined to use *heart* as the center of feeling and emotion. The pictograph for *levav* uses two letters: the symbol for tent and a shepherd's staff. Here Hebrew sees a tent to mean *in* or *within* and a staff to mean *authority*. Combined, these two letters may translate *heart* as *the authority within*. Benthien goes on to link Hebrew words for abdomen or heart, kidneys and living creature with mind, emotion, and soul,

---

33. 2 Samuel 6: 14—16.
34. Wilson, *Our Father Abraham*, 143.
35. Benner, *Ancient Hebrew Lexicon*, 103.
36. Rijstenberg, MATSATI.COM, "Thinking Hebraically," 2011.

respectively.³⁷ Viscerally speaking, the heart functions as the distributor of life-giving blood throughout the entire body.

While the common understanding of *shalom* is peace, Benthien associates it with the verb *shalam* to make restitution. For example, if someone stole another's cow, it is that person's responsibility to restore what has been stolen—to make restitution. So *shalom*, a noun associated with *shalam*, literally means "to make whole" indicative of how nouns in Hebrew may be used as words of action. "The noun 'shalom" means being in a state of wholeness . . . "³⁸

In sum, orality speaks of spoken and heard words derived from the dynamic nature of the Jewish people, a people always on the move. Literacy is the written and read word which visually displays what is spoken and heard using pictographs which indicate concrete action. The Bible may be thought of as an interactive continuum of revealed words handed down orally through generations. Eventually those spoken and heard words are written and read. We now turn our attention to what it may mean to think Hebraically. The written Hebrew language is the result of taking the visceral senses initially displayed in pictographs which form the basis for the Hebrew alphabet. Like any language, Hebrew uses its alphabet to form words that make sense.

Key Characteristics of Hebraic Thinking

We now consider the following key ways Hebraic thought distances itself from Hellenistic thinking with an analysis of revelation, oneness, image of God, time, kingdom of God, and the Sabbath.

Revelation

The *revelation of God* is uniquely Hebraic. Only the Jewish people claim a God who has revealed himself by speaking the universe into existence. Recall the Shema, "Hear, O Israel, The LORD is our God, The LORD is one . . . " No other religious ideologies claim to have a relationship with God through historical events over centuries. No other sacred literature, oral or written, possesses so consistent a message rooted in a

---

37. Benthien, "The Hebrew Language and Way of Thinking.
38. Ibid.

Shema-like prayer, conveyed by scores of authors, different genres, and finally compiled in a book, the Tanakh.

Global religions typically think of revelation as prophetic interpretations of events in the life of people or a prophet himself. Wisdom derives from humanity; but divine *revelation,* the essence of Judaism, derives from one God who gives life and breath.

Revelation may be thought of as God's self-disclosure to humanity. Creation may considered as natural revelation and covenant as special revelation. In creation, God reveals himself to Adam and Eve as one who blesses and as one who judges. In the Abrahamic Covenant, God reveals himself to be loyal and is initiated freely by himself.

Rabbi Kaufmann Kohler views Israel among all nations which "alone rose with the claim of having received the words of the living God and Ruler of the Universe as a revelation for all times and all generations of men."[39] He points out the genius of Judaism as a revelation from God to a plurality of recipients; not only to one person. One person might get it wrong. A continuity of theme over time heard, spoken, and written by a various authors is far more credible. "Israel's God is not called the God of Moses, David or Isaiah, but of Abraham, Isaac and Jacob, that is, of the fathers of the nation . . . "[40] Kohler equates revelation with the word of the LORD, *dabar*[41] *YHWH* [to formalize the name YHWH]. Here he includes more subjective conduits of revelation such as "oracles, signs, and dreams"[42] as part of Israel's instruction, Torah.

When Israel viewed creation, it didn't see Mother Nature. It saw God. The nation "heard" the skies declare the glory of God. "The heavens are not God, they are His witnesses . . . "[43] Creation is a *natural revelation* of God, the invisible One Ineffable God is separate from the created order, yet revealed by it. Any religion which conflates its god with nature is anti-Judaistic. Hebraic thinking rejects all forms of pantheism and nature-worship.

---

39. Kohler, "Revelation," *Jewish Encyclopedia.*

40. Ibid.

41. Benner, *Ancient Hebrew Lexicon*, Note: *dabar* is best translated as "An arrangement or placement something creating order; in our case, speaking a special arrangement of words or commands," 320.

42. Kohler, "Revelation."

43. Heschel, *Man Is Not Alone*, 116. The Psalmist also speaks of heaven declaring the glory of God in Psalm 19:1.

"The Bible, is first and foremost, God's *revelation* in history, and it is precisely this point that sets the Bible apart from other religious literature."[44] The special revelation of the Torah and Prophets in the Tanakh is a record of God's acts in history. Martin Buber said, "Divest the Bible of the acting character of God, and it loses its significance."[45] Hebraic thought emanates from both the natural and special revelation of God through Creation and the Bible. In each case, the voice of an invisible loving God is heard from the silence of a sunrise to the oral commandments Moses heard and received on Sinai. The silence of a sunset is no less revealing of God than the audible voice of God that Jeremiah heard when he spoke to the people about God's pending judgment.

Oneness

The Shema reveals God's *oneness*. Hebraic thinking presumes the one and only God which negates all pluralities of gods disinterested in humanity. "'God is One' . . . [means] . . . He is a being who is . . . both Creator and Redeemer; I am the Lord, thy God, who brought thee out of the land of Egypt" (Exodus 20: 2).[46] God is everywhere, "He is all here and all there . . . Rabbi Moshe of Kobrin once said, 'Do you want to know where God is? He took a piece of bread from the table, showed it to everybody and said, 'Here is God.'"[47] That is, God is sacramentally present in the ordinary. A Hebraic worldview includes living life with a God who is everywhere, yet personally related to a community and individual human beings. The oneness of God bespeaks God's unity and a unity of all humanity. "When God becomes our form of thinking we begin to sense all men in one man, the whole world in a grain of sand, eternity in a moment. To worldly ethics one human being is less than two human beings . . . "[48] However to the Hebraic mind if a man has caused one soul to perish, it is as though he had caused all humanity to perish, and if he has saved a single soul, it is as though he had saved a whole world [*Mishnah Sanhedrin*, 4, 5.] When Otto Schindler saved one Jew from a gas chamber, he saved all Jews from the gas chambers, because even though millions of Jews died in those

---

44. Wilson, *Our Father Abraham*, 163.
45. Ibid., 164 quoting Buber's *Israel and the World*, 99.
46. Ibid., 119.
47. Ibid., 121.
48. Ibid., 109.

deceitful showers of murder, surviving Jews were finally blessed with a permanent homeland, the State of Israel.

Image of God

The Torah states that God created all humanity in the *image of God*. "Let us make Man in Our image, after Our likeness."[49] The Hebraic view of the sanctity and dignity of all humanity is rooted in the Torah's phrase *image of God*; that is, the being of God embedded within each human being at creation. When any therapist works with the self-concept or self-image of a client, she's indebted to Hebraic thought about the worth and value of each person no matter what their socio-economic status, gender orientation, or ethnicity.

The Jewish people gave the world a theological and moral basis for the sanctity of all life. This is why responding to one person is a response to all persons. The unity of God is reflected in this unity of all humankind. Martin Buber put it this way: "In every sphere, everything that becomes present to us, we gaze toward the train of the eternal You, in each we perceive a breath of it; in every You we address the eternal You . . . "[50] Using Buber's threefold schema, we have You-eternal You, I-the Other, or I-God . . . as re-statements of his I-Thou. Each one of the three possibilities, links a person or persons with the image of God.

The Kingdom of God

Kingdom of God is not explicitly stated in the Tanakh. Yet implicit Kingdom of God imagery permeates Jewish literature.

The Kingdom of God is related to the image of God. Since God is eternal and the stamp of God is embedded within each human being, a broader view of God's imprint upon all creatures may be thought of as a future kingdom of God. Leo Baeck alludes to a future kingdom this way: "It is told in the Talmud: "May you see your *olam*[51] in your life,

---

49. Genesis 1: 26. Note in the Tanakh: "Moses wrote . . . this verse that there is more than one Creator, 'Sovereign of the Universe! Why do You . . . maintain that there is a plurality of divinities? . . . God replied . . . ' . . . the Creator . . . when He came to create Man He took counsel from the ministering angels.' (*Midrash*).

50. Buber, *I and Thou*, 57.

51. Benner, *Ancient Hebrew Lexicon*, Note: *olam* is usually translated as "land, the whole of the earth or region," 266; but here it's best associated with "age, a passing

and may your future be for the life of an *olam* to come . . . "[52] [author's italics]. Baeck translates *olam* as a rebirth where every life continues into the future.

While Baeck's analysis looks into a future Kingdom of God, Israel is exposed to the concept of kingdom while in Egypt. "Then a new king, who did not know about Joseph, came to power in Egypt."[53] The harmful impact of a visible king with power over a nation worked against Israel's possession of their one God, their own invisible king. God never intended for Israel to be ruled by visible kings. "When you enter the land the LORD your God is giving you . . . and you say, 'Let us set a king over us like all the nations around us, be sure to appoint over you a king the LORD your God chooses."[54] The key phrase is *and you say*. The history of Israel in its homeland included kings, a united kingdom, and then two divided kingdoms as God's concession which Moses here anticipates. The nation didn't wholly trust the God of the Shema, the invisible sovereign king of the universe who led them for forty years through a desert. Israel wanted what God never intended—a human king.

In his farewell speech, Samuel reminds the nation that they possessed a king because they wanted to be like other nations . . . "the LORD your God was your king . . . "[55] While visible kings do occur with Saul, David, Solomon and a host of kings in the divided kingdom, God's idea of a kingdom begins with Moses before Sinai.

Prior to Moses' reception of the Law, the Torah speaks of Israel as a "kingdom of priests and a holy nation."[56] This radical phrase establishes a theme for all of Scripture as to how God conceived a kingdom for Israel. It would be an invisible theocracy. The ineffable God who spoke in a misty Shekinah Glory was the king. Moses heard the king's voice and spoke the message to the people. No other neighboring nation possessed this quality. Even when the nation had its enthroned human kings, the prophets consistently reminded Israel that the Torah spoke of a kingdom of priests in the service of God.

In sum, what became the historic kingdoms of Israel was a far cry from God's intended design. The original Hebraic concept of a kingdom

---

through . . . time," 333.

52. Baeck, *This People Israel*, 248
53. Exodus 1: 8.
54. Deuteronomy 17: 14—15a.
55. 1 Samuel 12: 12b.
56. Exodus 19: 3.

of God meant having the invisible sovereign God and creator of the universe as Israel's necessary and sufficient ruler of the nation. That nation was holy; it was a kingdom, a community of priests, consecrated to serving the LORD.

Time

Hebraic thinking is concerned more about *time* than space. "Time is the heart of existence."[57] Judaism is rooted in the idea that history has an end game; that is, it's going somewhere—eventually toward the arrival of the kingdom of God, the messianic age. No other religious way of thinking has this. Christianity did not introduce the kingdom of God to humanity—Israel did. Professor Julius Guttman spoke of a future kingdom of God saying, "The blessedness of the world to come is understood as consisting of the pious enjoying the radiance of the presence of God.[58] Viewing this life as preparation for the next, he uses an excellent metaphor from the Talmudic saying, this world is like a vestibule in which a person prepares to enter the banquet hall of the world to come.[59] Hebraic thinking views time *within* God along with the historic interaction of God *in* time, each held in paradoxical tension with one another. Contradictory thoughts in tension characterizes normal Hebraic thinking.

Sabbath

Hebraic thought characterizes *Sabbath* as cyclical rest and renewal. If God needed the day after six days of labor to rest, how much more do we need one day to reflect totally on the presence of God. As Heschel said, "The Sabbath is the presence of God, open to the soul of man . . . God is not in things of space, but in moments of time."[60] During Shabbat worship it is as if time stands still. Readings from Torah, prayers, singing, proclaiming God's truth from the Tanakh—all these and more spiritual blessings bountifully flow during the hour when God's people are married to the Sabbath. Heschel states: " . . . we are within the Sabbath rather

---

57. Heschel, *The Sabbath*, 1.
58. Guttman, *Philosophies of Judaism*, 34 . . . quoting *Berakhot*, 17a.
59. Ibid., quoting *Pirke Abot* 4: 16.
60. Heschel, *The Sabbath*, xiv.

than the Sabbath being within us . . . we marry the day . . . on the seventh day God gave the world a soul . . . "[61]

There is a point in the Shabbat service where the congregation turns toward door to view the invisible bride of the Sabbath entering the sanctuary. Life's tangible necessities give way to the spiritual intangibilities enjoyed when celebrating the Torah's procession around the sanctuary. It is a reminder that something much larger and greater than us is present with us; for the Jewish people, it's the Shekinah Presence going back to the mobile Tabernacle tent.

Jonathan Sacks has a novel interpretation of *Shabbat* as "the antidote to the Golden Calf."[62] Aaron's idol was a costly alternative to worshiping the one true God. One context for the Sabbath is economic. He speaks of the Sabbath as a way of salvation from consumer culture. His focus is not on the *price* of things but upon their *value*. "It's the day dedicated to the celebration of things that have value . . . when we renew our sense of community in the synagogue . . . we listen to Torah together . . . and we thank God together for our blessings."[63]

In his *The Biblical Era*, William Bjoraker reflects on meaning of time where "the Sabbath is to remember the beginning of time (Creation) and the beginning of freedom (Redemption), as a people group and within each of us."[64] He points out that the Sabbath isn't about escaping time, but cherishing it. He agrees with other scholars who view time in God, not God in time in the same spiritual way that we are in the Sabbath, not the Sabbath in us.

Hebraic thought views God as the *I AM THAT I AM*.[65] He created in us the idea of time. The Torah starts with *In the beginning*. Since God created time, like everything created in those busy six days, God is separated from and precedes all that he created. Time, along with all creation, glorifies the Creator and declares his glory where the rest on the seventh day, the Sabbath, is the reward for the work. Our fatigued work-a-day world may be missing out on its reward. The idea of the Sabbath is unique in the world of ideas where eternity utters a day and a day represents eternity.

---

61. Ibid., xv.
62. Sacks, *Exodus: The Book of Redemption*, 261.
63. Ibid.
64. Bjoraker, *The Biblical Era*, 57.
65. Alter, *The First Five Books of Moses*, Note on Exodus 3: 14: This text may also be translated, "I Will Be Who I Will Be, " or "He who Brings Things into Being."

Thus far, we've considered the key characteristics of Hebrew thinking. Now we'll compare Hebraic thought to a Greek way of thinking. Since Jerusalem has nothing to do with Athens, we find a clear boundary between Hebraic thinking and Greek thought. Attempts to synthesize each together into one idea do not succeed. What results is not a synthesis where a combination of ideas retain their meaning to form a system, but a syncretism where the personality of each way of thinking loses its unique DNA.

Hebrew Thinking vs Greek Thinking

As an overview of how Hebraic thought specifically separates itself from Greek thinking, Brad Scott compares the Greek and Hebraic views of the nature of man. "To the Greeks, man is dual . . . made up of flesh (body, physical, material) . . . and soul (mind, spirit, invisible, eternal, that which is holy or godly)."[66] According to Scott, Greek thought views only the soul as redeemable . . . knowledge feeds the soul . . . only that which is spiritual is important. The physical body is not redeemable and inherently evil. Which is unfortunately why "commandments and laws from Scripture which deal primarily with the physical are irrelevant to the spiritual man."[67]

On the other hand, Hebraic thought positions man as an integrated whole and unity of body, mind, soul, and spirit, making no dualistic separation of each aspect of humanity's nature. "All is to be holy as YHVH is holy . . . all is to be redeemed . . . In Hebrew thinking, it is what a man does. The spirit, soul, and body are considered to be a man's life . . . the words for life, spirit, soul, and breath are used interchangeably."[68] All of life, so-called secular and sacred is redeemable. Given this critical background, we now consider specific comparisons of Hebrew and Greek thinking—all of which derive from the essential nature of humanity.

Hebraic thought is *concrete*. Greek thinking is *abstract*. A concrete word creates a word-picture related to seeing, hearing, feeling, tasting, or touching. Consider Exodus 17: 12 as an example:

---

66. Scott, "Hebrew Mind vs. Greek Mind: The Nature of Man," Lesson Ten, Wild Branch Ministry.
67. Ibid.
68. Ibid.

> But Moses' hands grew weary, so they took a stone and put it under him, and he sat on it, while Aaron and Hur held up his hands, one on one side, and the other on the other side. So his hands were steady until the going down of the sun.

The entire 51-word sentence creates a word-picture built upon these concrete words: *hands, stone, sat, side, steady* and *sun*. Now let's consider how this same text may appear using Greek [Hellenistic] thinking:

> Moses rested because of the heaviness of his hands and Aaron and Hur offered him a steadiness that lasted until darkness.

Note the abstractions of *heaviness, steadiness* and *darkness*. Which translation can you picture? It's not a question of right vs wrong, we're merely using two ways to express the same event from two very different cultural perspectives. Recall that the Hebrew language is constructed using pictographic letters. Culture isn't right or wrong; it's about learning how one culture views reality so that when we read the Bible written by Jewish people informed by Semitic culture, we do so accurately, without the misconceptions imposed by Greek distortions.

Hebraic thinking speaks of *function*. Greek thought emphasizes *appearance*. Here we have the difference between verbs and nouns/adjectives. Consider the Hebraic view of a godly person compared to a tree in Psalm 1:

> He shall be like a tree deeply *rooted* alongside brooks of water,
> That *yields* its fruit in season, and whose leaf never *withers*.

Note that the tree is pictured by action: *rooted, yields* and *withers*; three verbs which describe how firmly the tree is planted, how it grows its fruit in a timely manner, and how alive its leaves are. Using a Hebraic way of interpreting this text, we may understand a godly person intimately related to God as a source of life. This person is able to have an orderly stable life with built-in routines and habits which show up as admirable personal characteristics. Finally, this person values only that which is life-giving. Can you *see* this metaphor? Consider a possible Greek rendition of this same text:

> His essence is spiritually-centered characterized by eternal wetness of vitality characterized by timeliness.

Note the abstractions: *essence, spiritually-centered, eternal, wetness, vitality, timeliness*—these are descriptions [adjectives] and concepts [nouns], not behaviors or actions. Hebrew thinking views a godly person's active behavior in concrete action; Greek thought is limited to abstractions which require the passivity of nouns and adjectives.

Christian Overman uncovers premises and assumptions which influence the way we think and act. Maintaining the difference between Hebraic and Hellenistic [Greek] world views, he credits Judaism as the biblical source for morality, law, and ethics and the Greeks for philosophy, science, and politics. Overman points out the differences between Hellenistic and Hebraic assumptions about God, humanity, the image of God, and the sacredness of life. He asks, "Does freedom mean that we are free to do whatever we want whenever we want without being under obligation? No."[69] Ironically, *"To be free, then, is to submit oneself to the prescribed order of things, and function responsibly and creatively within the boundaries God has lovingly provided for our good and well-being."* [author's italics]. The Hebraic paradox holds together two apparent contradictions [freedom vs. boundaries] in tension as a *both-and*, not the dualism of Hellenism's *either-or*.

Further, Overman talks about a relationship between revelation and reason whereby reason submits to revelation. Greek thought pits one against the other concluding that meaningful intervention from a supernatural source doesn't matter to autonomous human beings who see themselves as the measure of all things. Hebraically speaking, the LORD is sovereign over all the earth and is in charge of what happens on the planet. However, what the LORD *allows*, is often not what he *intends* for living a good life.

Brian Knowles, in "The Hebrew Mind vs The Western Mind," quotes William Barrett to point out that the "Hebrew mind is concerned with practice, the Greek with knowledge; furthermore, the purpose of Greek knowledge is an end in itself, whereas the Jewish people view knowledge as a stepping stone to revere God."[70] Note Abraham Heschel's distaste for reducing the Bible to a series of principles which is like "trying to reduce a living person to a diagram."[71] Of course, we don't view a Judaism opposed to correct belief. But Judaism would also rightly confront the credibility of belief devoid of ethical behavior. Abraham took leaps of action. Kierkegaard took leaps of faith. Torah is instruction on how to *obey*

---

69. Overman, "Assumptions that Affect our Lives,"
70. Knowles, "The Hebrew Mind vs. The Western Mind."
71. Ibid.

the Shema's call to *love* God with all one's heart, soul, and mind which includes *loving* one's neighbor.

Henk Rijstenberg clarifies any misinterpretation of Torah as a type of legalism when he says, " . . . the Hebrew way of life was not a list of ethics and codes or lofty ideas."[72] Torah is instruction in "the way we should be walking before God . . . to pay close attention to the condition of our hearts as we interact with other members of the community and on the relationship with God especially while worshiping God."[73]

Elliptical Thinking

Probably one of the most difficult aspects of Hebraic thought is what Abraham Heschel called elliptical thinking. In stark contrast to the binary either-or model of Greek thought, he uses the geometric ellipse as a graphic model for Hebraic epistemology. Maintaining that philosophy of religion requires a tension between philosophy and religion, he states, "Philosophy of religion is involved in a polarity; like an ellipse it revolves around two foci: philosophy and religion . . . The failure to sense the profound tension of philosophical and religious categories has been the cause of much confusion."[74]

Ironically, apparent contradictions may be the source of order. While Greek thought pits one concept against another, Hebraic thought retains the tension. Take Creation for example. An invisible God spoke words to being matter from nothing to visible light, land, sea, plants, animals, and humankind. Invisibility and visibility are held together as opposites. The invisibility of God need not be an argument against created matter and all livings things. Heschel uses elliptical thinking to explain the unnecessary chaos surrounding any discussion of the Bible and science regarding Creation. "The Bible and science do not deal with the same problem."[75] Apples are different from oranges. He points out that science deals with space; Creation deals with time. Essentially, the Bible addresses a relationship between the Creator and the universe triggered by an *event*. Science, bounded by how things may have evolved, is concerned with

---

72. Rijstenberg, "Thinking Hebraically."
73. Ibid.
74. Heschel, *God In Search of Man*, 13.
75. Ibid., 16.

process, with no answer for first cause and clearly no subject interest in a relationship with God as first cause—Creator.

In this chapter we've sought to define Hebraic Thought focusing on the following important ideas: The Shema, orality and literacy, language, key characteristics and its differences with Greek Thinking. These pillars constitute the basis for how Jewish people think about the world. Our concern has not only been about knowledge; but more about *how we know* what we know.

We now shift gears from a formal treatment of thinking Hebraically to the story of Israel's forty-year journey through a desert. During this meandering trip, Hebraic thought regarding who God is and how He acts among His people continued to develop. The Story of Israel is next.

―― *Chapter 2* ――

The Story of Israel

IN THE PREVIOUS CHAPTER we introduced Hebraic thought. Now we will tell Israel's story by considering the *covenants* God made with the nation, its journey through a *desert*, and its arrival into the *land* God promised. We'll also get into key events, persons, and places shaped a community of tribes into a nation.

Scott McKnight says, "The Story of Israel, or the Bible, is the sweep of how the Bible's plot unfolds: the creation of the world as God's temple . . . Adam and Eve as divine image-bearers . . . God's [choice one person], Abraham, and then through him one people, Israel."[1] Abraham is the first patriarch of Israel who believed in one true living God and rejecting the surrounding polytheism of Mesopotamian gods and goddesses. He received the first covenant which informs all subsequent covenants to Moses, David, and Jeremiah. It reflects on the promises to Noah to never destroy all humanity ever again. We'll survey the following covenants: Noahic, Abrahamic, Mosaic, Davidic, and a new covenant predicted by Jeremiah.

---

1. Scott McKnight, *The King Jesus Gospel*, 35.

The Covenants

The Noahic Covenant

"God's relationship with Israel is most commonly described as a covenant . . . which conveys permanence, steadfastness, and mutuality . . . "[2] We may think of covenants as contracts between God and Israel, where each party holds the other accountable for keeping its side of the bargain. .

However, God's covenant with Noah is a one-way commitment of God to all humanity through Noah. God makes no explicit demand of Noah beyond building a large boat. After the annihilation of all creation through a global-flood, God promised the following:

> "I will establish my covenant with you and your descendants after you and with every living creature that was with you . . . Never again will all life be cutoff by the waters of a flood; never again will there be a flood to destroy the earth . . . This is the sign of the covenant . . . I have set my rainbow in the clouds, and it will be a sign of the covenant between me and the earth."[3]

Arnold R. Eisen states: "The generations leading up to Noah were *de*generations. God couldn't keep sending floods . . . Instead God turns to the more liberal solution: education. God will choose people, teach them God's way . . . give them perfect laws, and endow them with an abundant land . . . "[4] [author's italics]. God's covenant to Noah includes a removal of *de*struction, but the positive replacement of *in*struction—the Torah. He interprets the Noahic Covenant as a segue into God's second explicit covenant to Abraham, "the first Hebrew on earth."[5]

Yet, one key difference between the two covenants relates duration. Noah's ordeal lasts only forty days while the story of Israel involves approximately two millennia. The Noahic Covenant involves a brief encounter prompted by years of disobedience. The promise made to Abraham tells Israel's story with the back and forth of obedience and disobedience of God's laws.

---

2. Herschel, *The Prophets*, 90.
3. Genesis 9: 8—13.
4. Eisen, *Taking Hold of Torah*, 24.
5. Marvin R. Wilson, *Our Father Abraham*, 3. Wilson finds *Jew* and *Jewish* as interchangeable terms along with *Hebrew* and *Hebraic*, which we follow in this book.

The Abrahamic Covenant

God spoke the following to Abraham mentioned in three texts—Genesis 12, 15, and 17.

The first segment of the Abrahamic Covenant is a succinct statement of God's commitment to a people who will become a nation.

> "... I will make of you a great nation; I will bless you, and make your name great, and you shall be a blessing. I will bless those who bless you, and him who curses you I will curse; and all the families of the earth shall bless themselves by you."[6]

Partial fulfillment of the Abrahamic Covenant of Israel as a nation delivered from Egypt serves as a paradigm of freedom for all humanity. Future nations will understand the concept of liberty and freedom derived from God's liberation of Israel from Egypt—*you shall be a blessing*.

Jonathan Sacks points out that even during the oppression in Egypt, "What had been, at the end of Genesis, a family, has become a nation, just as God had said it would in his first words to Abraham ... "[7] He goes on to say that with the words of Abraham's covenant, "the very terms of Israel's existence are transformed."[8]

Second, the promise of land is offered in covenantal language :

> "I am HASHEM Who brought you out of Ur-kasdim to give you this land to inherit it ... HASHEM made a covenant with Abram saying, 'To your descendants have I given this land, from the river in Egypt to the great river ... "[9]

Following the multiple blessings of the first segment, and the land in this second segment, we address the covenant symbolized by circumcision in a third segment.

The *sign* of the Abrahamic Covenant is addressed in the following covenant statement echoing Genesis 12 with added promises and a *sign*:

> "I will set my covenant between Me and you, and I will increase you most exceedingly ... You shall be a father of a multitude of nations ... your name shall be Abraham[10] ... I will make

---

6. Genesis 12: 1—3.
7. Sacks, *Exodus*, 3.
8. Ibid.
9. Genesis 15: 7, 18.

10. *Abram* is changed to *Abraham* with this segment of the covenant like a king undergoing a name change when assuming a throne as that one who now will assume

> you most exceedingly fruitful, and make nations of you; and kings shall descend from you. I will ratify my covenant between Me and you and between your offspring . . . as an everlasting covenant . . . I will give to you . . . the land of Canaan—as an everlasting possession; and I shall be a God to them. Every male among you shall be circumcised. You shall circumcise the flesh of your foreskin, and that shall be the sign of the covenant between Me and you . . . And God said to Abraham. . I will bless Sarah and I will give you from her a son, and I will bless him, and she shall become nations, kings of peoples shall issue from her and you shall call your son, Isaac. I will establish my covenant with him."[11]

In the first segment, Abraham is promised to become the father of *one great nation*. In this third segment, God commits to making Abraham the father of a *multitude of many nations*. How was Abraham both the father of a great nation and many nations?

Of particular importance is the sign of the covenant: circumcision of the flesh. Abraham will be the father of many nations and Sarah will be involved with many nations and kingdoms through her son Isaac, this physical sign will permanently indicate that Jewish males are members of particular covenant made by God with Abraham. But what about the women of the nation? What will indicate that women, too, are members of the family?

Parenthetically, often neglected texts in the Torah may offer an answer? Leviticus 26: 41 connects disobedience of any member of the covenant with the unique phrase *uncircumcised heart*. What might this mean? Given the importance of the heart in Hebrews as the seat of one's mind, emotion, and will, an uncircumcised heart may be, as an invisible sign, a spiritual condition. Discussing the essence of the Law, Moses states in Deuteronomy 10: 16, "Circumcision, then, the foreskin of your heart, and do not be stubborn any longer." Such a cutting away may include any number sins obstructing the purity of a relationship with God which hinders the great command to love the LORD thy God with all one's heart.

Later in the context of God's faithfulness to Israel, Moses writes in Deuteronomy 30: 6, " . . . the LORD God will circumcise your heart and

---

full responsibility for the covenant. Also, both versions, Sarai and Sarah, mean *princess*. Alter, *The First Five Books of Moses*, 14.

11. Genesis 17: 2—19.

the hearts of your descendants . . . " Here God cut away the obstruction to anything which impedes obedience to the above command " . . . in order that you may live." God gives two commands related to circumcision—one physical as a permanent sign to remind Israel to whom it belongs, and one spiritual as a command to remove anything which obstructs complete obedience. Rabbi Bradley Shavit Artson interprets Deuteronomy 30: 6 to suggest that being alive means tearing "asunder the deadening wall encasing our hearts. In the words of the Torah, we must have the courage and the faith to circumcise our hearts anew."[12] He finds that the hard work of spiritual change will "open us to feel pain . . . Rooting that courage to circumcise in the presence of the Holy One, being nestled in the bosom of God, gives us the strength, the courage, and the faith to risk the pain, to feel the pain."[13]

The mention of Canaan in the second segment defines the geography of the *land* "from the river in Egypt to the great river the Euphrates,"[14] which is the land of ten nations. Rashi goes to the extent of saying that Abraham will become the father of all the world. Concrete land boundaries are really an expression of Hebraic thought going back to the Shema where only one true God exists and he is Israel's LORD. Also, the land referred to eventually includes the Persian Empire with King Cyrus playing a helpful role in the restoration of the nation after the Babylonian captivity. Marvin Wilson provocatively states that the Abrahamic Covenant is "only a preparation for the Sinaitic covenant into which it is absorbed.[15] Wilson's remarks taken in context suggest that a covenant is not a law, as sometimes thought, but "observance of the Mosaic Covenant is the opposite of an obstacle to a loving and intimate relationship with God. It is the vehicle and the sign of just that relationship."[16]

The mention of an *everlasting covenant with your offspring* is explained with the arrival of Isaac, who will father Jacob anticipating King David's eternal kingdom. A promise-command motif permeates the Torah, Prophets, and The Writings as a way of expressing *covenant*. Physical circumcision is a sign of belonging to a nation whose God is sovereign . Spiritual circumcision of the heart, with little mention in

---

12. Rabbi Bradley Shavit Artson, "The Soul of Sukkot: Circumcise Your Heart, " *Jewish Journal* (2023).

13. Ibid.

14. Genesis 15: 18.

15. Levenson, *Sinai and Zion*, 45.

16. Ibid.

the Torah, nevertheless is an invisible sign indicative of one's personal relationship with God.

In sum, the Abrahamic Covenant may be considered as the basis for all other covenants given to Israel, the next one of which we analyze now—the Mosaic Covenant.

The Mosaic Covenant

The promises given to Moses are more complicated than the clear statements of the covenant God made with Abraham. Most scholars agree that the six chapters of Exodus 19-24 contain the Mosaic Covenant. God's *covenant* given to Moses begins with the following statement in the Torah:

> "Now if today if you obey me fully and keep my covenant, then out of all nations you will be my treasured possession . . . you will be for me a kingdom of priests and a holy nation . . . "[17]

God continued with the Ten Commandments:

> "I am the Lord your God, who brought you out of the land of Egypt, out of the land of slavery. You shall . . . have no other gods before me . . . nor make for yourself an idol . . . nor bow down to them [idols] . . . nor misuse the name of the Lord your God . . . Remember the Sabbath day by keeping it holy . . . Honor your father and your mother . . . do not murder . . . do not commit adultery . . . do not steal . . . do not give false testimony . . . do not covet."[18]

God continued . . .

> "Whenever I cause my name to be honored, I will come to you and bless you."[19]

The practical stipulations covering a multitude of tasks and three festivals [Feasts of Unleavened Bread, Harvest, and Ingathering] are listed in Exodus 20: 22—24:

God continued with several *I will* statements:

> "I will be an enemy to your enemies . . . My angel will go ahead of you and bring you into the land . . . I will wipe them [your

---

17. Exodus 19: 5—6a.
18. Exodus 20: 2—17.
19. Ibid., 24b

enemies] out . . . God's blessing will be on your food and water . . . I will take away sickness from among you . . . none will miscarry or be barren . . . I will give you a full life span."[20]

We'll notice with the covenants that certain aspects are fulfilled within the span of the Elder Testament [Old Testament] and some remain unfulfilled. Clearly, the Ten Commandments remain intact as the basis for laws outside the Jewish community. Israel has given humanity the moral and legal basis for many laws across a diversity of cultures throughout world history.

Later, we'll get into those aspects of the Mosaic Covenant which are impacted by the absence of the Temple.

With the exception of the sacrificial penitential system of offerings [Exodus and Leviticus] of the Mosaic Covenant, all of God's covenants with humanity and Israel are eternal.

We now turn our attention to the covenant God made with David which extends to his son, Solomon.

The Davidic Covenant

God spoke the following Davidic Covenant through Nathan, a prophet during David's reign over Israel:

> " . . . I will make your name great . . . I will provide a place for my people Israel and will plant them so that they may have a home of their own and no longer be disturbed. Wicked people will not oppress them anymore . . . I will give you rest from all your enemies . . . the Lord will establish a house for you . . . I will raise up your offspring to succeed you, who will come from your own body, and I will establish his kingdom. He is the one who will build a house for my Name, and I will establish the throne of his kingdom forever. I will be his father, and he will be my son . . . my love will never leave him . . . Your house and your kingdom will endure forever before me; your throne will be established forever."[21]

The wording is similar to the Abrahamic Covenant . . . .I will make your name great . . . I will provide place . . . plant them so that they may

---

20. Exodus 23: 22b—26.
21. 2 Samuel 7: 9b—16.

have a home.[22] But there's much that's new. For the first time God speaks of establishing a house, which we understand to be the Temple. We must never forget that God requested only one thing from his people—the Tabernacle.[23] He never asked for a Temple.[24] Further, this Tabernacle, while designed with detailed specifications and very specific acts of priestly liturgy, was only temporary, while Israel traveled through the desert. It was never supposed to be permanent. Just as the wandering journey through a desert wasn't to last, neither was its mobile tent over which God spoke to Israel through Moses.

The house, a Temple, was a concession God granted to the nation. Even Solomon, its builder, questioned the confinement of the Temple for the God of Abraham, Isaac, and Jacob. During the Temple's dedication, he says, "But will God really dwell on earth? The heavens, even the highest, cannot contain you. How much less this temple that I have built!"[25] We see that the initial statements in the Davidic Covenant are fulfilled—David's name is known all over the civilized world, Israel has its homeland in a united kingdom, and the nation gets its desired Temple.

But nowhere in Israel's history do the wicked stop oppressing the nation—right up to today. This part of the Davidic Covenant has yet to be fulfilled and appears to track with another unfulfilled prophecy—regarding Solomon, God states he will grant him an eternal throne and kingdom, and in some way, even the "house" [Temple] will be eternal. In no place within Israel's story are these elements of the Davidic Covenant fulfilled. No note in the Tanakh attempts to explain the eternal aspects of a throne, Temple, and kingdom. The Tanakh *does* record the destruction of the Temple and the loss of David's kingdom. Robert Alter, one of Judaism's exegetical scholars, makes no attempt to explain this future eternal characteristic of David's kingdom. It remains an open question within both revealed and rabbinic literature.

So far, we've considered three explicit Covenants given to Abraham, Moses, and David. We now turn our attention to a new covenant that God gives to Prophet Jeremiah.

---

22. These "I will" statements echo the blessings from Genesis 12 and 15

23. Exodus 25: 8 "Then have them make a sanctuary for me, and I will dwell among them,"

24. 1 Samuel 7: 1—7. It is only David who longs for the Temple, not God. God never complained to Moses about not having a dwelling place with cedar walls.

25. 1 Kings 8: 27.

A New Covenant in Jeremiah

A new covenant [*brit hadashah*][26] is given to Jeremiah in the following words:

> "The time is coming when I will make a new covenant with the house of Israel and the house of Judah . . . This is the covenant that I will make with the house of Israel at that time. I will put my law in their minds and will write it on their hearts. I will be their God and they will be my people . . . they will all know me . . . I will forgive their wickedness and will remember their sins no more."[27]

Note the usage of *heart*. Might Jeremiah implying a circumcision of the heart?

After the exile from Babylon, echoing the words of Jeremiah, God said to the prophet Ezekiel:

> "I will give you a new heart and put a new spirit in you; I will remove your heart of stone and give you a heart of flesh. and I will put my Spirit in you and move you to follow my decrees and be careful to keep my laws."

Ezekiel also picks up on The Torah's earlier reference to a heart without any impurities which may impede one's relationship with God. But he doesn't go further to explain what this new heart might be other than the metaphor of a soft heart of flesh compared to a stone's hardness. *New spirit* and *Spirit in you* represent language never before used in the Tanakh to explain the covenants. What might Ezekiel's new vocabulary mean?

We've begun our look into Israel's story with a brief analysis of God's *covenants* to Noah, Abraham, Moses, David, and Jeremiah.

We now focus upon the nation's meandering journey through a *desert*.

"Although it's less than two hundred miles from the Suez in Egypt to Israel, it took Moses and the Israelites forty years to get there."[28]

---

26. Alter, Lit., "new covenant," noted by Alter as "designation for the Christian Scriptures ("New Testament"), *The Prophets*, 966.
27. Jeremiah 31: 31—34.
28. Zaslow, *Exodus*, 40.

The Desert

The covenants God revealed to Israel began through the patriarch Abraham and continued with Moses as he led God's people to the promised land. God, named YHWH,[29] led Israel out of slavery in Egypt through the halved[30] Red Sea. We will now survey of Israel's forty-year journey through a desert. Of particular interest are the following key events and places: a *burning bush, Passover, Exodus, Red Sea, bread, water, meat, the Law from Mount Sinai, Sabbath,* and *Tabernacle.*

The *burning bush*[31] is a key event where God established YHWH, the LORD, as his true name. This event is important as that place where God first states the coming exodus based upon his notice of Israel's suffering as slaves. "I have come down to rescue them . . . I have seen the way the Egyptians are oppressing them. So now, go. I am sending you to Pharoah to bring the Israelites out of Egypt."[32]

The *First Passover*[33] and the *Exodus*[34] are two pillars of remembrance in the story of Israel. Without the blood sacrifice of a perfect lamb, the angel of death would have killed Israel's firstborn. The blood of a lamb signaled that the angel would literally *pass over* that house. Jonathan Sacks' spiritual interpretation as the blood sacrifice may apply to Moses when he said, "This is the blood of the covenant that the LORD has made with you in accordance with all these words."[35] Note the connection between blood and covenant. Without the Exodus prompted by

---

29. R. Kendall Soulen, *Irrevocable*, 1. Soulen urges the use of YHWH, the unspoken Tetragrammaton acronym for "the unspoken personal proper name of God," the Ineffable God of Abraham, Isaac and Jacob and the God of Matthew, Mark, Luke, John, and the Apostle Paul. The one true living God named himself as the "I am that I am," when speaking to Moses through what appeared to be a burning bush. Soulen however cites the LORD, that Is YHWH [Exodus 3: 15], as the real name which was revered as the unspoken name, "The Name," for God.

30. Sacks, *Exodus*, 116. Sacks speaks of sacrifice as passing through the two halves of a slaughtered animal. This idea of passing in between the two halves of a dove or young pigeon begins in Genesis 15: 9—18 as the ratification of a covenant between two entities previously divided now united. While in Egypt, Pharoah owned Israel. When Israel passed through the "halves" of the Red Sea, they became God's people.

31. The real miracle in this event, which occurred on Mt. Horeb which is also called Mt Sinai, was that *Moses heard God's voice for the first time.*

32. Exodus 3: 8—10.

33. Exodus 12. The familiar stories about the plagues culminating in the Passover change Pharoah's mind and he releases the nation to the desert under Moses' leadership.

34. Exodus 13.

35. Exodus 24: 8.

plagues and Moses' intervention with Pharoah, it is highly likely that the nation might have been snuffed out by the Egyptians in revengeful genocide. That would have ended Israel's story. The story of Jewish survival began with the Exodus. That survival story continues today.

Passing through the *Red Sea* is both physically and spiritually important. The physical aspect of this milestone is obvious in that the nation literally passes through deep waters. Spiritually, God's abiding presence through a most harrowing experience continues to guide Israel on it journey.

Bread, meat, and water play a significant part in Israel's journey. A sticky substance of flakes on the desert floor provided their daily bread when baked into cakes. Quail offered them meat. Water, a necessity while walking through the heat, came out of a rock when Moses hit it with his staff. In all three events it is God's voice which is the supernatural element going back to when He spoke Creation into existence.

The *burning bush*, which was located on Mount Horeb [Mount Sinai],[36] anticipates a key event in the nation's trek through a desert— the giving of the Law.[37] After three months of travel, Israel camped at the foot of Mount Sinai [Exodus 19: 2], where God confirms his covenant to Abraham saying, "Now if you obey me fully and keep my covenants, then out of all nations you will be my treasured possession . . . you will be for me a kingdom of priests and a holy nation."[38] God's part of the bargain was to make Israel a special nation; Israel's part was obedience to God's commands.

Remembering the *Sabbath* became embedded in the life of Israel. "The day of rest is one of the great Jewish contributions to the comfort and joy of mankind."[39] Paul Johnson adds that "it was a holy day . . . being increasingly associated in the minds of the people with the belief

---

36. While no explicit biblical reference equates Mount Horeb and Mount Sinai, the biblical evidence suggests they are the same. Mt. Sinai is where God gave Moses the two tablets of testimony [Exodus 31:18]. The Israelites worshiped a golden calf at Horeb and we know that they did this at Mount Sinai [Exodus 32: 8].

37. Deuteronomy 1: 5 summarizes God's revelation of "this law" after 40 years of travel. A NIV note states that "this law" is the Ten Commandments and other laws given at Mount Sinai and recorded in Exodus 20—24, Leviticus, and Numbers.

38. Exodus 19: 5, 6. These words restate what God's first words in the covenant to Abraham about Israel becoming a great nation as a "kingdom of priests and a holy nation." This is an early statement of the Kingdom of God, an example of Hebraic Thought in and of itself which is borrowed by Christianity centuries later.

39. Paul Johnson, *A History of the Jews*, 38.

in the elect nation of God . . . "[40] As noted, the Hebrew people had no problem retaining paradox, while all other commandments instruct *how to behave*, the imperative to keep the Sabbath holy involves the *absence of any behavior*. *Remembering* and *keeping* are spiritual activities of the mind and spirit. This commandment is the only one explicitly linked with Creation where obedience requires resting as God did after six straight days of labor.[41]

Jon D. Levenson speaks of a Book of the Covenants, a Levitical law-code, and very long code in Deuteronomy 12—26.[42] Levenson weighs in on the vital importance of the *Sinai event*—"Sinai is not the final goal of the Exodus, but lying between Egypt and Canaan, it does represent YHWH's unchallengeable mastery over both."[43] God is king over Israel and all nations. Each area of sovereignty emanates from the Abrahamic covenant given in two parts: for Israel, Genesis 12 and for all nations, Genesis 15. Levenson concludes his discussion of Sinai emphasizing the voice of God: "There is, therefore, no voice more central to Judaism that the voice heard on Mount Sinai. Sinai confronts anyone who would live as a Jew with an awesome choice . . . whether God is or is not king . . . Sinai demands that the Torah be taken with radical seriousness . . . But alongside the burden of choice is . . . the love of YHWH for Israel, of a passionate groom for his bride . . . the intersection of love and law . . . the link between a past together and a future together."[44]

Then God makes a startling request. "Then have them make a sanctuary for me, and I will dwell with them. Make this *tabernacle*[45] and all its furnishings exactly like the pattern I will show you."[46] Practically speaking, any place of worship for a people constantly on the move

40. Ibid.

41. Exodus 20:8.

42. Levenson, *Sinai and Zion*, 18. He defines the Book of the Covenant as those laws contained in Exodus 20:22 –23:33, the Levitical code in Leviticus 17—26. All of these may possibly be part of *this law* from Deuteronomy 1: 5 as an elongated series of revelation dedicated to the nation's worship and lifestyle

43. Ibid., 23.

44. Ibid., 86.

45. The Hebrew pictograph for *tabernacle* uses symbols which refer to the shining light reflected off a tent as a guiding "star" when traveling . . . *shine* and *star* are original meanings of *tabernacle*, Benner, 104. The tabernacle was a mobile tent with intricate details for its construction and furniture. God chose to be present in a cloud over the Tabernacle when he spoke to Moses. The gathered people around Moses would actually be able to hear God's voice.

46. Exodus 24: 8, 9.

could not be stationary. Sacks entitles his discussion of the Tabernacle: *A Portable Home*.[47] He extols the merits of this temporary mobile tent that had a lasting memory linked to the future Temple, which while "intended to be permanent proved to be temporary—until, as we pray daily, it is rebuilt."[48]

The Tabernacle was uniquely adapted to people traveling through a wilderness, as pilgrims, in between Egypt and Canaan. The people pitched their tents and the Tent of Meeting throughout their journey. God dwelled among his people in and over the Tabernacle in the *Shekinah*,[49] a cloud through which YHWH spoke to Moses. The Shekinah Presence hovered over the Tabernacle. "The Tabernacle was erected in order that the Shekinah might dwell on earth and it actually entered the Holy of Holies."[50] Spiritually, we can derive genuine lessons for living as ordinary people of faith with our feet on the ground as sojourners just as the Jewish nation did. According to Stephen F. Olford, the Tabernacle "was always pitched on the sand . . . no provision was ever made to cover the sand. The contact of the priest's feet with the sand was a reminder that they were on a journey and had not reached their final destination."[51]

Hebraic concreteness is at work in the desert. Here we find a flaming bush, hearing God's voice emblematic of the Shema, the visceral concerns for the body by the people going hungry and thirsty in a wilderness of sand, the Sabbath as a day of bodily rest, and the Tabernacle as a dynamic place to worship. Though the Tabernacle was an important place to worship God, "Security belongs not to place but to person, not to a physical space on the surface of the earth, but to a spiritual place in the human heart."[52] Abraham's nomadic lifestyle as a sojourner without

---

47. Sacks, *Exodus*, 189.

48. Ibid.,191.

49. "Shekinah is the English name of God in its feminine, motherly manifestation. The original word means the dwelling or settling, and denotes the dwelling of settling of the Divine Presence of God . . . ," "I shall rest My Presence among the Children of Israel, and I shall be their God." Exodus 29: 45, Tanakh. "And I shall abide in the midst of the Israelite," Alter's translation of Exodus 29: 45. Alter, *The First Five Books of Moses*, 333.

50. Kohler and Blau, "Shekinah (lit., "the dwelling"), *Jewish Encyclopedia*. Kohler and Blau also mention the multiple ways to name the Shekinah: "God, the Name, light and the Holy Spirit." Finally, they state that, " . . . God took refuge under the wings of the Shekinah [Shab. 31]."

51. Olford, *The Tabernacle: Camping with God*, 16—7.

52. Sacks, *Exodus*, 324.

an inheritance or citizenship on earth found its security in a futuristic mystical Jerusalem.[53]

In sum, having looked into key milestones of Israel's long journey through a *desert*, we now turn our attention to that final phase of Israel's story—the *land*.

The Land

Rashi interpreted Israel's right to the land as the answer to why the Tanakh begins "with stories about trials and tribulations, the loves and losses, of ancestors. What bearing could Adam and Eve, the flood, and genealogies galore . . . possibly have on the yeses and noes of everyday life?"[54] That is, one interpretation of Rashi's explanation is that Israel deserves its own homeland for all that the nation has encountered. However, Israel's homeland involves God's undeserved grace to his beloved people. Grace is not about what anyone does or doesn't deserve. Grace is God's *hesed*,[55] his nature.

A Jewish homeland first occurs in the Abrahamic Covenant [Genesis 12: 1], "HASHEM said to Abram, 'Go for yourself from your land . . . to the land [Ur of the Chaldees] that I will show you.'"[56] A next mention of the land occurs in Genesis 13: 17 where YHWH essentially restates the original promise, "Go, walk through the length and breadth of the land, for I am giving it to you."[57] Scriptural references to a promised land, the holy land, or the land of Israel certainly constitute the concreteness of land as vital to the Jewish people. "For indeed, the major witnesses of Jewish theology see 'the Land as of the essence of Judaism.'"[58] God continues his conversation with Abraham in language reminiscent of the Torah's reminder that YHWH brought Israel of the land of Egypt. Here God says, "I am the LORD who brought you out of

---

53. Wilson, *Exploring Our Hebraic Heritage*, 91.

54. Eisen, *Taking Hold of the Torah*, 1.

55. Benner, *Ancient Hebrew Lexicon*, 338, "lovingkindness, as a bowing the neck as a sign of kindness . . . "

56. Alter notes that " . . . Abram becomes an individual character, and begins the Patriarchal narratives . . . ," *The First Five Book of Moses*, 40.

57. Alter explains a significant aspect of this text pointing out that the physical walking the dimensions of a piece of land was common legal ritual in the Near East going back to the thirteenth century B.C.E., 44.

58. Wilson, *Our Father Abraham*, 261, quoting W.D. Davies, *The Territorial Dimensions of Judaism*, 53.

Ur of the Chaldeans to give you this land to take possession of it."[59] Fast forwarding several centuries, Moses' career as journey leader concludes by handing off of the baton to Joshua for entrance into Canaan, which he calls "a land of hills and valleys."[60] Mountains, a river, the Mediterranean Sea, and the desert formed natural boundaries for this new land making it adaptable to unite tribes together as a whole.

The story of Israel continues as a function of God's covenants, the nation's journey through a desert, and entry into the promised land. The *land* is the tangible fulfillment of God's *covenants* with Israel and is the destination of a trip through a *desert*. Doing a rapid survey, we now consider the selected key milestones of Israel's history in the land from the thirteenth century to fifth century B.C.E. In each milestone we'll notice that settling down in the promised land didn't mean the end of conflict. Israel's story in the land includes *war, judges, kings* and *prophets, deportation, captivity*, and the restoration of a *city* and a *temple*.

Joshua ran an important leg in the relay race of Israel's entry into the promised land. He reflected his mentor's [Moses] faith as the moon is a reflection of the sun. No small amount of misunderstanding exists about the devastating *war* General Joshua waged obeying God's command to destroy everything in each city they conquered.[61] The penalty for retaining anything of value was punishable by death as told in the story of Achan. Why such devastation and execution? Could not the nation have entered and possessed the land peacefully? When the city of Ai was destroyed, Joshua murdered all women and children, impaled the king on a pole and piled stones on his body.[62] Ironically, in the very next verse the Tanakh states that Joshua built an altar to HASHEM . . . and he carved in stone the words of the Torah . . . and read them to the people.[63] This pattern of pillage and devastation of thirty-one Canaanite cities is documented in the first eleven chapters of Joshua. "The land then rested from war."[64] Admittedly, juxtaposed bloody wars no different from any conquering nation over another along with religious rituals of worship are problematic for many. That said, this apparent contradiction may find

59. Genesis 15: 7b.
60. Deuteronomy 11:11.
61. Joshua 6: 24, Everything in the city of Jericho was burned.
62. Alter, *The Prophets*, 537, Alter explains how dishonorable it was to hang someone on a tree, a sure sign of God's curse upon the victim.
63. Ibid., vv30—35.
64. Joshua 11: 23.

its resolution within a Hebraic epistemology which can retain tension and paradox in how it thinks.

Possession of land was incomplete without Israel's promise to maintain a wholehearted worship of God and "not to come into these nations which still remain with you; you shall not mention the name of their gods . . . "[65] During his farewell speech, Joshua tells the story of Israel to the people reiterating the removal of any foreigner's gods which remain and urges them to "direct your hears to HASHEM, the God of Israel."[66] The slaughtered people and destroyed cities with their many gods were examples that a holy and jealous God is sovereign. Polytheism would not be tolerated in the land of Israel. He emphasized the presence of a holy and righteous God among his people, One who consistently fought for the nation. God was to be the only God in the land of his people. The story of Israel included a faithful God who punished any nation who oppressed Israel. Joshua instructed Israel to worship the only God who is One.

Regarding the uniqueness of Israel's historical record, Paul Johnson asserts: "The Jews are the thus the only people in the world today who possess a historical record . . . "[67] The Book of *Judges* documents Israel's transition from a conquering army to a loose confederation of tribes. It "illuminates the essentially democratic and meritocratic nature of Israelite society."[68] It does so through a series of uniquely charismatic persons, not the least of which are women. "Certainly the Song of Deborah, which constitutes Chapter 5 of the Book of Judges . . . [includes a] . . . multitude of feminine images—a triumphal vindication of female strength . . . "[69] Women modeled constructive leadership in Israel's story.

The *judges*, typically one per tribe rather than a panel in charge of all the tribes, were not part of any formal aristocracy. Rather, they came from the lower classes, "semi-criminal types, outlaws and misfits, who become by their exploits folk-heroes and then in time religious heroes."[70] The left-handed Ehud, a juvenile delinquent Samson, poor and lowly Gideon whose son, the monster Abimelech, slaughtered seventy of his father's male children. Israel's disunited tribal system gave

---

65. Joshua 23: 7.
66. Joshua 24: 23.
67. Johnson, *A History of the Jews*, 6.
68. Ibid., 45.
69. Ibid., 15.
70. Johnson, *A History of the Jews*, 47.

rise to a chaos where "everyone did what was right in his eyes rather than what is right in God's eyes."[71]

Israel's disobedience in following other gods from the only partially-conquered cultures within its borders persisted as the nation's chief problem. While professing to be a theocracy, the story of Israel never includes one sustained period during which its people consistently obeyed the Shema and the first commandment about worshiping only the One true God. In "Canaan Israel had quickly forgotten the acts of God that had given her birth and had established her in the land . . . [where] the fundamental issue was the lordship of God in Israel . . . uniquely established by the covenant at Sinai."[72] The stage was set for a *king* to replace judges as a form of government; but this was not a solution to Israel's continuing spiritual battle to love God with all their heart. Samuel, Israel's greatest prophet-judge, provided a needed transition from the period of the judges to the establishment of a monarchy.

God never wanted either judges of *kings* to lead Israel. Each form of government emerged from the people. The establishment of Israel's monarchy exemplifies God's sovereignty—for what God doesn't intend, he often allows. Politically pressured to be like its surrounding nations, the people pushed Samuel to give them a king. Samuel appealed to God who told him, "'Listen to their voice, and crown a king for them.'"[73]

Even though God didn't command a *king* for Israel, he arranged the circumstances where Samuel would anoint the nation's first king—Saul. Samuel "hesitated to make him *melek* or hereditary king"[74] [author's italics]. Johnson describes Saul as a "dark, saturnine character . . . an unpredictable oriental potentate—bandit, alternating between sudden generosity and unbridled rage . . . always brave and clearly gifted, but often hovering on the brink of madness and sometimes slipping over it."[75] Saul was no Joshua. As guerilla fighter, the new king was unable to develop a strong military.

The turning point in his reign was Israel's perennial problem of disobeying YHWH's voice by pitying a defeated enemy rather than fully destroying it. Because Saul retained the spoils of war, namely the best of

71. Exodus 15: 26. Tanakh.
72. Davis and Herbert Wolf, NIV Introduction to Judges, "Theme and Theology," 325.
73. Ibid., 1 Samuel 8: 22.
74. Johnson, *A History of the Jews*, 53.
75. Ibid., 52-3.

the enemy's sheep he wished to sacrifice, he fell out of favor with God, who told Samuel, "I have reconsidered My having made Saul king, for he has turned away from Me and has not fulfilled My word!"[76] Saul preferred the sound of bleating sheep in his ears rather than the voice of God. The process of deposing Israel's first king exemplifies a lesson for both Israel then and all persons of faith now. "To obey is better than sacrifice."[77]

Saul substituted religion for the Shema. That is, he replaced genuine faith in the only LORD with false piety and didn't recall the mandate to "Hear, O Israel . . . " which always meant that the people should prove they've heard God's voice by doing the right thing. Would that Israel have learned this lesson early in their experience as a united kingdom ruled by one king, who in Saul's case proved to be an unmitigated disaster. But God did not fault the nation either for its desire for a king or because it put Saul in power. Instead, God selected David, a least likely candidate for a king and the nation anointed him in Jerusalem after Saul's death in battle. "All the elders of Israel came to the king at Hebron, and King David sealed a covenant with them in Hebron before HASHEM, and they anointed David as king over Israel."[78]

Recall that the Davidic Covenant included that Solomon, not he, would build Israel's first temple, but even more importantly, "Your dynasty and your kingdom . . . [and] your throne will remain firm forever."[79] There's a certain irony to the tension between not building the temple while at the same time being told about *your* eternal throne. We've already observed how Hebraic thought allows for holding two apparently contradictory facts in tension. What is surprising about so important a text is that no note in the Tanakh nor in Alter's commentary makes any reference to so great a claim—the eternal kingdom and throne of David. History records that David's kingdom officially ended when Solomon became king. Any apparent earthly continuation of David's throne clearly vanished when the kingdom split into two kingdoms, Judah and Israel. Each had its own assortment of good and bad actors as monarchs. All of which begs the question: When would David's kingdom and throne become eternal? The Tanakh is silent on this question.

Solomon's reign continued to fulfill the Davidic Covenant, but without his father's heart for God. "Where David was passionate, rash,

---

76. 1 Samuel 15: 11.
77. I Samuel 15: 22b.
78. II Samuel 5: 3.
79. II Samuel 7: 16

willful, sinful but repentant, conscious of sin, ultimately pure in heart and God-fearing, Solomon was a secular person: a man of his world and age to the bottom of his heart . . . "[80]

The Tanakh lists eight categories of historic literature under the heading, "The *Prophets*," beginning with Joshua's entrance into the promised land concluding with the prophet Malachi.[81] A complete analysis of the reasons for the united kingdom under the name Israel evolving into two kingdoms is beyond the scope of this book. In a sentence, Solomon's disobedience of intermarriage with its idolatry[82] was the spiritual reason for the split accompanied by political issues related to taxes, forced labor, and refusal to submit to King Rehoboam, Solomon's son, who reigned over the one-tribe southern kingdom Judah. Israel, the northern kingdom was comprised of ten tribes. The split occurred in 930 B.C.

The *prophets* spanned the reign of several kings for each kingdom. For example, Isaiah prophesied in Judah "during the reigns of Uzziah, Jotham, Ahaz and Hezekiah,"[83] and Jeremiah was prophet to Judah from "the thirteenth year of Josiah . . . Jehoiakim . . . to the fifteen month of the eleventh year of Zedekiah."[84] The kingdom of Israel began in 909 B.C. ended in 722 B.C when the Assyrians forced the people to relocate to other parts of their empire while Assyrians relocated into the conquered territory.

The southern kingdom began in about 913 B.C. and ended in 586 B.C. when Babylonian King Nebuchadnezzar deported 10,000 Jews to his capital in Babylon.[85] During Israel's two centuries of eighteen kings, the issues were both spiritual, ethical, and political involving the accommodation of foreign gods—a precedent set by King Solomon.

For example, in Israel, "Ahab . . . did more to provoke the LORD, the God of Israel, to anger than did all the kings of Israel before him."[86] That is, he violated the name of Israel's one God by worshiping the god of Sidon, marrying Jezebel, the king of Sidon's daughter, and set up temple and altar to Baal making it the official religion of Israel. The *prophet* Elijah ministered in Israel and prophesied the consequences of Ahab's idolatry

80. Johnson, *A History of the Jews*, 59.
81. Tanakh, 515.
82. 1 Kings 11: 11—13, 29—39.
83. Isaiah 1: 1.
84. Jeremiah 1:1—3.
85. Ibid.
86. I Kings 16: 33b.

saying to him, "As the LORD, the God of Israel, lives, whom I serve, there will neither dew nor rain in the next few years except at my word." This pattern of kingly disobedience and prophetic response occurred throughout both kingdoms.

The assimilation of the Israel into Assyria and the *deportation and captivity* of Judah to Babylon mark the end of each kingdom. The "first great mass tragedy in Jewish history took place"[87] with the Assyrian assimilation and deportation of Israel. The annihilation of Israel occurred with a forced march to Assyria where "the ten tribes of the north moved out of history and into myth . . . losing their faith and their language . . . In Samaria, Israelite peasants . . . intermarried with the new settlers . . . In the eyes of Jerusalem and its priests, the northerners had always mingled with the pagans."[88]

The Babylonian Captivity of Judah was not as severe as the Assyrian Deportation. "There was . . . one vital difference between the Babylonian conquest of Judah and the Assyrian descent on the north. The Babylonians were much less ruthless. They did not colonize . . . the poor people could cling to their religion . . . cities were left intact . . . it was a diaspora as well as an exile . . . many fled to the north, to Samaria . . . or to Egypt."[89]

The continuation of the kingdom of Judah maintained the covenant given to Abraham—that God would continue to bless Israel and all nations on earth through his chosen people.

Two key figures, Ezra and Nehemiah, surface in about 530 B.C. after the release of Judah from captivity by Persian King Cyrus who the Tanakh records is anointed[90] by God to *restore* his people. "In the first year of Cyrus, king of Persia, in order to fulfill the word of the LORD spoken by Jeremiah, the LORD moved the heart of Cyrus the king of Persia to make a proclamation throughout his realm: "The LORD, the God of heaven, has given me all the kingdoms of the earth and he has appointed me to build a *temple* for him at Jerusalem in Judah."[91] What an amazing shift in response to God's people by a foreign king! What can only be attributed

---

87. Johnson, *A History of the Jews*, 70.

88. Ibid., 70—1.

89. Ibid., 78.

90. Heschel, *The Prophets*, 772. Alter frames *anointed* in this verse as more a political than theological term; however, what's special is that God has a unique role for Cyrus to play in the historical restoration of the Jewish people.

91. Ezra 1: 1—2.

to God's sovereignty, Jerusalem and its walls would now be supported with finances and materials for the needed reconstruction.

Ezra oversaw the rebuilding of the *temple*; Nehemiah managed the reconstruction of Jerusalem's *city* wall. The book of Ezra states: "Then the people of Israel—the priests, the Levites and the rest of the exiles—celebrated the dedication of the house of God with joy . . . and they installed . . . priests and the Levites for the service of God . . . according to what is written in the Book of Moses."[92] When the city walls were completed, the book of Nehemiah records, "At the dedication of the wall of Jerusalem, the Levites were . . . brought to Jerusalem to celebrate joyfully the dedication with songs of thanksgiving and with the music of cymbals, harps and lyres."[93]

We began the story of Israel with God's revelation of the *covenants*, wanderings in a *desert,* and entrance into the promised *land*. The Noahic promise of a rainbow signaled no future global flood for all humanity. The covenants given to Abraham, Moses, David, and a new covenant mentioned by Jeremiah were uniquely designed for the Jews, God's selected people. In between the uniqueness and universal impact of certain covenants, we can rightly observe that a blessing was intended for all humanity through the Jewish people.

Moving on from the covenant to the *desert,* we noted several supernatural events all characterized by a person who actually heard the LORD's voice without ever seeing him—from a burning bush to clouds on the top of Mount Sinai. Finally, we briefly surveyed the history of a fledgling nation in their own *land*. There, Israel went from a loose confederation of tribes led by an assortment of judges to a kingdom unified under three kings only to become fractured into two separate kingdoms, each with its own set of prophets and good or bad kings. A common theme among all prophets no matter the kingdom was the need to return to God to maintain the purity of worship of the God who gave them the Shema, the Tabernacle, the Shekinah Presence, and all the commandments.

We now make a significant shift in genre from philosophical thought and historical narrative to a prominent rabbinic teaching method which combines both thought and story– the Hebraic parable.

---

92. Ibid., 6: 16. 18.
93. Nehemiah 12: 27—8.

Chapter 3

The Hebraic Parable

So far, we've discussed how Hebraic thought informs the adventurous story of Israel. This chapter addresses the medium through which Hebraic Thought and Israel's history were orally handed down throughout its generations using parables and stories.

The Parable

In his robust tome, *Stories with Intent*, Klyne Snodgrass states that any parable "in its broadest sense refers to an expanded analogy . . . Such analogies . . . are *used to explain or convince*.[1] [author's italics]. He dismisses the historic reduction of parables to allegories or mere illustrations. He cites "a first-century definition of fable . . . – the genre to which parables belong—as 'a fictitious saying picturing truth,' . . . "[2] Better yet, Snodgrass compares parables to imaginary gardens containing real toads.

Warren W. Wiersbe talks about parables in three ways: a *story* about a situation, a *mirror* of insight reflecting on a hearer's life, and a *window* through which the hearer may envision God. Amy-Jill Levine says, " . . . that parables and tellers of parables were there to prompt them [hearers] to see the world in a different way, to challenge, and at times to indict."[3] Levine's frank perspectives are especially helpful given her Jewish roots

---

1. Snodgrass, *Stories With Intent*, 2.
2. Ibid., 8.
3. Levine, *Short Stories of Jesus*, 4.

as a professor of New Testament in a Protestant divinity school. Bill Bjoraker's definition of parables as story speaks of their Hebrew and Jewish roots informed by "the master story of the universe by which all smaller stories are given their meaning."[4] He states that the theology of Israel is based on story, and that "*Hear O Israel* is fundamental to human communication."[5] [my italics]. This is a prime example how the *Shema* may be applied to parables. Bjoraker emphasizes the importance of orality as a medium which conveyed the truth of God's master story. Stories are first heard and then written. "There are regions of the human brain that have neurons that light up and retain memory of story and song longer and deeper than most of the propositional prose that a person reads. God has 'wired' us as human beings to connect at a deeper level than the cognitive."[6] Susan Niditch, supporting Bjoraker's focus on orality, says that "an oral aesthetic infuses Hebrew Scripture as it now stands. Without an understanding of this aesthetic . . . we cannot fully appreciate the literature of ancient Israel preserved in the Bible."[7]

Linguistically, *parable* is derived from the Greek verb *paraballo* [lit., "compare, to throw together"]. Confining *parable* to its Greek origins limits a more complete understanding which is better rendered by the Hebrew *mashal* which may be translated as parable, but also more widely as a song, saying, oracle, taunt or proverb.[8] Jeremy Schipper stresses that a mashal is best defined "not by its type and form, be it a proverb, a parable . . . or a song. Rather, we should concentrate on its content and function."[9] Unlike a traditional approach, Schipper concludes that parables may be drawn from *any* genre, not necessarily from a *specific* type of genre.

There are two technical terms associated with a parable: the *mashal* and the *nimshal*. A *mashal* is a story; a *nimshal* may be defined as "the reality portrayed by a parable."[10] A nimshal is the moral of the story. Nimshals are the applications, actions or decisions a hearer is to

---

4. Bjoraker, "The Place of Story and Storytelling in Messianic Jewish Ministry: Rediscovering the Lost Treasures Hebraic Narrative."

5. Ibid.

6. Ibid.

7. Niditch, *Oral World and Written Word*, 24.

8. Schipper, "Breaking Down Parables: Introductory Issues," from *Parables and Conflict in the Hebrew* Bible.

9. Ibid.,

10. Rabbi Ben Zeev, Niddah 17b—"So, What's the Nimshal." *Core Emunah*.

take having heard the mashal. For example, there's a story about a lame man and a blind man who were unable to protect vineyard. The lame man couldn't get around the entire vineyard and the blind man couldn't see whether the grapes were ripe or not. So the owner said each could keep his job if the blind man put the lame man on his shoulders working together to protect the vineyard. That's the mashal. The nimshal of the story may be that collaborative work is better than working alone. Typically only one main nimshal exists for each mashal. The mashal is designed to get a hearer's attention; the nimshal is the persuasive force which often demands an act of justice.

Hebraic parables were initially delivered orally and only later written down. Recall the *Shema* summoning Israel "Hear, O Israel! . . . not Read, O Israel!"[11] Bjoraker derives his thinking from Creation where God *speaks* everything into existence. For example from Creation, trees were spoken into existence. It may have been like, "Hear, O Earth, it's time for trees to appear!" The spoken parable ushers meaning into existence giving life to words communicating the need to act. Taking the entire Bible as story, its nimshal may be that "The purpose of the Book of the Lord is to know the Lord of the Book."[12]

Susan Niditch concludes that an "interplay between oral and literate mentalities emerges beautifully in the writings of the Hebrew Bible."[13] Niditch gets into Daniel's way of discovering nimshals from mashals using wordplay—"a technique used for dream interpretation in the Near East."[14] She maintains that a particular image in a dream may apply to the life of the hearer. To that extent, dream interpretation may fall under the notion of nimshal as the call to decision for action. "Dreamers dream of Torah passages that require explanation and application to their life situations . . . "[15] We find common ground between parables and dream interpretation to the degree that both pertain to one's life. Given the wide range of meaning that accompanies a nimshal, the prophet *Ezekiel himself becomes a parable* as the medium of communication. God says to the prophet, "Open your mouth and eat that

---

11. Bjoraker, "The Place of Story and Storytelling in Messianic Jewish Ministry: Rediscovering the Lost Treasures of Hebraic Narrative."

12. Ibid.

13. Niditch, *Oral World and Written Word*, 133.

14. Ibid., 81.

15. Ibid.

which I give you."[16] What the prophet digests, he speaks to the people. This is an extreme example of a prophet's role as a communicator of God's word designed to get the attention of hearers.

"In Jewish thought, parables belong to a style of teaching known as *agadah* . . . or story-like . . . approach to theology . . . a highly effective tool for communicating subtle aspects of the biblical texts . . . "[17] [author's italics]. *Halakah* refers to specific laws of ritual and purity. Parables are more useful for conveying aggadic thought than halakic laws. "The *aggadah* leaves Scripture in its representative form . . . and closer to an understanding of the common man . . . adapting Scripture to the understanding of the masses . . . "[18] [author's italics]. "Halakah is ultimately dependent upon agadah . . . its ultimate authority."[19] Heschel compares halakah to the tension between the lawgiver and the psalmist or between inwardness and outward behavior. Without aggadah, Judaism becomes a letter of the law; without halakah, it is reduced to light-blocking inwardness. The Hebraic parable seeks to retain both law and light, principle and obedience, and teaching with action.[20] Another example of a *both-and* in Hebraic thought.

No small debate surrounds the difference between allegory and parable. Essentially, an allegory is a fictionalized writing of symbolic features where each represents something other than itself. That is, an allegory requires an outside referent. Amy-Jill Levine says, "A parable requires no external key to explain what its elements mean; an allegory does."[21] As we analyze the parables more closely, it is important not to fall into the trap of assigning specific meaning to each character in the story as symbolic of something outside the parable. For example, recent biblical scholarship demonstrates that the Song of Songs in The Writings of the Tanakh is simply an erotic love story between a man and a woman. It need not symbolize the love between God and Israel or between God and the individual soul. "Through allegorization the reader will no doubt receive some kind of communication; but it is highly doubtful that it will be what the author intended to say . . . the allegorization of the Song of Songs was

16. Ezekiel 2: 9.
17. Young, *Meet the Rabbis: Rabbinic Thought and the Teachings of Jesus*, 33.
18. Guttman, *Philosophies of Judaism*, 341.
19. Heschel, *God in Search of Man*, 338.
20. Young, *The Parables: Jewish Tradition and Christian Interpretation*, 8. Note: Young quotes Heschel's *God in Search of Man*, 336-37.
21. Levine, *Short Stories of Jesus*, 7.

not the original . . . it was a later development."[22] However, this is not to say that Scripture doesn't make good use of allegories.

Given a brief definition of the Hebraic parable and a cursory discussion of its characteristics, we'll now discuss the parables in the Tanakh and Talmud.

Parables in the Tanakh

When authors of the Psalms told Israel's story to their children, they spoke in parables. "Listen, my people to my teaching . . . I will open my mouth with a parable. I will utter [and explain] riddles from antiquity . . . He [HASHEM] established a testimony in Jacob and set down a Torah in Israel . . . "[23] Rabbi Hirsch has this comment: "Rather than 'parables' . . . in the usual sense, the psalm reviews the events of Jewish history. The events of Israel's history are parables in the sense that they are objective lessons for all time."[24] Furthermore, the personal histories of *any* human being are parables, for they tell a story, offer insight into oneself, and suggest a way to envision God. The parable of one's life may be considered a mashal in which a moral, decision, or ethic is communicated as a nimshal. Your life may offer others an insight into themselves; it may also provide someone a new vision of God.

The following story from The Writings speaks of a human being who wants to live *the good life*:

> Praiseworthy is the man who walked not in the counsel of the wicked, and stood not in the path of the sinful, and sat not in the session of scorners. But his desire is in the Torah of HASHEM, and in His Torah he meditates day and night. He shall be like a tree deeply rooted alongside brooks of water, that yields its fruit in its season, and whose leaf never withers; and everything he does will succeed. Not so the wicked; rather [they are] like chaff that the wind drives away. Therefore the wicked shall not be vindicated in judgment, nor the sinful in the assembly of the righteous—for HASHEM attends the way of the righteous, while the way of the wicked will perish.[25]

---

22. Fields, "Early and Medieval Jewish Interpretations of the Song of Songs," *Grace Theological Journal*, 231.

23. Psalm 78: 1—4, Tanakh note.

24. R'Hirsch, Tanakh, Note on Psalm 78: 2.

25. Psalm 1.

Admittedly, this is an extended simile and metaphor, not a parable in the true sense of the word. Yet, we find a mashal in a story of a person whom God's chooses to bless based upon his righteous desires and lifestyle. Psalms were first heard in congregational Temple worship sung by Levite priests as part of Israel's Oral Tradition. Composer King David was "the harp upon which his own emotions sing or weep . . . everyone can see himself mirrored in David's psalms."[26] The takeaway, the nimshal, may be that "the keys to good fortune are to shun evil and to study the Torah.[27] Or, a moral of the story may be that pursuing righteousness leads to enjoying God's presence in your life. David's psalms express sorrow, grief or frustration as well as joy, thanksgiving or resolution. A thematic nimshal common to all aspects of his life may be that no matter what his experience, God's presence assured him that he never went through any situation alone.

The prophet Ezekiel uses an allegory whose symbolic fictional characters are a lioness and her cubs.

> Oh how your mother was a lioness . . . rearing her cubs among the young lions. She raised one of her cubs and made him into a young lion. He learned how to prey . . . the nations were mustered against him . . . she raised another cub . . . and he devoured men . . . They put him in a collar with hooks and brought him to the king of Babylon.[28]

The lioness is the Congregation of Israel; her two cubs are Kings Jehoahaz and Jehoiakim, sons of Josiah.[29] A possible nimshal might be that God disciplines his people for disobedience. Without the stated interpretation, the allegory would be difficult to take beyond a story about lions with the unique comparison of someone's [your] mother to a lion. History, as an outside reference, is required to determine that the two cubs are the mother's two sons Jehoahaz and Jehoiakim fathered by King Josiah. So the mother is Israel whose family is carted off to Babylon. We know that Ezekiel himself was one of those taken captive. Beyond extended metaphors, similes, and allegories, we can now show how parables differ as unique genres in the oral tradition of Israel. That is, rather than

---

26. Tanakh, "Introduction to the Psalms," 1437.
27. Ibid., Note.
28. Ezekiel 19: 1—4.
29. Tanakh note on Ezekiel 19:2.

drawing from one particular genre, parables may possibly employ several genres, or constitute their own genre.

Let's take a look at a classic Tanakh parable about the prophet Nathan and King David from a paraphrased version of 2 Samuel 12: 1—7:

> There were two men in one city; one rich and one poor. The rich man had very many sheep and cattle, but the poor man had nothing except one small ewe that he had acquired. He raised it and it grew up together with him and his children. It ate from his bread and drank from his cup and lay in his bosom; it became like a daughter to him. A wayfarer came to the rich man. He was reluctant to take from his own sheep or cattle to prepare for the visitor who had come to him, so he took the poor man's ewe and prepared it for the man who had come to him.

David was livid with the injustice of the rich taking from the poor and said to Nathan "As HASHEM lives, any man who does this deserves to die! And he must pay fourfold for the ewe, because he did this deed, and he had no pity." To which Nathan replied, "You are that man!"[30] The mashal is fictional, but gets David's attention. However, the nimshal is jarring for David who is obviously blindsided and ends up indicting himself. Note that Nathan didn't go directly to David with an accusation of adultery and murder—David committed adultery with a general's wife and purposely sent her husband into battle so that he might be killed. Nathan uses a parable to get a difficult point across to a king who may think he's above the moral law of Torah. Nathan has obviously set David up to make the point. At the same time, since David indicted himself, Nathan didn't have to. "The shock of Nathan's parable is that the one condemned is the parable's intended target, David himself; he was able to recognize, finally, the gravity of his sin."[31] David now knows he must do something. The nimshal has taken effect. He needs to make a decision, which is the successful outcome for any effective parable. We know that his decision was admission and confession. In Psalm Fifty-One David writes, "Have mercy on me, O God. according to your steadfast love . . . blot out my transgressions. Wash me thoroughly from my iniquity, and cleanse me from my sin . . . Then I will teach transgressors your ways, and sinners will return to you." While the parable brings David to his knees, there are consequences. He marries Bathsheba; the

---

30. 2 Samuel 12: 5—7a.
31. Levine, *Short Stories of Jesus*, 6.

birth of their son conceived in adultery dies. Scripture records that David consoled his wife in the loss of their baby.

The preceding parable is rather straight forward, unlike the one below taken from the prophet Isaiah.

> If one plows to sow, does he plow all day, [endlessly] opening and furrowing his land? Surely when he smooths its surface he will scatter black caraway and throw around cumin; he will place wheat by measure and barley where designated and spelt by its border!... For not with a threshing board is black caraway threshed, nor does a wagon wheel roll over cumin; rather it is with a staff that black caraway is beaten, and cumin with a stick. [Wheat for] bread is pounded; but not forever does one thresh it, for even if he rolls his wagon wheel with its implements until they fall apart, he will not have milled the wheat ... [32]

Rashi's explains a nimshal this way: God's admonitions are likened to plowing and his punishments to sowing. Farmers don't continuously plow without planting, so God doesn't warn unless He is ready to carry out His threats. The purpose of the threat is to prompt repentance, and its degree varies with the receptivity of the sinner. Sinners are like cumin and caraway [they require a minimum of threshing, and wheat requires more threshing, but not endlessly, because too much threshing can damage the wheat for flour]. In all three cases, God uses only what's needed in the appropriate degree to prompt repentance.[33]

Finally, the prophet Hosea issues a parable to graphically demonstrate Israel's unfaithfulness to God just as a husband who marries an adulteress. Hosea *is* the parable. He marries Gomer, a prostitute, giving birth to three children whose names express God's harsh treatment of a nation requiring *teshuvah*—a return to God. This is the story of his life. His ordeal is a parable which holds up a mirror such that Israel may gain an insight into its spiritual adultery and unfaithfulness to God.

We paraphrase the mashal below:

> When the LORD began to speak through Hosea the LORD said, Go marry an adulterous woman and children of unfaithfulness because the land is guilty of the vilest adultery. So he married Gomer and she bore him a son, named Jezreel which means 'God scatters.' Gomer then had a daughter named Lo-Ruhamah which means 'God shows no love.' Gomer then had another son,

32. Isaiah 28: 23—29.
33. Ezekiel 28: 23—29, Tanakh, Rashi note.

Lo-Ammi, which means 'You are not my people.' God said that he would end up loving Israel after he disciplines her and call the nation 'sons of the living God.'[34]

The context of Hosea's entire prophecy is twofold—God's punishment of Israel for its sins of unfaithfulness and idolatry and then by his mercy and grace, God restores the kingdom. A succinct nimshal of this parable modeled by Hosea's life may be: Because God is just, disciplines and restores sinners. Just like Isaiah's parable about the farmer above, God's punishment is a means to an end; that is, He punishes so that his people may see their need to return to Him. God is not out to break an individual or an entire nation. He desires repentance leading to reconciliation. God's motives are always pure. His means *do* justify the ends.

Brad H. Young refers to Hosea's parable as "The King Who was Reconciled with His Wife."[35] There is no parable in all of Scripture which better exemplifies the tension that accompanies apparent contradictions. For example, Jezreel, "God scatters," is reconciled when the LORD tells Hosea, "The people of Judah and the people of Israel will be reunited."[36] Later, the second child, Lo-Ruhamah, 'not my loved one,' is later reconciled, "I will show love to the one I called 'Not my loved.'"[37] Finally, Lo-Ammi, "you are not my people," is later reconciled, "I will say to those I called, 'not my people,' You are my people."[38] There is no apparent reason for God's change of heart in the three above reconciliations. The first two chapters in Hosea are riddled with first-person statements by God about how harshly He will act toward both northern and southern kingdoms. This mashal speaks of Hosea reconciling with his adulteress wife even though she is loved by another man. God asks his prophet to do what is unheard of; that is, to get back together with his adulteress wife while she's involved with another man. God asks Hosea to play His part in the drama of the nation's estrangement from Himself even when Israel continues to worship other gods. A nimshal? Maybe the love of a sovereign God for his covenant people is steadfast even when they don't uphold their end of the bargain.

34. Hosea 1: 2—10.
35. Young, *Jesus and His Jewish Parables*, 75ff.
36. Hosea 1: 4, 11a.
37. Ibid., 1: 6 and 2: 23b.
38. Ibid., 1: 9 and 2: 23c. Note how soon after God's rejection of Israel as his people does He then say in 1: 10b, "they will be called 'sons of the living God.'"

THE HEBRAIC PARABLE 53

The Torah, Prophets, and Writings are replete with statements about God's sovereignty as LORD over the world. Parables in the Tanakh show nimshals which address God's control over and involvement in the universe as a sovereign King. We now turn our attention to parables in the Talmud and Oral Tradition which often help to interpret those stories in the Tanakh.

Parables in the Talmud

Just as the Tanakh records the revealed sacred literature of the Jewish faith, the Talmud may be considered commentary as the record of Judaism's rich Oral Tradition. In this section, we'll get into Talmud's fictional stories authored by writers who "believed in the pedagogic importance of the parable, and regarded it as a valuable means of determining the true sense of the Law . . . "[39] A correct understanding of the Torah includes study of halakah, haggadah and parables. Parables convey the existence of God and His method of retribution, His faithful governance, His impatience with injustice and His relation to Israel. "Thus parables dealing with kings were frequently chosen to illustrate God's relation to the world in general and to Israel in particular."[40]

For example, a pagan philosopher once asked Rabbi Gamaliel why God is angry with idolaters and not with idols, where upon the rabbi answered, "A King had a son who raised a dog which he named after his royal father; and whenever he was about to swear he said, 'By the life of the dog, the father.' When the king heard of this, against whom did his anger turn, against the dog or against the son? Surely only against the son."[41] Here we have a quite simple parable in response to a particular question. A possible nimshal might be a warning against blame shifting, rather than owning one's own sin.

The following Talmudic parable tells a story about an emperor who asked a rabbi how punishment could exist after death since the body and soul were separated and could not blame each other for sins they were unable to commit. Recall that it was in a garden that the first sin of humanity was blaming another rather than taking responsibility for one's

---

39. Bacher and Jacob Zallel Lauterbach, "Parable."
40. Ibid.
41. 'Ab. Zarah 54b.

own disobedience. Here's an extended version of a story about a lame and blind man in a garden:

> A certain king had a beautiful garden in which was excellent fruit; and over it he appointed two watchmen, one blind and the other lame. The lame man said to the blind one, 'I see exquisite fruit in the garden. Carry me there that I may get it; and we will eat it together.' The blind man consented and both ate of the fruit. After some days the lord of the garden came and asked the watchmen concerning the fruit. Then the lame man said, 'As I have no legs I could not go to take it'; and the blind man said, 'I could not even see it.' What did the lord of the garden do? He made the blind man carry the lame, and thus passed judgment on them both. So God will replace the souls in their bodies, and will punish both together for their sins.[42]

This mashal contains its nimshal as the last sentence. The togetherness of body and soul is a key Hebraic concept. It counters Greek Gnosticism which always seeks to divide soul and body by defining salvation as the escape of the good soul from the evil body. As we've already noted, the *Shema* speaks of loving God holistically; that is, physically, mentally, and spiritually. The lame man tries to absolve himself of wrongdoing using his physical inability to go anywhere near the fruit. The blind man's self-justification is that he cannot see the fruit. Taken separately each alibi appears reasonable. However, there can be no split or division because all persons are created in God's image as wholly integrated human beings in body, mind, soul, and spirit.

Brad Young offers another interpretation. He sees the two workers as resurrection and final judgement. "The question concerning the bodily resurrection and the judgment of the soul was intriguing to the minds of Israel's sages."[43] Hebraic thought always allows for holding together two apparently opposite concepts [Heschel's elliptical thinking]. Judaism consistently resolves apparent contradictions looking through a *both-and* lens rather than the Greek *either-or* way of thinking.

Here's a brief Talmudic parable from the fourth century which, like many Talmudic parables, interprets a truth from the revealed Tanakh:

> There was one who sat at the crossroads; one path was smooth at its beginning, but its end was thorny, and the other path was thorny at the beginning, but its end was smooth. He would tell

---

42. Sanh. 91a, b.
43. Young, "The Parables of Talmudic Literature," *Jesus and His Jewish Parables*, 66.

those who were coming and going, 'You see this path which is smooth at its beginning? For two or three steps you walk in it smoothness but it ends up in thorns. You see this other path which is thorny at its beginning. For two or three steps you walk in thorns, but it ends up in smoothness. He encouraged the travelers to take the path which begins with thorns.[44]

The two texts from which this parable comes are Deuteronomy 11: 26 and 30: 19: "I have set before you life and death, blessing and cursing and you shall choose life, so that you may live, you and your offspring . . ." The nimshal from the Torah is to choose blessing by worshiping God and not by following other gods; that is, to choose life. A possible nimshal may not even involve a choice as much as the awareness that even a prickly beginning to living doesn't necessarily mean one's life will end in difficulty. At the same time, one cannot assume that just because living begins without problems that it will end that way. This parable implies having faith to trust God despite life's negative circumstances. In his farewell speech to the nation, Moses instructed Israel to choose life.

Young offers the following different Talmudic parable with a similar nimshal:

> One was traveling along the road. He encountered a wolf and was saved from him. So he kept on telling the story of the wolf. Then he encountered a lion and was saved from him. So he forgot the story about the wolf and told the story of the lion. He then encountered a serpent and was saved from him. So he forget the story about the lion and kept on telling the story of the serpent. So it is with Israel. Later troubles cause the former ones to be forgotten.[45]

Young's nimshal is that God has miraculously delivered Israel . . . [from] . . . the perilous dangers that a traveler may encounter. He suggests that the story is about Israel's exodus from Egypt and "at the same time gives the description of God's redemption from the past a present application."[46] Thus, Israel's initial thorny beginning ends in the relatively smooth end by both its exodus out from under slavery and journey through the dry ground of the Red Sea. Slavery is forgotten because of the more significant salvation of the exodus. When the Jewish people recount

---

44. Sifre Devarim-Sefaria, "Parable of the Two Ways."

45. Young, *Jesus and His Jewish Parables*, quoting Rabbi Simeon bar Yochai, "The Traveler and His Perils," 63.

46. Ibid., 64.

their history, they never forget this story which eventually results in its destined entry into the promised land. Israel looks back at its thorny past and realizes God's faithfulness. They then thank Him for the freedom to enjoy the good life thought thorny or smooth experiences along the way—by continuing to love God with all their heart, mind, and soul.

Talmudic parables tell stories which employ both haggadah and halakah genres. "In Heschel's thinking, haggadah inspires the people while halakah deals more with details."[47] One might say that haggadah is more accessible to the common person than halakah. Rabbis took full advantage of the ways to compare each mode of Jewish literature using parables. For example, when it appeared that the serious issues of halakah law took precedence over the inspiring haggadic stories, Rabbi Abbahu used this parable:

> To what may the matter be compared? It may be compared to two men. One of them was selling precious stones and the other various kinds of small ware. To whom do the people rush? Is it not to the seller of various kinds of small ware?[48]

At first glance the nimshal could be to seek after the more valuable things in life. Yet, Rabbi Abbahu used this story to emphasize the popular appeal of haggadah because it is within the grasp of the common folk, for the small ware may possess an unseen value which is absent in the precious stones.

The parables make sense out of the inconsistencies of life even when they reflect inherent inconsistencies themselves. For example, take the following parable about which came first, the creation of heaven or earth:

> It may be compared to a king who first made a throne and then his footstool, for it is written, 'The heaven is my throne and the earth is my footstool' [Isaiah 66: 1], [or] it may be compared to a king who builds a palace only after he built the lower story did he build the upper story, for it is written, 'In the day that the LORD God made earth and heaven' [Gen. 2:4].[49]

The question may be asked: Which text in the Tanakh is correct about the order of creation? We see here another example of Hebraic thought expressed in a parable; for the idea of contradiction is tolerated within

---

47. Heschel, *God in Search of Man*, 336-67.

48. Young, *The Parables: Jewish Tradition and Christian interpretation*, 66, from b. *Sota* 40a and parallels.

49. Ibid., 33, *Gen. Rab.* 1:15 (ed. Albeck, 1:13); *Midr. Sam.* 28b.

Judaism. Is the real issue that God spoke heaven and earth into existence with no concern for sequence?

"The same parable may be revised and used to support a very different argument."[50] Parables are works of art subject to varied interpretation. We suggest that the question pursued by both rabbis is possibly beside the main point of the parable; that is, it's not about the order in creation, but the fact that God is the Creator. The timing God may have used is His business, not ours. Recall that time is in God, not the other way around.

In this chapter, we've briefly analyzed a cross-section of Hebraic parables informed by Hebraic thought. We've noted that Judaism's parables emerge organically from stories which may be considered parables. That is, Israel's dynamic history echoed in its Oral Tradition offers the hearer an opportunity to reflect upon one's own life akin to looking into a mirror. Overall, the main point of Israel's story is a communication of the *Shema*—that the Lord is its God who is One and we are to love Him holistically with heart, mind, soul, spirit and all our resources.

We drew upon both the revealed Tanakh and its human interpretation located in the varied stories from the Talmud. We located the story itself, the mashal, and its one main point, the nimshal, which calls for a hearer's decision to act. We agree with David Stern's summative statement about Hebraic parables—"the mashal represents the greatest effort to imagine God in all Rabbinic literature."[51] A possible nimshal to go with Stern's view of parables may be that the it urges hearers to worship the God of Abraham, Issac, and Jacob. Recall that hearing means obeying. Imagining God means loving him with all one's heart, mind, body, and soul.

We now turn our attention to a key Hebraic theological concept—the Kingdom of God—as communicated through Jewish parables rooted in Hebraic thought lived out in Israel's story.

---

50. Young, *The Parables*, 13.
51. Stern, *Parables in the Midrash: Narrative and Exegesis in Rabbinic Literature*, 93.

Chapter 4

The Hebraic Kingdom of God

IN THE LAST CHAPTER we analyzed Hebraic parables located in the revealed and oral traditions of Judaism; that is, in the Tanakh and in the Talmud, respectively. We defined a parable as a story [mashal] with one main point [nimshal]. We characterized the parable as a mirror reflecting back to a hearer insights into his or her own life and a window through which one may see a vision of God.

In this chapter we have two major objectives. First, to define a Hebraic view of the Kingdom of God as it appears in both the Tanakh and the Talmud noting that the term *Kingdom of God* never explicitly appears, but is implied throughout both documents. Second, we'll discover how Hebraic parables in both the Tanakh and the Talmud convey the Kingdom of God.

The Kingdom of God in the Tanakh

A Hebraic view of the Kingdom of God begins at creation. God launched his kingdom by creating light, sky, water, heavenly bodies, animals and plants, and human beings made in His image.[1] God, the ruler of all creation, gave human beings the power to rule fill, subdue, and care for the earth.[2] That is, God gave persons the privilege and the responsibility

---

1. Genesis 1 and 2.

2. Genesis 1: 28. The Hebraic view of Creation predates any present-day discussion of ecological care for the planet and environment. Mother Earth is an inadequate term

to sustain all life—the most significant being to perpetuate the human species.

William D. Barrick states, "God began His program at creation ... "[3] The context for this statement is that God rules and molds all matter into a well-ordered whole. Following Hebraic thought, creator and creation are distinct from one another. God's sovereignty creates no space for a pantheistic syncretizing of creator and creation. Trees don't contain God. Only God can make a tree. Like any part of creation, a tree is a participant in the universe which provides the ingenious production of oxygen helping humanity to breathe. Human beings are the highest form of life designed to bear God's likeness on earth.[4]

The Tanakh linguistically reveals the kingdom of God using the Hebrew root *mlk* used thousands of times to mean kingship, human kings, and kingdoms. Jeff Benner defines kingdom as God "walking among the people."[5] For example, king David reminds us from The Writings that humanity is simultaneously frail, yet God created us "slightly less than the angels ... [with] ... dominion over all Your handiwork ... "[6] David's title reflects God's kingship over Israel, God's kingdom people on earth. The nation reflects an intended well-ordered community of persons who realize that God is sovereign.

Before Israel became a nation, all nations were established are under God's sovereign rule,[7] with or without their acknowledgement. Parenthetically, as nations were being formed after the flood, the term for Ashkenazi Jewish persons came into being and is derived from Noah's great-grandson, Ashkenaz.[8] Often, reference to the kingdom of God is implied. For example, the Song of Moses, sung after Israel passed through

---

to name what God, the invisible author, has created out of nothing, *creation ex nihilo*. If humanity claims any ability or right to impact climate and weather, it's because a sovereign king of Creation gave us the concept and power to care for his dominion.

3. Barrick, "The Kingdom of God in the Old Testament," *The Master's Seminary Journal*, 174.

4. Genesis 1: 26.

5. Benner, *Ancient Hebrew Lexicon*, 367.

6. Psalm 8: 5—7, Alter, *The Writings*, 39. Alter comments that this text suggests a hierarchy with God at the top, ... celestial beings below Him, then man, and below man the whole kingdom of other living creatures," affirming creation as the kingdom of God.

7. Genesis 10 names all nations derived from the sons of Noah after the flood

8. Genesis 10: 2. The family tree begins with Noah's son Japheth, grandson Gomer who gave birth to Ashkenaz.

the divided Red Sea, uses the normal term for kingdom in its last line, "HASHEM shall reign for all eternity!"[9]

The Covenants convey the Kingdom of God. According to Rashi the Kingdom of God comes when the Messiah arrives. "The scepter shall not depart from Judah ... until Shiloh arrives and his will be an assemblage of nations."[10] Rashi identifies Shiloh as the Messiah to whom the kingdom belongs. The Abrahamic Covenant includes nation, a massive number of descendants, land, and possession of Israel's enemies. Overall, the future fulfillment of this covenant mandates a sovereign king who rules over not only his people, but also over all nations. The Mosaic Covenant states that Israel will be to God a kingdom of ministers.[11] The concept of the Kingdom of God includes the advent of Israel's first king, Saul, and is most fully realized in the Davidic Covenant which states, "Your dynasty and your kingdom will remain steadfast before you before for all time; your throne will remain firm forever."[12]

While The Prophets imply aspects of the Kingdom of God, Jeremiah explicitly states: "At that time people will call Jerusalem 'The Throne of HASHEM,' and all the nations will be gathered to her in the name of HASHEM—to Jerusalem."[13] Zechariah includes many references to the Kingdom of God which include a future kingdom inhabited by a governor and a priest on separate thrones;[14] and that all "nations who had invaded Jerusalem will come up every year to worship the King HASHEM ... and to celebrate Succos."[15] A brief reference to the kingdom of God concludes the short prophetic book by Obadiah who claims a vision of Messiah's arrival at that point in time when all nations are judged. "And saviors will ascend Mount Zion to judge the Mountain of Esau, and the kingdom will be HASHEM'S."[16]

---

9. Alter, *The First Five Books of Moses*, 277.

10. Genesis 49: 10 Tanakh Note: " . . . the sense of the verse is that once Messiah begins to reign, Judah's blessing of kingship will become fully realized" (Rashi).

11. Exodus 19: 6.

12. 2 Samuel 7: 16.

13. Jeremiah 3: 17.

14. Zechariah 14: 12—13.

15. Zechariah 14: 16.

16. Obadiah 1: 21. Note: Messiah and his colleagues will exact retribution from the Edomites for their
cruelty, and then God will be recognized as the Sovereign of the entire universe (Radak).

The unique book of Daniel from The Writings makes a clear statement of a future kingdom of God. Daniel states: "Then, in the days of these kingdoms, the God of Heaven will establish a kingdom that will never be destroyed nor will its sovereignty be left to another people; it will crumble and consume all these kingdoms, and it will stand forever."[17] Reminiscent of the eternal kingdom in the Davidic Covenant, Alter identifies this kingdom with the messianic age. "The establishment by God of an eternal kingdom on earth is a strongly messianic idea."[18]

Recall the outlandish role the prophet Hosea played to graphically portray the steadfast love of a *sovereign God* even when his people are unfaithful. In a way, Hosea models how one person may at times be called upon to vicariously bear the sins of an entire community to achieve reconciliation with God. Hosea ushers in the reconciliation and restoration which characterizes the Kingdom of God.

There can be no question that the idea of the Kingdom of God is deeply rooted in Hebraic thought as documented in the revealed Tanakh. Having seen how the Hebraic concept of the Kingdom of God appears in the Tanakh, we now turn our attention to how rabbinic scholarship has represented the Kingdom of God in the Talmud.

The Kingdom of God in the Talmud

Having briefly surveyed the Kingdom of God in the Tanakh, we now turn our attention to the human interpretations in Judaism's Oral Tradition. We'll cite several rabbinic authors' commentary on the Tanakh located in the Talmud.

In his book, *This People Israel: The Meaning of Jewish Existence*, Leo Baeck devotes an entire chapter to the Kingdom of God. From Daniel he talks about how the kingdoms of the world continued to rise and fall throughout Israel's history. He raises the question, "When would the true kingdom appear, 'the kingdom of all times', 'the kingdom of the Almighty', 'the kingdom of Heaven', 'the kingdom of God?'"[19] Baeck's midrash on Daniel includes a prayer for the future kingdom of God:

> And, behold, there came with the clouds of heaven
> One like unto a son of man,

---

17. Daniel 2: 44.
18. Alter, *The Writings*, 758.
19. Baeck, *This People Israel: The Meaning of Jewish Existence*, 246.

>   and he came even to the Ancient of Days,
>   and he was brought near before Him.
>   And there was given to him dominion . . . [20]

Baeck's comment: "The times of the wild animals are ended, the time of humanity has dawned. Those in this people who have remained 'holy' will share in it. They are preserved for a future which is firmly established."[21]

He then defines *olam* using the Talmudic reference to a future fulfillment . . . a "personal renewal . . . rebirth . . . the true history of men and peoples . . . the kingdom of the Almighty had become a reality to them [teachers]."[22] Given such hope for the future despite the events of deportation and captivity, *kavanah,* an inner harmony and serenity would characterize the Jewish people.[23] Baeck defines *tikkun* within the context of prayer as the old word for *order* stated in the *aleinu* [it is incumbent upon us] which a congregation prays on New Year's Day . . . "give the world a harmony, an 'order' through the kingdom of the Almighty . . . "[24] [author's italics]. Putting Baeck's definitions together, *tikkun olam* may be translated as the orderly renewal associated with the kingdom of God, which happens to contain along with harmony, unity, and inner serenity, the action associated with bringing about justice for the marginalized—a Hebraic way to unify being and action.

Leo Baeck concludes his robust analysis of the kingdom of God by saying that Jewish existence was "a history for the sake of the kingdom of God."[25] He employs paradox to speak of the kingdom requiring patience for the future which presently exists. The existence and history of the Jewish people is not only for the sake of the kingdom but, "it was also within the kingdom of God at all times."[26]

Kaufmann Kohler wrote a thoroughly researched article on the Kingdom of God for the *Jewish Encyclopedia.* In that article he states, "Upon the Red Sea, Israel first sang the praise of God's Kingdom."[27]

---

20. Ibid, 247, Daniel 7: 13—14, Note: Rashi names the son of man as the Messiah; Alter mentions the angel Michael whose arrival ends the rise and fall of the world's kingdoms ushering in the kingdom of God, *The Writings,* 778—79.

21. Ibid.

22. Ibid., 248—49.

23. Ibid., 257.

24. Ibid., 267.

25. Baeck, *This People Israel,* 288.

26. Ibid.

27. Kohler, *Jewish Encyclopedia,* (Malkuta de-Adonai"), literally, "The Kingdom of

THE HEBRAIC KINGDOM OF GOD

This is his comment on the Tanakh's mention of Moses, Miriam, and the entire nation singing about God's mighty arm which delivered them from slavery in Egypt: "I shall sing to HASHEM for He is exalted above the arrogant, having hurled the horse and with its rider into the sea."[28]

Regarding the Mount Sinai event, Kohler adds that "they accepted the yoke of God's Kingdom, just as Abraham did, making Him King upon the earth... The yoke of God's Kingdom—the yoke of the Torah—grants freedom from other yokes... it was the principle of... the Zealots not to recognize asking anyone except God... the prayer: Abinu Malkenu—'Our Father, our King, we have no King except Thee!' "[29] The last line of the article states that "'In the world to come there is neither eating, nor drinking, nor procreation, nor strife; but the righteous encrowned and enjoy the splendor of Shekinah' "(*Ber.* 17a).[30]

Yoke in the above references has a significant relationship with the Kingdom of God.

Benner traces its origin back to its pictographic roots meaning a green branch which may be bent to a desired shape and be left to dry.[31] Bearing the yoke of God's Kingdom, the yoke of the Torah, implies adherence to God's rule in one's particular life-situation. Submitting to the Torah sets a right path for all persons. Another way to think of *yoke* is the more common illustration of two oxen joined together to plow a field. The yoke serves to guide both animals forward to plow a straight path in a field. That is, the yoke of the Torah "is a light unto my path,"[32] to help one clearly see a way through dark situations. Finally, Ichael F. Bird speaks of nine nuances of the Kingdom of God, one of which he calls spiritual. In later rabbinic writings the socio-political connotations of kingdom are displaced by ethical horizons so the 'kingdom

---

God."

28. Exodus 15: 1b. Note: Moses *led* the song, but all the people sang responsively with him {*Sotah* 30b). The uniqueness of this Song was that an entire nation—not merely its prophets, scholars, and leaders—could Rise to a state of prophecy. Also, from *Sotah* 11b commenting on 15: 20-21, The Talmud teaches about the special role of women to maintain the spirituality of Israel "who had greater faith than the men that there would be an eventual redemption, accompanied by miracle pf great magnitude."

29. Kohler, "The Kingdom of God."

30. Ibid., (*Rab*),

31. Benner, *Ancient Hebrew Lexicon*, 167.

32. Psalm 119: 105. Related to this idea is Psalm 16: 11a, "You will show me the path of life..."

of heaven" could be equated with accepting the yoke of Torah and its profession of God's oneness."[33]

Julius Guttman speaks of the Talmud's role in formulating Judaism's basic ideas. He states, "The faith of Talmudic Judaism rests completely on biblical foundations. Central to it are the simple . . . ideas of the Bible concerning a transcendent God, the Torah as the embodiment of his moral demands . . . the relationship between God and man, the wisdom and justice of divine providence, the election of Israel, and the *promise of the coming kingdom of God.*"[34] [my italics]. Judaism speaks of a coming messianic age where future promises of the prophets were foundational for the Jewish community. "The individual hope for an eternal life was thus combined with the idea that past generations too, would share in the promise of the kingdom of God."[35] However, one need not wait for death as the entrance into the enjoyment of eternal life.

Unlike other rabbinic voices, Guttmann distinguishes between the world to come and the kingdom of God. He locates the world to come existing from eternity as a reality outside of time. He employs Hebraic thought's ability to retain in tension two opposing views as a dialectic. That is, given Guttmann's definition of an eternal world to come "faces a double opposition, on the one hand between the present reality of history and the future kingdom of God, and on the other, between life on earth and life beyond. The two orientations do not necessarily exclude each other."[36] A simile from the Talmud may resolve the paradox: "this world is like a vestibule in which man should prepare himself for entering the banquet hall of the world to come."[37]

Franz Rosenzweig, arguably Judaism's leading scholar in the twentieth century, believes that prayer hastens the coming of the Kingdom of God. "Eternity . . . must be hastened, it must always be capable of coming as early as 'today;' only through it is it eternity. If there is no such force, no such prayer that can hasten the coming of the Kingdom, then it does not come eternally, but—eternally does not come."[38] Delaying the Kingdom of God is the result of violating the command to not

---

33. Bird, "Jewish Views About The Kingdom of God," *Ber* 2.2; 13b; *Pirke Aboth* 3.70.

34. Guttman, "The Religious Ideas of Talmudic Judaism," *Philosophies of Judaism*, 31.

35. Ibid., 33.

36. Ibid., 33-34,

37. Ibid., 43, *Berakhot*, 17a.

38. Rosenzweig, *The Star of Redemption*, "About the Kingdom," 306.

do to others what you would not have done to you [Hillel]. "The zealot the sectarian, in short, all tyrants of the Kingdom of Heaven, instead of accelerating the coming of the Kingdom sooner delay it; by leaving the nearest . . . [the neighbor] . . . unloved . . . "[39] Rosenzweig's vision of the kingdom is beautifully expressed in this statement: "For the Sages are the only ones who dare to describe the eternal bliss of the future Kingdom; the only conception that proposes a bliss in it other than the peace constantly renewed, which the lonely soul found in God's love; the pious ones seated, crowns upon their heads, and their eyes are turned toward the brilliance of the divinity become manifest."[40]

In this section we've analyzed several texts from the Talmud referenced by the rabbinic community to define a Hebraic view of the Kingdom of God. With this brief background of the Kingdom of God from both the Tanakh and the Talmud, we now turn our attention to how Judaism's oral tradition and written literature portray a sovereign God in parables.

The Kingdom of God in Hebraic Parables

This section addresses how Hebraic parables portray the Kingdom of God from both the revealed Tanakh and human interpretations in the Talmud.

In sum, the following statements itemize criteria for locating the Kingdom of God in Hebraic Thought. First, the Kingdom of God presents God as creator, sustainer, and sovereign over all creation. Second, He is Lord over the nation of Israel as a kingdom of ministers and priests with whom he has made covenants and given commandments. Third, the Kingdom of Heaven is a present reality as God walking among the people where entering the kingdom is to take on the yoke of the Torah. Fourth, it is the future hope of a messianic age characterized by the inner serenity of *kavanah* and ordered personal rebirth known as *tikkun olam*.

As we navigate the Tanakh and the Talmud we will cite those parables which are explicit or implicit conduits of the Kingdom of God. For each parable, we will link a parable's nimshal, with the Kingdom of God beginning with the Tanakh.

---

39. Ibid., 289.
40. Ibid., 271.

The Kingdom of God in the Tanakh Parables

As an introduction to how rhetorical devices may be used to communicate Hebraic thought in general and the Kingdom of God in particular, we reference a metaphor that spans all Scripture, "the finger of God." We first locate this metaphor's conveyance of the Kingdom of God during the Egyptian plagues when Pharoah's magicians couldn't produce gnats and said, "This is the finger of God."[41] That is, God's power in creation enabled Moses and Aaron to produce gnats by striking the ground with his staff. Here, the Kingdom of God is associated with creation. God initially spoke gnats into existence and empowered Aaron to bring them out of the ground. A second reference in the Torah refers to the God's etching of the commandments onto—"the two Tablets of Testimony, stone tablets inscribed by the finger of God.[42] While not a parable in the formal sense, this metaphor highlights concrete Hebraic thinking, dynamic action, and exemplifies God's sovereignty and control of the universe. A nimshal may be that God displays his power in creation as Lord of the Universe. Creation is the first evidence of God's kingdom.

God's kingdom uses judgment and discipline to restore, not to punish for no reason. Its desired result is reconciliation. Nathan's parable brought David to his knees in admission, confession, and repentance. God restored David's relationship with Himself. The Kingdom of God is characterized by a community of reconciled persons at peace with God and with one another. This meets the criterion where God's people joyfully take on the yoke of the commandments.

With justice as its theme, the parable about a farmer already discussed portrays the Kingdom of God where the Lord of the universe employs proportionate discipline, not designed to break or destroy, but to heal and to reconcile. The Prophets include the story of God's meting out discipline only in the amount required to bring about repentance. The King of the universe is fair.

In sum, the Tanakh's explicit and implicit parables portray the Kingdom of God with God as a righteous King and judge who consistently disciplines Israel and all nations such that justice will characterize their earthly kingdoms. The Prophets regularly confronted individual kings in either Israel or Judah about the injustices in their communities. They consistently challenged Israel's kings to restore God's ethics of

---

41. Exodus 8: 19.
42. Exodus 31: 18.

loving the neighbor. We now turn our attention to those parables in the Talmud which speak of God's Kingdom.

The Kingdom of God in the Talmudic Parables

There are far more parables in the Talmud than in the Tanakh covering a wide variety of subjects including faith, fear, speech, war, divine service, the world to come, humility, *tzedakah* [gift-giving], rewards, punishment, Torah, prayer, repentance, and redemption.[43]

Rabbi Bronstein's extensive coverage of Talmudic parables includes a section entitled, "This World and the World to Come." Taking a futuristic view of the Kingdom of God, his parable, *This World Is Like a Vestibule*, is introduced with a statement we've already seen—"This world is like a vestibule before the World to Come: prepare yourself in the vestibule so that you may enter the banquet hall."[44] The following paraphrase suggests the foolishness of worrying about enjoying life in this present world.

> A wealthy man hired an architect to build a lovely new home with a large living room and a spacious foyer as well. The architect informed him that there was not enough space for both a large living room and a large foyer and that the home owner needed to choose which should be larger. Based upon his experience with other homes, the architect suggested he make a large living room and a small foyer.[45]

Thinking of the foyer and living room as living in this world and the later world of the Kingdom of God, respectively, we may infer from this parable that life is better spent in preparing for the next. But how do we do this? "Through fulfilling the Torah and its *mitzvos!*"[46] [author's italics]. This parable stresses the Torah's importance for living a committed Jewish life—in this life, the good life. From Moses' farewell speech to Israel, he urges the community to choose life and the good . . . to love God, to walk in His ways, to observe His commandments . . . then you will live and multiply . . . and your God will bless you in the Land to which you come, to possess it . . . your God . . . is your life

---

43. Rabbi Bronstein, *Jewish Parables: A Mashal for Every Occasion*, 5—9.
44. Ibid., 144, *Avos* (4:21).
45. Ibid.,
46. Ibid., 145

and the length of your days . . . [47] Moses is not talking about the world to come, but life in the here and now. The foyer appears to be the same entrance either to experience the good life in this present world or in the next world to come. Torah is central to both. As we've seen earlier, Hebraic thought allows for apparent contradiction and paradox such that the same parable may be revised to communicate a different important aspect. What if the foyer were larger than the living room? Could a similar parable illustrate Moses' command to live the good life on earth? Could not the promised land be a present view of the Kingdom of God where the people would live under the sovereign rule of God as King of the universe, and yet look forward to an eternal Kingdom of God? The same parable may offer an equally-valid nimshal, as we've just seen.

Bronstein includes the following parable to remind us that God meets all the needs of his creatures whose response should be gratitude:

> A man received a gift from the king's treasury, and was granted enough money to comfortably support himself for the duration of the year. Before he went to the marketplace each day to purchase his household necessities, he would make his way to the king's courtyard, stand there for a few moments and only afterwards head to the marketplace. "Why must you trouble yourself each day to travel to the king's courtyard?" asked his friends. He answered, "Despite the fact that I take this money out of my own pocket, it is not truly mine; rather, it is a free gift from the king. In order to constantly recall this fact and feel gratitude towards the king, I am accustomed to spending a short while in his courtyard each day before I set out for the marketplace. In this way, my family and I remember from whom this kindliness has emanated.[48]

The nimshal is that we must be grateful that God, the King of kings, meets all our needs. "When a man has accepted upon himself the yoke of Heavenly sovereignty, he will recall and feel gratitude for His abundant kindness."[49] Our focus in the above nimshal is on the *yoke of Heavenly sovereignty*. Recall that the metaphor of the yoke in Judaism goes right to the Kingdom of God. One enters the Kingdom of God by taking on the yoke of the Torah. Bronstein's nimshal explicitly links *yoke* with *God the King*. We're reminded that living under the rule of God and His sovereignty is

---

47. Deuteronomy 30: 15—20.
48. Bronstein, *Jewish Parables*, 251—52.
49. Ibid.

to choose life and the blessing of God. We're to "stand in God's courtyard" every day thanking Him for giving us our daily bread.

Brad Young, a student of Rabbi David Flusser,[50] has written three books on Hebraic parables which describe the King of heaven and earth who judges his people and exists without any created form. The following parable illustrates a king's judgment:

> When our forefathers stood at Mount Sinai to accept the Torah for themselves, they saw no form resembling a human being, creature or anything that has breath . . . they saw only God, the one God . . . the Lord of lords . . . whose kingdom stands in heaven and on earth as well as in the highest heaven of heavens. And yet you say that God is fire and no more than a rod to punish human beings. The story is told that a king used a rod to threaten his children so that they turn away from sin and repent. When the children did not behave properly, the king growled at them like a bear and roared at them like a lion and seemed to be coming as the angel of death. In this way, the Lord thy God is a devouring fire.[51]

A twofold nimshal may be that hearing God's voice is all we need to know his commands. Or, that God often judges his people that they might return to Him. This parable is closely linked with the Tanakh and uses simile and metaphor to get the point across.

Young finds the following vivid parable an example of punishment:

> Two brothers were identical twins. One was the king of the entire world and the other one went out and joined a band of robbers. Eventually they caught the one who was a robber. They crucified him upon a cross. Each one who passed by exclaimed, 'That one crucified looks just like the king?' Thus it was said, ' . . . for a hanged man is accursed by God.'[52]

He suggests that "even a criminal may be considered a divine twin because every person is created in God's image . . . As Jewish haggadah,

---

50. Young, *Jesus and His Jewish Parables*, 38. Rabbi Flusser's research on parables introduced what may be called the "classic parable," often related to an ethical or moral issue and is less likely to be connected to a text from the Tanakh. Rather, such parables are linked with popular anecdotes and story illustrations. The classic variety of parables appear quite frequently in texts called homiletical midrashim derived from historic sources.

51. Ibid., 93-4.

52. t. *Sanh.* 9:7

the parable reveals the divine nature in startling metaphor/description based upon common human experience."⁵³

Rabbi Bronstein's voluminous arsenal of Talmudic parables includes the following paraphrased parable:

> Jealous citizens decided to spread vile rumors that a wealthy merchant was forging money. He was sent to prison while awaiting trial. False witnesses conspired together against the merchant appeared in court, and he was found guilty, sentenced to torture in the town square, and exiled to a labor camp in a desolate country. Among the townspeople who came to see him was a business colleague who vouched for his integrity to the ruler of the city knew the prisoner and thought highly of him. The ruler stopped the punishment until the matter could be further investigated. The false witnesses vanished but reasonable doubt never went away. The merchant received only a reduced sentence removing all torture and labor; he would however be exiled to a different land, live like a free man, but could not return to his home. Even with the reduced sentence, the exiled merchant wept bitterly at being so lonely unable to return home to his family.⁵⁴

Here's Bronstein's suggests this nimshal: In the future the day will arrive when sinners will be punished on account of their wrongdoings. Once they have been dealt their punishment, they will sit and cry over not having performed more *mitzvos* in this world. But by then it will be too late for in the World of Truth one is unable to amass *mitzvos* and good deeds. It is unclear from this parable what the World of Truth really is. Is it heaven? A place of eternally damnation? The best this parable offers is a reduced sentence, not acquittal. The merchant's eternal future was based upon a rumor and false witnesses! No wonder that this innocent man wept bitterly as a free man in a foreign land falsely deprived of his homeland.

This chapter has had two objectives. First, to define a Hebraic view of the Kingdom of God. Second, to locate parables which communicate the Kingdom of God in both the Tanakh and the Talmud.

Chapter 4 marks the end of Part One, whose topics have included Hebraic Thought, The Story of Israel, Hebraic Parables, and The Kingdom of God in Hebraic Parables.

---

53. Young, *The Parables: Jewish Tradition and Christian Interpretation*, 11.
54. Ibid., 192–93.

In Part Two we will use a similar four-chapter model to analyze Christianity. That is, we'll discuss Christian Thought, tell the Story of Jesus, analyze a cross-section of Jesus' Parables, and The Kingdom of God in Jesus' Parables.

PART TWO
Thinking Christianly

Chapter 5
Christian Thought

THIS CHAPTER LAUNCHES PART Two: "Thinking Christianly." We'll cover Christian thought, tell the story of Jesus, discuss his parables, and analyze how Jesus used parables to convey the Kingdom of God.

Alister McGrath states, "Christianity is . . . a sustained response to the questions raised by the life, death, and resurrection of Jesus Christ."[1] No Christian thought exists without Jesus Christ, the Savior and Lord of all creation. All Christian worship, community, and mission center upon the person and work of the historical Christ who is at the same time the Jesus of faith. Were Jesus only historical [code for human-only, not supernatural, not God], there would be no more reason to obey him than to follow Socrates, Darwin, or Bertrand Russell; conversely, were Jesus only a mystical being who never walked on the planet, no one could relate to him humanly.

We'll discuss Christian thought in terms of the Lord's Prayer, his Manifesto, his Sermon on the Mount, and finally Jesus' claims about who he was and what he came to do. We'll also point out, where appropriate, how Hebraic thinking has influenced Christian thought.

The Lord's Prayer

Rachel Levine states, "The central prayer of Jewish liturgy is known as the Amidah (which means standing) or the Shemoney Esreh (which

---

1. McGrath, *Christian Theology: An Introduction*, 322-323.

means eighteen), second only to the Shema, the basic Jewish affirmation of faith . . . when the rabbis discussed [the Amidah] among themselves, they referred to it as the Tephillah—"The Prayer;—and not by name."[2] The Hebraic roots of the Lord's Prayer derive from a rabbinic desire to offer Jewish worshipers a minimal version of the entire Amidah. "There are many Talmudic discussions as to what this minimum may be in certain situations, and it was not until the sixth century C.E. that a consensus was reached."[3] It's conceivable that as a rabbi, Jesus would have wanted to increase public participation. His alignment with the Pharisees would have shared their belief that Judaism needed to be practiced by uneducated people and not confined to synagogue leaders, Temple teachers, and scribes.

Levine links specific benedictions of the Amidah to Jesus' statements in the Lord's Prayer. For example, *Our Father*, speaks of the fatherhood of God linked with the Amidah's first of eighteen benedictions, Avinu, our father. This one Hebrew word is frequently found at the beginning of prayers of petition . . . the Tanakh prayers often include *our Father* [e.g., David prays "Blessed by Thou O Lord, the God of Israel our Father for ever and ever . . . "][4] *Hallowed be your name* or . . . better, *may your name be sanctified*, related directly to the third Amidah blessing: "Thou art holy and Thy Name is holy and the holy praise Thee daily."[5]

Jewish prayers consistently include two basic characteristics of God, Fatherhood and Kingship. *Thy Kingdom come, [thy will be done]* refers to Amidah blessings eleven, thirteen and fourteen which speak of God's righteous reign; that is, David's and a messianic king, respectively. Peter and John went into the temple to pray the Amidah at the hour of prayer. Along with corporate recitation, private prayer for specific individuals exists within the Amidah. For example, a prayer that asks God to heal a specific person is done by saying the person's Hebrew name, then his or her mother's name such as 'Joseph ben Sarah,' or 'Miriam bat Sarah.' To summarize, David Bivin specifically identifies Jesus' format, the Lord's Prayer as the shortened form of the Amidah.[6] The Lord's Prayer may be translated:

---

2. Levine, "The Lord's Prayer and the Amidah: A Comparative Analysis."
3. Ibid.
4. I Chronicles 29: 10.
5. Ibid.
6. Bivin, "The Amidah Prayer: A New Translation," En-Gedi Resource Center, 2019,

Our Father, who art in Heaven
may your name be sacred.
May your kingdom come and your will be done
On earth as it is in Heaven.
Give us this day our daily bread.
Forgive us our debts as we forgive our debtors.
Lead us not into temptation, but deliver us from evil.
For thine is the kingdom and the power and the glory forever.
Amen[7]

Given the Lord's Prayer as background, other sayings of Jesus form the basis for Christian thought. Early in his ministry, Jesus explicitly claimed to fulfill words from The Prophets. In so-doing, he launched his ministry by reading from Isaiah in his hometown synagogue. Many scholars refer to it as a manifesto—a publicly-stated plan of action indicating his motivation and vision for building the Kingdom of God on earth.

Jesus' Manifesto

"The spirit of my Lord, HASHEM/ELOHIM, is upon me Because HASHEM has anointed me to bring tidings to the humbled; He has sent me to bind up the brokenhearted, to proclaim freedom for captives and release from bondage for the imprisoned, proclaim a year of favor unto HASHEM and a day of vengeance for our God, to comfort all mourners . . . to give them splendor instead of ashes, oil of joy instead of mourning, a cloak of praise instead of a dim spirit. They will then be called 'elms of righteousness,' the planting of HASHEM in which to glory."[8]

What would this reading have meant to Israel and Judah? Answer: hope, comfort, and peace. Judah, the Southern Kingdom, knew about neighboring Assyria's ruthlessness at scattering the Northern Kingdom among idolaters. Then came Babylon about to exile Judah *en masse* to be their slaves. The above text referred to a future restoration, where "this time the army would be wiped out."[9] Isaiah's poetic style comes through here where the same Hebrew consonants for *splendor* are rearranged

---

7. A compilation of Hebrew translations from both the rabbinic and Christian communities.

8. Isaiah 61: 1—3.

9. Ibid., Tanakh Introduction to Isaiah, 953.

to mean *ashes*.[10] Only the joyful would rub his body with oil; only a mourner would place ashes on her head. Referencing Torah,[11] Isaiah predicted that a day would come when captive Israel would finally experience lasting freedom.

Isaiah speaks on behalf of God. He is literally not that person upon whom the Spirit of God rests. He is *not* the speaker. "[Isaiah] always lets his own person fall back into the shade . . . Isaiah's 'anointing' is as a prophet, not as a king . . . "[12] His prediction is *partially* fulfilled when Babylon is finally defeated by Persia King Cyrus, who champions Israel's cause to reconstruct its Temple [the second Temple] surrounded by new city walls. That second Temple would be destroyed by a first-century Roman army. Isaiah's prophecy was *yet to be completely* fulfilled.

Unlike Isaiah who was only a mouthpiece for God, Jesus is both the speaker and the one upon whom the Spirit of God resides. The Spirit of God descended upon Jesus at his baptism. He knew the Holy Spirit's presence, not as some private spiritual experience to be hoarded, but as the power needed to identify with the poor and the imprisoned in body, mind and spirit, where the poor are worthy recipients of the good news. Jesus consistently identified with the vulnerable and disenfranchised in society. His manifesto focuses upon the marginalized.

The reader of the Prophet Isaiah, a hometown lad from insignificant Nazareth, claimed to be the one speaking through Isaiah centuries before. He read the exact words from Isaiah and concluded by saying: 'Today, this scripture has been fulfilled in your hearing.'"[13] Understand that Jesus was not an invited outside speaker with a vast reputation as a Tanakh scholar. His hearers taught him in Hebrew school; they watched him grow up in their synagogue. They quibbled that this was just Joseph's son, yet they were proud of their local boy.

Jesus' message of liberty, healing and joy was not only confined to the Jewish community, but also to non-Jewish people, the Gentiles. That's when his Temple audience turned on him. The selfish audience couldn't fathom the transition Jesus was making. His coming kingdom would be for *all* humanity. *Jesus* was the message. *Jesus* was that servant of the

---

10. Alter, *The Prophets*, 827.

11. Ibid., Alter sees captivity to freedom as a recurring theme both literal [Year of Jubilee] as well as a metaphor for exile in Isaiah 40—55.

12. Keil—Delitzsch, *Commentary on the Old Testament*, Vol. VII, *Isaiah*, trans., James Martin, Grand Rapids: Eerdmans, 1976, 424 –25.

13. Luke 4: 21.

Lord about whom Isaiah spoke. Just as Israel and its covenants were to serve the well-being and flourishing of all humanity, Jesus, the embodied human-divine person, came to seek and to save the lost.

What might Jesus' words have meant to his audience? Comfort and trouble. It would be that way for the remainder of his brief time on earth. It would be a new-norm. Having laid out his manifesto at the beginning of his ministry, Jesus added one radical component at the end of his public ministry. Not only would Jesus care for the poor, downtrodden, imprisoned, and marginalized. Jesus claimed *to be* the poor and marginalized. At the end of his ministry recorded in Matthew 25, when he thanked his followers for ministering to him, he stated that *he* was the hungry, thirsty, sick, imprisoned, and lonely person. Of course, they helped him feed thousands and they were there during the miracles and healings. But when was the healer sick, when did he go to jail, and when was the Living Water thirsty? That's when Jesus said, "Truly, I say to you, as you did it to one of the least of these my brethren, you did it to me . . . as you did not do it to one of the least of these, you did not do it to me."[14] Employing Hebraic thought, by expressing the thought both positively and negatively, Jesus equated himself with the lowest of the low. The message was simple. The beggar at the corner is Jesus. The homeless person asleep on the floor of a police station is Jesus. The person waiting for the local food pantry to open is Jesus. The one locked up for murder is Jesus. Mysteriously, Jesus appeared to be the worst criminal imaginable crucified on a Roman cross who was at the same time the second person of the Trinity, the Son of God.

Along with Jesus' teaching on prayer and his manifesto for ministry, the Sermon on the Mount is a detailed extension of Jesus' manifesto.

The Sermon on the Mount

Though two versions [Matthew and Luke] of Jesus' sermon exist, we will focus our analysis on the more-Hebraic rendering by Matthew.

At the outset, we need to tackle the following question related to the Sermon on the Mount: "What is the Meaning of the Sermon on the Mount?" Is it a "perfectionist conception, an impossible ideal, or an interim-ethic."[15] Jeremias debunks each response as mere versions

---

14. Matthew 25: 40—45.
15. Jeremias, *The Sermon on the Mount*, London, Athone, 1961. Pbk.ISBN:

of a legalism which miss the Gospel. "The first conception makes Jesus a teacher of the law; the second a preacher of repentance; the third an apocalypticist."[16] He says that when reading the Sermon on the Mount, one must always interpret it in light of something which has preceded it to avoid confining Jesus' teaching to legalism. That *something else which precedes* the sermon is "... *the proclamation of gospel; and it was preceded by conversion, by a being overpowered by the Good News.*"[17] [author's italics]. Later, Jeremias states, "Every word of the Sermon on the Mount was preceded by . . . the preaching of the kingdom of God . . . If I may express it with a touch of exaggeration, it is as if to every saying of the Sermon on the Mount we must supply . . . 'Your sins are forgiven.' . . . "[18]

The Sermon on the Mount presupposes grace. It is not self-help. It's about gift, not onerous demand. Since Jesus spoke of the presence of the Spirit of the Lord as he outlined his manifesto, he anticipates the need for the power of the Holy Spirit who energizes the Christian to obey difficult commands.

Finally Jeremias explicitly states that "... the Sermon on the Mount is not law, but gospel."[19] It is not a legal yoke, but the Hebraic *yoke of the commands* which according to rabbinic interpretation is the way to enter the kingdom of God. Jesus doesn't oppose rabbinic tradition; rather, he fulfills the intent of the Law and the Prophets. The ethical demands he proposed *are* possible to follow in a lived faithful relationship with him. Jesus becomes the Torah. His notion of ethical monotheism was not some type of perfectionism, nor an interim ethic for a later age. The Sermon on the Mount is the normative here-and-now lifestyle for all Jesus-followers. The gift of the Gospel and the Spirit precede the demands. He concludes that one may now experience the city of God "out of the thankfulness of a redeemed child of God [within whom] a new life in the Spirit is growing. That is the meaning of the Sermon of the Mount."[20] Having presented an overview of the Sermon on the Mount, we now turn our attention to segments of Jesus' sermon which may be categorized as 1. *The Promises,* 2. *The Law and the Prophets,* 3. *New Interpretations,* and 4. *Commands.*

0485143127, 33.

16. Ibid.
17. Ibid.
18. Ibid., quoting Matthew 9: 2.
19. Ibid.
20. Ibid.

The Promises

Jesus begins his sermon with The Beatitudes—statements which assign promises to spiritual qualities. Jesus' statements are embedded within Hebraic thought. That is, the Beatitudes explicitly use language reminiscent of the Torah's motif—promise-command. The good life for Israel is promised by adhering to the covenants and obeying the commands of Yahweh. For example, in his farewell address to the nation, Joshua says, "If you violate the covenant . . . you will perish . . . from the good land he has given you."[21]

Historic scholarship on the Beatitudes has typically focused upon their *qualities* at the expense of the *promises*. It has neglected the Hebraic thought behind the Sermon on the Mount. For all his detailed comparative analysis of the sermon with rabbinical-Pharisaic piety, his focus on origin, insightful grasp of the *precedence of something else*, and his understanding of the Sermon on the Mount as Gospel, not Law, Jeremias nowhere highlights the promises associated with the Beatitudes.[22]

However, John Piper's exposition of the Beatitudes states, "Notice the promise of the first beatitude . . . And notice the promise of the eighth beatitude . . . Both of them have the identical promise, 'For theirs is the kingdom of heaven.'"[23] Piper's analysis is replete with Hebraic promise-command motif, even if he doesn't explicitly identify it as Hebraic Thought.

The Law and the Prophets

Jesus said, "Do not think that I have come to abolish the Law or the Prophets, but to fulfill them."[24] Jesus affirmed both the Torah and the Prophets; that is, the words of Moses and all the prophets from Samuel to John the Baptizer. He encouraged ordinary Jewish citizens to practice their faith daily while simultaneously challenging the Pharisees' misinterpretations of the Law.

Abolish is rather self-evident, but the more difficult issue, *fulfill*, needs clarification. Might *fulfill* imply some deficiency in the first books of Moses, the Torah? No. While affirming the Law's necessity, Jesus

21. Joshua 23: 14ff.
22. Jeremias, "The Sermon on the Mount."
23. Piper, "The Beatitudes and the Gospel of the Kingdom."
24. Matthew 5: 17.

advocates the spirit of the Law to render it sufficient, not confined to keeping the letter of the Law. What might this mean?

Literally, *fulfill* is best translated in one of the following two ways: "do, carry out or bring to full expression . . . [or] . . . show it forth in its true meaning."[25] Pharisees taught the Law and often failed to practice it. Jesus said, " . . . whoever teaches and practices [the Law and its commandments], this one will be called great in the kingdom of heaven . . . unless your righteousness exceeds that of the scribes and Pharisees you may never enter into the kingdom of heaven."[26] The Pharisees did not practice what they taught. Jesus had no time for hypocrisy. He added a new interpretation of the Law involving intent and motive rather than displaying perfunctory religious motions. Hebraically, hearing involves behavior—Jesus adds attitude and the condition of the heart. He does so citing six examples which we now consider.

New Interpretations

Jesus prefaced his new interpretation of six commands from the Torah and rabbinic sayings with these words: "You have heard that it was said . . . But I say to you . . . "[27] He speaks of murder, adultery, divorce, oaths, retribution, and love for one another. Each category comes directly from the Tanakh. While not abolishing behavioral aspects of the Law and the Prophets, Jesus adds the important component of inner *attitude, intent,* and *motivation*. Implied in his critique is the half-truth of obedience without the spirituality, a circumcision of the heart.

In and of itself, murder is wrong; after all it's mentioned the Ten Commandments. But Jesus speaks of anger, which when allowed to fester leads to a desire to eliminate someone. Murder is a behavior prompted by an inner attitude, anger. A similar motif exists for adultery which Jesus extends to lust, a spiritual condition of the heart. He qualifies divorce with a specific behavior, fornication. When Jesus challenges oath-taking, informed by two texts from the Torah, he's speaking of lying about a vow without doing it. Testifying "under oath" in court means telling the whole truth succinctly; that is, with a *yes* or a *no*. Rather than resisting an evil person who physically abuses you, Jesus challenges a

---

25. Bauer, Arndt and Gingrich, *English Lexicon of the New Testament*, 677.
26. Matthew 5: 19b—20.
27. Matthew 5: 21, 27, 31, 33, 38 and 42.

retributive justice of *quid pro quo;* that is, matching of offensive behavior with another—an eye for an eye, a tooth for a tooth. Metaphorically, he suggests replacing retribution with restoration, matching negative behavior with a positive one. The new interpretation involves the Hebraic concept of "pouring coals on another's head."[28]

Robert Alter comments that pouring coals mean treating one's enemy with humanity, or, better, treating a foe inhumanly may bring on the same treatment of oneself by the Lord.[29] Jeremy Myers explains this difficult concept from a culturally Hebraic understanding. He interprets feeding one's enemy by generously giving them the ability to cook their own food. "When this Proverb was written people . . . cooked with fire. But sometimes a person's fire would go out during the night, and before they could cook breakfast, they had to go to a neighbor's house to get a coal to . . . restart his fire. Giving a person coals in a pan 'on his head' was a kind neighborly act; it made friends, not enemies."[30]

Finally, a new interpretation of the Torah is about going beyond loving your neighbor and hating your enemy.[31] Jesus says we are to love our enemies. It's too radical for most; yet, loving an enemy may mean gaining a new friend. It is with a right spirit of the heart that empowers Jesus followers to grasp God's love for all humanity, the just and the unjust. In sum, Jesus introduces attitude as a fulfillment of Jeremiah's and Ezekiel's mention of the heart.[32]

Commands

The bulk of Jesus' ethics resides in Matthew 6 and 7. Detailed analysis of these two chapters is beyond the parameters of this book and is well addressed by a myriad of authors. We'll briefly treat Jesus' warnings and commands.

Matthew Six warns against hypocrisy. First, "Be careful not to do your 'acts of righteousness before men, to be seen by them . . . when you give to the needy, don't announce it with trumpets . . . but do not

---

28. Proverbs 25: 22.
29. Alter, *The Writings*, 432.
30. Myers, "How do you heap burning coals on the heads of your enemies?"
31. Leviticus 19: 18,
32. Jeremiah 31:33b and Ezekiel 36:26.

let your left hand know what your right hand is doing. ."[33] Earlier, Jesus challenged his disciples to exceed pharisaic righteousness [religion for show]. Jesus never faulted the Pharisees for giving to the needy. He decried their motive to be seen doing it in public. Their giving did not originate from the heart. Whether in private humility or grandiose religious piety, the needy will receive what they need. Jesus takes giving to another level emphasizing not only the act, but also the attitude with which a gift is given. Here we have a clear example of how Jewish thinking has informed Jesus' teaching about gift giving.

"The Torah's word for the act of giving to the need, *tzedakah*, although commonly translated as 'charity,' more accurately means 'justice.'"[34] Jesus' essential challenge to Second Temple Judaism in his day wasn't about written law as much as it was about one's heart-felt attitude toward the recipient. Loving God with all one's heart presented itself by loving one's neighbor. While affirming Sinai's command not to covet a neighbor's possessions, Jesus added a spiritual component centered in motive. "Maimonides (Rabbi Moses be Maimon, 1135-1204) formulated a list of eight levels of giving, correlating to the degree to which the giver is sensitive to the needs and feelings of the recipient."[35] Beginning with the lowest form of giving to the highest his list is as follows:

1. Giving grudgingly with a sour countenance.
2. Giving less than you can afford, but doing so pleasantly.
3. Giving generously, but only after being asked.
4. Giving before you are asked.
5. The recipient knows the giver; but the giver does not know the recipient.
6. The giver knows the recipient, but the recipient does not know the giver.
7. Giving anonymously, where neither giver nor recipient knows each other.
8. Helping someone become self-sufficient.[36]

---

33. Matthew 6: 1—4.
34. Suchat, "Eight Degrees of Giving."
35. Ibid.
36. Ibid.

Jesus said, "Seek first the kingdom of God, and all these things will be added unto you."[37] Clearly, living a sacred life includes *tzedakah* where its blessing may eventually return to us.

Second, Jesus says more about prayer. "But when you pray, go into your room, close the door, and pray to your Father."[38] Praying privately where only God knows about it is the norm. Earlier we saw that one's yes must yes and no must be no. It follows that prayer be succinct. Since God knows what we need, He doesn't require long drawn out conversations. Recall that the Lord's Prayer is an abbreviated version of the Jewish Amidah. Within the context of the Lord's Prayer, there follows an apparently contradictory statement about forgiveness: "For if you forgive men when they sin against you, your heavenly Father will also forgive you. But if you do not forgive men their sins, your Father will not forgive your sins"[39] This sounds like God's forgiveness is conditionally based upon what I do to earn personal forgiveness making Christ's work on the cross unnecessary. How might this apparent contradiction be explained?

This apparent problem may be cleared up by realizing the difference between a *singular and plural context* about forgiveness. The Lord's Prayer states that we are to understand that God's forgiveness of us means we are to follow suit and forgive our debtors. The *context is plural* and doesn't speak to individual sins. Our understanding for forgiveness means we should remind anyone that forgiveness applies to all sins—murder, adultery, idolatry, etc. The issue is understanding God's gracious forgiveness and then applying that same grace to others.

Forgiveness is *defined* in the Lord's Prayer and *applies* forgiveness in a *singular context*. If someone sins against you, that sin is forgiveable. Because of the plural context of a global forgiveness, all sins committed against an individual in a singular context are forgiveable as well. The Christian who has experienced God's forgiveness knows no alternative but to unconditionally forgive when sinned against. God's unconditional forgiveness of us implies our unconditional forgiveness of all others whether they are stuck in *any* sin [applied to all of us in a *plural* context] or in a sin against us *individually*.

Further, a detailed method to forgive one who has sinned against us involves going directly to that person to express being offended to receive forgiveness from the other person, and if needed, followed by doing so

37. Matthew 6: 33.
38. Matthew 6: 6.
39. Matthew 6: 14-15.

with two or three others. If all that doesn't work, then the church must be involved. Finally, anyone who remains stubborn and doesn't realize the Gospel, must be removed from the blessings of the community. In sum, forgiving is one of the most important, and sadly one of the least effectively practiced, Christian behaviors.

Third, Jesus addresses fasting as a good thing. However, just as in giving and praying, fasting is to be hidden. Rather than display ashes as the public sign that you're fasting, Jesus recommends using oil as a sign of joy and gladness so as not to appear self-righteous and hypocritical. It is up to us to find modern updates to ashes and oil on our faces when fasting.

In each of the above devotional acts of giving, prayer, forgiveness and fasting, one's worship need not resort to religion-for-recognition.

The final section in Matthew Six may be summed up by having faith in God's provision according to a verse we've already considered. Accumulating wealth and anxiety about one's daily bread and devoting one's energy to greed are merely illusions of the good life. However, Jesus followers strive to obey this verse: "But seek first the kingdom of God and his righteousness and all these things shall be yours as well."[40] Note that this text answers the question about God's righteousness, not that of the Pharisees. Public piety is replaced by private devotion; self-righteousness is replaced by God's righteousness, the only way to enter into the blessings of God's kingdom.

Matthew Seven is the final chapter devoted to the Sermon on the Mount. It is a *pot pourri* of categories including judgment, holiness, God's good gifts, difficulty at attaining genuine life, discerning truth, being known by Christ as the criterion for entering the kingdom of heaven, and the wisdom of obeying Christ's commands to live the good life. Each category deserves a detailed analysis which is beyond the scope of this book. We briefly offer the following two perspectives which undergird what Jesus says about each ethic.

First, Jesus makes this summative statement: "So whatever you wish that men would do to you, do so to them; for this is the Law and the Prophets."[41] This is not a religious statement per se, but one confined to human relationship. Rabbi Hillel, whose primary years of ministry [30 BCE to 10 CE] pre-date the three years of Jesus' ministry, employed

---

40. Matthew 6: 33.
41. Matthew 7: 12.

Hebraic language: "That which is hateful to you do not do to another; that is the entire Torah, and the rest is its interpretation. Go study."[42] By implication loving God with all one's heart, spirit, soul, and mind must be reflected in loving the neighbor as oneself goes right to treating as others like you would want to be treated. The so-called Golden Rule implies the great command to love God. Loving God and being a neighbor go hand in hand; you simply cannot have one without the other.

Here's the last verse in the Sermon on the Mount—"Now when Jesus had finished saying these things, the crowds were astonished at his teaching, for he taught them as one having authority, and not as their scribes."[43] Jesus conveyed his message with passionate assurance. The authority of the teachers of the law was dependent upon the group think of the priests, scribes, teachers and other subgroups within Second Temple Judaism. Jesus was obligated to no one except his Father in heaven. That's what got him in trouble. Jesus repeatedly explained that he came only to do his Father's will. He didn't tow any party line. His sayings were new and vibrant. "Jesus taught as one who had independent authority, unlike a normal teacher of the law."[44]

Having discussed key areas of the Sermon on the Mount, we complete our analysis of Christian thought with a summary of Jesus' radical claims.

Jesus' Claims

Jesus made the most radical claims of any religious leader in history. Since Christianity is the daughter of Judaism, Jesus' claims are Hebraic and derive from the Tanakh or the oral tradition. Note that Jesus doesn't use simile or metaphor. He doesn't say, "I am *like* a resurrection." He says "I *am* the resurrection." *I am* connotes *essence*; *like* merely makes an *analogy* or a *correspondence*. Jesus doesn't merely correspond to living water. He *is* living water. Hillel may have been a better story-teller than Jesus. But Hillel made no claim to be one with God. Was Jesus self-deceived, knowingly lying, or telling the truth? Jesus is the truthful way to the good life.

---

42. Hillel, *Shabbat* 31a.
43. Matthew 7: 28.
44. NRSV Note on Matthew 7: 28, 24.

All of Jesus' claims derive from " . . . before Abraham was, *I am*."⁴⁵ [my italics]. To a Second Temple Jewish worshipper, this was blasphemy! Like all Jesus' claims, we must decide whether he was self-deluded, lying or telling the truth. We believe Jesus was telling the truth. Jesus was in his right mind. Jesus was not a liar. We will proceed through each of his claims taking a trajectory from the *I am* in a conversation God has with Moses. Moses knew that the people would ask in whose name he spoke. God replied, "Say to the people of Israel, 'I AM' sent me to you."⁴⁶

Six of Jesus' claims emerge from ordinary elements of daily life. He claims to be *living water* [implied], the *bread of life*, *light of the world*, the *door*, the *good shepherd*, and the *true vine*. Each metaphor connotes the spiritual nourishment available to all humanity through a personal relationship with Jesus himself. Our analysis locates its New Testament and Old Testament origins and, where possible, its mention in the Oral Tradition.

Living Water

One day Jesus took the risk of speaking with a Samaritan woman at a well in the heat of noon. Their discussion began with water, continued with the differences between Second Temple Judaism, and her Samaritan faith. Jesus talked about the advantages of water which originate from a flowing stream, not still water.⁴⁷ Both Jesus and the woman had a religious context for the term living water from the Jewish ritual of cleansing.⁴⁸ It had to do with baptism which needed to be flowing water from a spring or stream. Jesus said that the need for a running stream of living water can originate within a person. The calm water of a well, which could not be used in the purification ritual of *tevilah* using a *mikveh*, would not suffice.⁴⁹ Only living water could be used for ritual baptism. Jesus claimed to be that living water; that is, *spiritual* water which only He could provide, for God is spirit implying that He was divine and greater than Jacob. Samaritans focused upon *where* one worshiped. It had to be on the top of

---

45. John 8: 58b.
46. Exodus 3: 14b. The Tanakh translation is "I SHALL BE AS I SHALL BE."
47. John 4: 10—14.
48. Leviticus 15: 13 uses "fresh water," Lev. 11: 36 uses "spring, cistern" with comment from Sifra regarding full body immersion.
49. *Tevilah* refers to any regulation involving full body immersion; a *mikveh* is the device used for the immersion.

a mountain. Jesus said that the more important issue had to do with *who* one worshipped by revering God in spirit.

Bread of Life

Jesus said, "I am the bread of life[50] . . . I am the living bread that came down from heaven. If anyone eats of this bread, he will live forever. This bread is my flesh, which I will give for the life of the world."[51] When Jesus claims to be the bread of life, living bread from heaven, he's talking about spiritual need, not physical hunger.

One day Jesus' followers challenged him to do a miracle, so they could really believe in him. Knowing Jesus' use of Scripture, they referred him to the famous miracle of manna during the exodus in the desert. Jesus separated the miracle of manna in the desert with true bread which comes from his father, and Jesus is that bread.[52] Jesus claimed to be the bread of life [*lechem*[53]], for bread from God gives life to the world. Spiritually speaking, Jesus is the bread of life.

We find that both the Tanakh and Talmud use metaphors which anticipate that Jesus fulfills spiritual thirst and hunger. Jesus claimed to be the bread of the Presence on the table in the Tabernacle anticipating his profound statement while holding bread, "This is my body given for you, do this in remembrance of me."[54] Jesus claimed to be the sacrificial *lechem* for the world. He was born in the House of Bread [Beth-lehem] to become the Bread of Life [*lechem*] to feed both the physically and spiritually hungry.[55]

Light of the World

Jesus said, "I am the light of the world. Whoever follows me will never walk in darkness but will have the light of life."[56] During the healing of a blind man, Jesus said, "As long as I am in the world, I am the light of

50. John 6: 35, NIV.
51. John 6: 51, NIV.
52. John 6: 32
53. Often used in the Tanakh for *food*, especially when offered as a sacrifice.
54. Luke 22: 19b, NIV.
55. Fisher, "Lechem: BREAD of Life," *Hebrew Word Lessons*.
56. John 8: 12, NRSV.

the world."[57] No one can adequately define *light*, but everyone knows the difference between light and darkness. We can't see light, but we become aware of its presence when it allows us to see other things. Darkness is just the opposite. We become aware of its presence when we can't see anything. The testimony of the blind man was not that he could define the concepts of light and darkness, but was " . . . though I was blind, now I see."[58] Greek thought deals in concepts. Hebraic thinking requires action. Christian thought is Hebraic.

The Tanakh makes metaphorical use of light in the Writings: "Thy word is a lamp unto my feet, and a light to my path."[59] "A mitzvah is a candle, and the Torah is light."[60] Any Jewish hearer would have easily connected having one's path lit while following a pillar of fire in the desert during the night.[61]

The Apostle John introduces Jesus as the world's savior with "in him [the Word], was life, and that life was the light of men. The light shines in the darkness, and the darkness did not *overtake* it . . . "[62] [my italics]. Rabbi Lauren Eichler Berkun illuminates the powerfully spiritual metaphor of light in the Jewish tradition. ""Light is one of the enduring symbols for God in our sacred texts . . . We cannot see God, but we become aware of God's presence when we see the beauty of the world, when we experience love and goodness of our fellow human beings. (Eitz Hayim Commentary, p. 503) . . . as the light of the menorah[63] illuminates our homes and the flowing faces of our loved once, we can contemplate God's bountiful blessings." Jesus is the Menorah of the world.

The Door

Jesus said, "I am the door of the sheep . . . through me if anyone enters he will be saved . . . "[64] Here Jesus illustrates the spiritual truth of

---

57. John 9: 5, NRSV.
58. John 9: 25b, NSRV.
59. Psalm 119: 105.
60. Proverbs 6: 23.
61. Exodus 13: 21.
62. John 1: 5.
63. The Menorah [Lampstand] was a seven-candle, pure gold structure in the Tabernacle (Exodus 37: 17—24). Later Jewish tradition focused on its use in the Hanukkah celebration of the dedication of the Temple after the Maccabean Revolt, 167—160 BCE.
64. John 1: 7.

salvation from local agriculture. His hearers would have had no trouble understanding the safety of sheep led into a stone-walled fold for protection. The Writings employ the context of the sheepfold to render Jesus' claim as door *to* the sheep which may also include the sense of Jesus as the door *to* the Father.[65] [my italics]. The pictorial symbol for door in Hebrew includes the staff of a shepherd.[66]

Jesus used *gate* in another context to convey the commitment, even the hardship, often required to follow in Jesus' steps. "Enter through the narrow gate, for the gate is wide that leads to destruction, and there are many who find it. For the gate is narrow and the road is hard that leads to life, and there are few who find it."[67] In what way might Jesus be the narrow gate that leads to life. The text from Psalm 118: 19, 20 states: "Open for me the gates of righteousness; I will enter them and thank God." Natan Lawrence likens entering into worship, the context of Psalm 118, through a gate which may anticipate what Jesus says in the closing words of his Sermon on the Mount in Matthew 7: 13.

In sum, Jesus, Yeshua is the gate or straight narrow way of life and truth, the door to salvation and the way to the Father in heaven. He is the Word of Elohim[68] made flesh as an incarnation of the Torah. Jesus has fulfilled the Torah, by *being* the Torah in the flesh who tabernacled among us.

Good Shepherd

Jesus said, "I am the good shepherd. I know my own and my own know me."[69] The pictograph for *shepherd* combines the symbols for an eye and the head of a man. "Combined these mean 'man watches,' the shepherd watched over his flock, often they are his only companion."[70] Benner

65. Psalm 118: 19, 20, *A Greek-English Lexicon of the New Testament and Other Early Christian Literature,* Bauer, Arndt, Gingrich, 366.

66. Benner, *Ancient Hebrew Lexicon,* 422.

67. Matthew 7: 13, 14,

68. Elohim is a plural noun for deity In Hebrew understood to be singular by Israel's one true God. Mark Sameth Speaks of Elohim as a singular noun of a dual-gendered deity, *The Name: A History of the Dual-Gendered Hebrew Name for God,* Eugene: Wipf & Stock, 2020. Consequently, Genesis 1: 27, "Let us . . . ." cannot be a proof-text for the Christian doctrine of the Trinity. Any notion of multiple gods is foreign to the Tanakh. The Trinity is better defined by New Testament texts.

69. John 10: 14.

70. Benner, *Ancient Hebrew Lexicon,* 263

goes on to add how the shepherd-sheep relationship becomes personal. "One who provides and protects the flock and *takes desire in them*."[71] [my italics]. Jesus is the good shepherd because he provides for his people and because he wants to befriend them.

The Tanakh makes repeated us of *shepherd*. When Jacob [Israel] blessed his sons, he said, "May the God before whom my fathers Abraham and Isaac walked, the God who has been my shepherd all my life to this day . . . bless these boys."[72] Toward the end of the Babylonian captivity, Isaiah spoke this way about God: "He is like a shepherd who grazes his flock, who gathers the lambs in his arm, who carries them in his bosom, who guides the nursing ewes."[73] While sheep represent animal life common to local culture, Jesus also introduced plant life into his claims—vines, its branches and fruit.

True Vine

Jesus said, "I am the vine, the true one and my father is the vine-grower."[74] The metaphor models the authentic relationship between the Father and the Son. As vine-grower, the Father nurtures the Son. This text goes on to say that the Son in turn nurtures us as the branches. We might even say that the Holy Spirit who indwells the Christian is symbolized in this metaphor.

The Tanakh speaks of the confusing role of a vine in Jonah's life. God told Jonah to prophesy God's pending judgment against a city of sin. When "God saw . . . that they repented of their evil ways, God relented concerning the evil He had said He would bring upon them, and did not do it."[75] Jonah's apathy toward the repentant Nineveh resulted in self-pity and anger. He chose to miss the value of God's grace toward repentant sinners. Despite his wrong response, God nurtured and cared for him in his discomfort and grew a vine to shade him. He was happy to receive God's grace. Then God responded to Jonah's anger and destroyed the vine resulting in his feelings of possible suicide: " 'It would be better for

---

71. Ibid., 264.
72. Genesis 48: 15-16.
73. Isaiah 40: 11.
74. John 15: 1, paraphrased NRSV,
75. Jonah 3: 10.

me to die than live."⁷⁶ God displayed his judgment toward a disobedient Jonah rather than a city which returned to God. God's nurturing absence may be felt during our disobedience as well.

We continue by considering four more claims Jesus made about himself: the *way*, the *truth*, the *resurrection*, and the *life*. Unlike the above concrete six claims, these four claims tend to be abstract; yet we must keep in mind that Hebrew nouns often function as verbs.

Way

Jesus claimed to be the way; that is, *the* way . . . the *only way* to the Father.⁷⁷ [my italics].

The first believers were called *The Way*.⁷⁸ [my italics]. The prophet Isaiah warned Israel against saying to him: "'Do not see true visions for us! Speak pleasant things to us; see fantasies for us. Veer from *the way*, stray from the path. Remove from our presence [the word of] the Holy One of Israel!'"⁷⁹ [my italics]. The Tanakh uses *way* far more than the Younger Testament testifying to the robust Hebraic context of Jesus' claim. As the way, Jesus helps us to see.

Truth

Jesus said, "I am . . . the truth . . . "⁸⁰ Not *a* truth . . . but *the* truth. Jesus' claims about himself are absolute and unique. All truth is God's truth, but the only way to the Father is through the truth about Jesus Christ. It is not enough to say, "I believe in Jesus." *What* do you believe about Jesus Christ? The answer for Christians is that we believe Jesus Christ is the way, the truth and the life and that no one comes to the Father except through Him.

All four authors of the Gospels repeated this sentence from Jesus— *I tell you the truth*. It may be about his words being fulfilled,⁸¹ forgiving

---

76. Jonah 4: 8
77. John 14: 6, paraphrased, NRSV.
78. Acts 9: 2
79. Isaiah 30: 10-11.
80. John 14: 6.
81. Matthew 5: 18.

sins,[82] receiving the kingdom as a child,[83] or about seeing the kingdom of God without being born from above.[84] Virtually all of the Apostle Paul's letters mention some aspect of truth. Paul is particularly concerned about denial of the truth. "The wrath of God is being revealed from heaven against all godlessness and wickedness of men who suppress the truth . . ."[85] Finally, in three of the shortest letters in the New Testament, the Apostle John references *truth* twenty-one times. "We are from God, and whoever knows God listens to us . . . This is how we recognize the Spirit of truth . . ."[86]

Resurrection

Jesus also said, "I am the resurrection . . ."[87] Jesus raised two people from the dead during his ministry. A synagogue leader's daughter,[88] and his good friend Lazarus.[89] At the raising of Lazarus Jesus claimed to be the resurrection . . ."[90] The resurrection of Lazarus was the last public event of Jesus' ministry right before the last week of his life.

Resurrection explicitly appears in the Tanakh. Elisha, a prophet, raised a boy from the dead.[91] The closest the Tanakh comes to the *idea* of resurrection is found in Daniel's forecast " . . . at the time of the End . . . at that time . . . Many of those who sleep in the dusty earth will awaken . . ."[92] Alter commenting on Daniel's prediction: "This is, famously, the first and only clear reference to resurrection in the Hebrew Bible . . . Bodily resurrection after burial is here accompanied by reward for the righteous and punishment for the wicked . . ."[93] *The bodily resurrection of a* divine-human *being is uniquely Christian.*

---

82. Mark 3: 28.
83. Luke 18: 17.
84. John 3: 3.
85. Romans 1: 18.
86. 1 John 4: 6.
87. John 11: 25.
88. Mark 5: 21—24; 35—43.
89. John 11: 1—44.
90. John 11: 25.
91. 2 Kings 4: 32—37.
92. Daniel 12: 2.
93. Alter, *The Prophets*, 797.

The Apostle's Creed concludes with this statement of belief: "in the resurrection of the *body* . . . "[94] [my italics]. In the first sermon of the church, Peter linked David's psalm,[95] to the resurrection of Jesus Christ when he said, "But God raised him from the dead."[96] The Apostle Paul proclaimed the resurrection of the Jesus Christ throughout his letters to churches summarizing the Gospel in his letter to the believers in Rome. "Paul . . . set apart for the gospel of God . . . regarding his Son . . . who through the Spirit was declared to be the Son of God by his resurrection from the dead: Jesus Christ our Lord."[97] Jesus claimed to be not only *the* resurrection, but also, *the* life.

Life

Jesus said, "I am . . . the life . . . "[98] Resurrection and life go together. "I came that they might have life, and have it abundantly."[99] The Apostle John takes it further when he speaks of *eternal life*. God's love for humanity has eternal life as its ultimate goal,[100] eternal life is knowing Jesus Christ,[101] and the purpose of John's Gospel is "that through believing you might have life in his name."[102]

From the Torah we have Moses' powerful farewell speech reminding the nation to choose life.[103] From creation God put the breath of life into Adam's nostrils "and he became a living being.[104] The Writings remind us that God's desire is for his creation have life. One of the rare references to resurrection in the Jewish Bible refers to everlasting life.[105] Job's friend Elihu reminded him—"The spirit of God has made me, and the breath of the Almighty gives me life."[106] The role of the Holy Spirit as a life-giver

94. *The Apostle's Creed.*
95. Psalm 16: 8—11
96. Acts 2: 24; 3: 15.
97. Romans 1: 1—4.
98. John 14: 6.
99. John 10: 10.
100. John 3: 16.
101. John 17: 3
102. John 20: 31.
103. Deuteronomy 30: 20.
104. Genesis 2: 7.
105. Daniel 12: 2.
106. Job 33: 4.

is anticipated in the Jewish Scriptures with the arrival of Messiah Jesus as we've noted in the Gospels. In Galatians 6: 8 Paul writes, " . . . the one who sows to please the Spirit will reap eternal life." Further, the role of the Holy Spirit in the life of the believer is restoration. Benner finds this idea of restoration and renewal anticipated in the Hebraic understanding of life which impacts "The whole of a person, the body, breath, and mind."[107]

As we've seen so many times in both the Tanakh and the Younger Testament, Hebraic thought is often the root of Christian thinking. Our investigation of the radical claims of Jesus Christ bears this out.

We now summarize our study of Christian thought with Jesus' first words about his ministry to bring God's kingdom to earth.

Summary of Christian Thought

In this chapter we have focused on the person and work of the Jesus of history who is simultaneously the Christ of faith. We've analyzed his sayings and his claims. We now conclude with the very first words Jesus said when he began his ministry: "The time is fulfilled, the kingdom of God has come near, repent and believe in the good news."[108]

The Time

Judaism is essentially about events in time, not places. Because he was Jewish, Jesus focused upon time. *What* time is fulfilled? To what *event* might Jesus be referring? The event is his arrival from heaven to earth; for it was time to fulfill the Law and the Prophets. *He* was the event. *He* ushered in the *Kingdom*. Jesus came that all might *repent* and return to God. Jesus is the Good News of the *Gospel*. Christianity is *not about places* either. There aren't any pilgrimages to Bethlehem, Golgotha, or Jesus' burial place. But Christians do *remember the events* of Jesus' birth, his healings, his suffering and death, the resurrection, his many appearances, and his Ascension. The New Testament sums up all things in Christ.[109]

---

107. Benner, *Ancient Hebrew Lexicon*, 382.

108. Mark 1: 15, NRSV. Other renderings include: *has approached, is at hand* or *near*.

109. For example, Ephesians 1: 10 talks about a dispensation of the fullness of times where Christ recapitulates all things in heaven and on earth into himself.

The Kingdom

The Kingdom of God was the theme of Jesus' teaching and preaching. Jesus consistently spoke about the kingdom. At times about its *nearness*, that it is *in you,* that it *is yours* and, that it is *yet to come.* Jesus spoke more about the Kingdom of God than any other topic. If Christianity is to become *Christian* again, it must return *to* Jesus and his words, not merely on what others said *about* Jesus. The Church must give up submitting to every wind and wave of culture's constant shift and changing tides. As time goes on, the Church will need to settle on its counter-cultural position rooted in Scripture, not in "religious correctness." Since Jesus is the fulfillment of that time for which all humanity has been waiting, Jesus' main concern, the Kingdom, must be the unsullied essential message of the church. The Church only distorts the Kingdom of God by accommodating a secular culture into its liturgy, fellowship and outreach.

The Gospel

The Gospel is the good news of God's forgiving grace. The Gospel is bad news for anyone who rejects it. When Jesus says *repent*, he's not rubbing someone's nose in their sin, but laying down the behavioral Hebraic tracks for returning to God. The Gospel is taking a leap of action [repent] *and* taking a leap of faith [believe]. You can't have one without the other. *Repent—believe* together form a motif using two of the most important verbs in Christianity thought.

This chapter launched us into Part Two: "Thinking Christianly" by analyzing Christian thought as represented by the life, death, resurrection, ascension of the historic Jesus who is at the same time the Christ of faith—one person with two natures: human and divine. We got into The Lord's Prayer, Jesus' Manifesto, The Sermon on the Mount, and Jesus' radical claims.

We now focus on the story of Jesus as the fulfillment of the story of Israel.

─── *Chapter 6* ───

The Story of Jesus

JUST AS WE INVESTIGATED the key *sayings* of Jesus as the basis for Christian thought, we now tell the *story of Jesus* focusing on key *events* in his life. Our main sources include the synoptic [lit., "seeing/summarizing the same events"] Gospels [Matthew, Mark, and Luke] along with the theological commentary of John's fourth Gospel. The key events in Jesus' ministry tell the story of his life. The Gospel narratives are biographical focusing primarily on the last three years of Jesus' life.

Scot McKnight says, "... *the gospel Story of Jesus Christ resolves or brings to completion the Story of Israel* ... "[1] [author's italics]. That is, Jesus' story doesn't hang out in space disconnected from the Tanakh; rather, Jesus' story is anticipated in the story of Israel which creates the historical and cultural context for *Jesus' birth, the Temple dedication, the Passover pilgrimage, his baptism, his temptation, miracles, the transfiguration, the Last Passover, the cross, the resurrection, appearances, and the ascension.*

Jesus' Birth Story

Luke 1:26—56; 2:1—20

The historical Christ and the Jesus of faith are one and the same divine-human being born to an unsuspecting teenage Mideastern woman named Mary of Nazareth. The agent of Jesus' conception was God the

---

1. McKnight, *The King Jesus Gospel*, 50.

Holy Spirit as Luke records in a conversation between the angel Gabriel and a bewildered young woman. "The Holy Spirit will come upon you, and the power of the Most High will overshadow you: therefore the child to be born will be called holy, the Son of God."[2]

Jesus' birth symbolizes the intimacy of a God-human relationship. Mary's unique pregnancy anticipates the presence of the Holy Spirit for any human being. She was the first person whose body was filled with the Holy Spirit. Mary's firstborn was Christ, "the first-born of all creation;"[3] Mary was the conduit humanity needed to see God. By giving God a body, she made Him visible.[4] Mary's baby boy was God-made-visible or as the Apostle John states: "And the Word became flesh . . . "[5]

Jesus' birth was scandalous. The salvation of humanity doesn't succeed without the heresy of God-in-the-flesh according to first-century Judaism—the religion of Joseph and Mary.

YHWH, the invisible one God could never become visible. Certainly not as a human being. Christianity's key teaching of the Incarnation was a major Jewish heresy. A holy spirit impregnating a young human being was blasphemy according to the religion of the time and ludicrous to any understanding of conception. Mary's pregnancy became gossip at Nazareth's water well.

The term *virgin birth* fails to capture the deep theological meaning of Jesus' birth as the unique divine-human being who is the " . . . Son of the Most High [who] will reign over the house of Jacob forever . . . [whose] . . . kingdom will have no end."[6] Virgin birth merely describes conception which doesn't require male participation. The term only addresses what the miraculous birth of Jesus *was not*. The miracle *was* a mysteriously invisible divine-human interaction which resulted in Mary's baby, the Son of God. The Holy Spirit contributed nothing to Jesus' humanity; Mary contributed nothing to Jesus' divinity. It's not about *how* Mary's baby came into the world; it's *who* her baby is that matters . . . "For a child has been born for us, a son given to us, . . . he is named Wonderful Counselor, Mighty God, Everlasting Father and Prince of Peace . . . "[7]

---

2. Luke 1: 35.
3. Colossians 1: 15.
4. Bischoff, *Mary Gave God a Body*, 1—8.
5. John 1: 14.
6. Luke 1: 32-33.
7. Isaiah 9: 6.

Temple Dedication

Luke 2:21—40

The next key event in Jesus' story occurred when Joseph and Mary presented their baby boy to God following the Torah's command: "Sanctify to Me every firstborn holy to the Lord . . . "[8] *Firstborn* in the Tanakh implies first male child. Scripture doesn't describe a service of dedication for Jesus in the Temple. As far as we're told, no teacher of the law or elder in the Temple participated in Jesus' dedication. It was about what two *unofficial* inhabitants of the Temple said about Jesus. The Spirit-led conversation of Simeon and Anna, two inhabitants of the Temple, with Mary and Joseph marks this event. The Temple Dedication focused upon *who* Jesus is, not *how* he arrived. This event reveals Messiah not only to the Jewish community, but also to the nations. A venerable Jewish man of deep faith would affirm the angel Gabriel's words about her son.

How did Simeon know that the baby brought by Joseph and Mary to the Temple was the "consolation of Israel . . . the Lord's Messiah . . . a light for revelation to the Gentiles and . . . glory to your people Israel."[9] Scripture tells us that the Holy Spirit revealed the identity of Mary's baby to him. Mary was stunned by Simeon's prophetic words. She may have been especially perplexed when he said, "This child is destined for the falling and rising of many in Israel . . . [he] will be opposed . . . "[10] These were not the usual words spoken over a child being blessed at a Temple dedication. They were certainly not uplifting. *How* would people oppose her son? If Jesus were the consolation of Israel, why would *many fall*?

Then there was Anna, a prophetess, who "worshiped there with fasting and prayer night and day."[11] How did she know Mary and Joseph's boy was the Messiah? We can safely assume that, like Simeon, the Holy Spirit led her to Jesus causing her to break out in joyous praise. An eighty-four year old widow was about to evangelize a crowded Temple—Jerusalem's redeemer was being dedicated!

God used two senior citizens to reveal his Son as the Lord and Savior to not only the Jewish people, but to all people outside the specific covenants and promises made to Israel. This key event in Jesus' story partially

---

8. Exodus 13: 2, 12, Tanakh, Note: The term *firstborn* refers only to the male species.
9. Luke 1: 25, 26, 32.
10. Luke 2: 34.
11. Luke 2: 37.

fulfilled the Abrahamic Covenant which speaks of Israel being a blessing to all humanity. We never hear about Simeon or Anna again. Their one-time behind-the-scenes role set a precedent for all future Jesus-followers whose silent faith continues to sustain the church to this day.

Anna's role is especially significant as a woman in a patriarchal society. Luke uniquely names women [Elizabeth, Mary, and Anna] in Jesus' early years. A publicly vocal woman, even as a prophetess, proclaiming the identity and role of Jesus would have been highly suspicious during Second Temple Judaism, whose ideas about the messiah differed from the words Simeon and Anna spoke in the Temple that day.

Simeon tied God's promises and blessings to the Gentiles stated in Abraham's Covenant and reinforced by the prophet Isaiah: "I will give you [Israel] as a light to the nations (or, Gentiles), that my salvation may reach to the end of the earth" (Isaiah 49:6).[12] The story of Israel is consummated in the story of Jesus.

Passover Pilgrimage

Luke 2:41—51

The Gospels continually include Jewish events to tell Jesus' story. His Jewishness derives from his parents who were practicing Jews who followed the Torah's commandments. The next significant milestone in Jesus' biography is his dialogue with the Temple scholars and teachers of the law during the family's pilgrimage to celebrate Passover in Jerusalem.

This event had to be awkward for his parents. Jesus described his father in ways that had to be awkward for Joseph. The pilgrimage would only reinforce what Joseph had come to realize as his supportive role in ushering Messiah into the world. Like any normal mother who finally locates her lost child, Mary was exasperated! She didn't know whether to hug him or scold him! "Child, why have you treated us like this? Look, your father and I have been searching for you in great anxiety?"[13] Mary doesn't seem proud that her son is conducting a seminar with the Temple teachers. Luke doesn't domesticate Mary, but allows us to identify with her as a human being.[14] As human as Mary's question is to her son, his answer raises more

---

12.
13. Luke 2: 48b.
14. Bischoff, *Mary Gave God a Body*, 43—48.

questions than it answers. "Why were you searching for me? Did you not know that I must be doing the things of my Father?"[15]

Jesus' response frustrates his parents even more. Think for a moment about how Joseph must have felt when Jesus implied that he belonged in his Father's house. Might that have been a bit confusing for Joseph in whose house Jesus was to grow up to become a carpenter? Beyond this awkward event, we find the peripheral events of the Passover pilgrimage as antecedents to how Jesus would introduce the kingdom of God. That is, in typically enigmatic style, he's letting his parents and Temple leaders know that things are about to change now that he's here. For the second time[16] Luke tells us that Mary treasured and pondered all that had transpired between her son's birth and dedication. What would it be like raising a teenage boy who was God?

Baptism

Luke 3:21—22

Just as we focused upon *what Jesus said about himself* to develop Christian thought, we now get into *what others said about Jesus*. Jesus' baptism includes powerful words from Israel's last prophet, John the Immerser[17], and from God his Father. All three synoptic Gospels and John's Gospel mention Jesus' baptism. Luke offers a robust historical and cultural context beginning with John's identification with the prophet Isaiah's earlier comforting words about returning to Jerusalem after the Babylonian captivity.[18] He provides a new meaning for baptism from physical to spiritual purification

---

15. Luke 2: 49. This is a literal Greek translation of Jesus' words. Many translations use *house* as in "I must be in my Father's house. *House* does not appear in the Greek. Other translations supply *business*, as in "I must be about my Father's *business*.

16. Luke 2: 19, 51.

17. Rabbi Leynor, "The Meaning of Baptism in the Jewish Culture." Ritual immersion for purification. The person must undergo total immersion in either *mayim hayyim*, a river or sea; or, a *mikveh*, water brought together by natural means, not drawn. The person would need to be clean and naked. Ritual immersion would change the status of the person from impure to pure. Impurity resulted from leprosy, issue from sexual organs, and the dead bodies of certain animals.

18. Isaiah 40: 3—5.

and cleansing,[19] and most importantly predicts that "one more powerful than I . . . will baptize you with the Holy Spirit and fire."[20]

John's words provide a major transition within Judaism from the outward physical purification of baptism to an inner spiritual purification for repentance of all sins. Nothing in the Tanakh explicitly links the *forgiveness of sins* with baptism. Such a shift begins with John, the Baptizer even though Ezekiel's words anticipate water which purifies Israel. "Then I will sprinkle pure water upon you that you may be cleansed . . . I will give you a new heart and put a new spirit within you . . . I will put My spirit within you and I will make it so that you will follow my decrees."[21] This language is foreign to Judaism, yet uniquely Christian.

John the Baptizer's most significant words are: "Here is the Lamb of God who takes away the sin of the world . . . I saw the Spirit descending from heaven like a dove, and it remained on him. I myself did not know him, but the one who sent me to baptize with water said to me, 'He on whom you see the Spirit descend and remain is the one who baptizes with the Holy Spirit.'"[22]

Jesus' baptism launched his ministry. Jesus' new baptism of the Spirit fulfills Jeremiah's and Ezekiel's words about the heart. The Psalmist link both heart and spirit in his profound confession: "Create a pure heart in me . . . and a steadfast spirit . . . and take not your Holy Spirit from me."[23] From here on, the signs, miracles, and wonders of Jesus healing ministry of body, mind, and spirit point to the Holy Spirit who makes ongoing repentance, renewal and restoration possible.

Jesus' baptism is all about doing God's will and hearing his approval for doing so. "And a voice came from heaven, 'You are my Son, the Beloved [One]; with you I am well pleased.'"[24] There is no son who does

---

19. Luke 3: 3, 10—14. Note that in vv10 -14 John responds to a questioning crowd by defining behavioral repentance resulting from forgiveness of sins. No longer is baptism limited to physical purity; it now involves sins of the heart which present as sharing resources with the needy, accurate taxation, and the absence of threats. This approach to baptism is entirely new to Judaism.

20. Luke 3: 16

21. Ezekiel 36: 25—27. This statement echoes Jeremiah's, " . . . I will place my Torah within them and I will write it onto their heart . . . " [Jeremiah 31: 32b]. Both prophetic words emphasis the inner condition of the heart beyond physical contact with outward impurity.

22. John 1: 29—34.

23. Psalm 51: 12—13b.

24. Luke 3: 21-22. I have supplied *One* from the actual Greek.

not want to hear such affirming from his father. Before he accomplished anything in the way of preaching, teaching, performing miracles, or healings, God the Father expressed confidence in his Son.

The next important event in Jesus' story is his confrontation with Satan, We'll notice how important both Word and Spirit were to Jesus during the enemy's various temptations.

Temptation

Luke 4:1—13

Jesus returned from the Jordan and was led by the Spirit in the desert where for forty days he was tempted by the devil.

Parenthetically, recall God's dealings with Israel while they, too, encountered temptation, in a desert. Jesus' story intersects with Israel's story. But here we'll notice that while the journeying nation regularly forgot God's Word, Jesus consistently used the Torah to ward off the devil.

Why did Jesus not immediately go right into teaching, preaching, healing and performing miracles to demonstrate his power and glory? That would have been the rational thing to do. Rather, he exposes himself to the devil's tricks and hubris. Not only that, it's the Holy Spirit who leads him out into desert to be tempted. It almost seemed like a rite of passage preparing the Son of God for ministry.

From his birth on, everything about Jesus' life is a descent from privilege, security, and comfort. Jesus' identity with humanity required that he meet us where we are. Opening himself up to temptation was part of that descent which ultimately cost Jesus his life. Just as future followers would be harassed and hampered by Satan, Jesus endured it first to demonstrate that God's Word and power always win out.

Jesus is vulnerable and hungry. Satan senses his human need and starts talking about bread and sarcastically affirms Jesus' ability to turn stones into bread. But Jesus doesn't fall for Satan's entrapment and quotes the Torah. "It is written, 'Man does not live on bread alone.'"[25] Jesus fought his spiritual battles armed by the Torah to defeat the enemy. The context for his Torah quote finds Israel led by God into a desert, also hungry, for forty years, not just forty days. The parallel is obvious. Knowing Israel's story, Jesus realized exactly what was going on and

---

25. Deuteronomy 8: 3c. Luke uses only part of this verse in response to Satan in Luke 4: 4.

dismisses a ridiculous challenge with "every word that comes from the mouth of the Lord."[26] Israel's desert story anticipates Jesus' temptation in a desert. Jesus knew his Torah.

Satan then ludicrously proposes to give back to Jesus what he had already created. Jesus sees right through all this narcissism and pride and once again quotes the Torah: "It is written: 'Worship the Lord your God and serve him only.'"[27] The context for this quote is the all-important Shema—there would be no better quote from the Torah to identify Jesus with Israel. Jesus knew that Israel's God was One and that only God was to be loved with all one's heart, soul, and strength.

Satan has one more card to play. He tries to defeat Jesus at his own game. Now *he* will be the one who quotes the Tanakh. Note that Jesus didn't directly challenge Satan's quote from The Writings about how angels guard the godly to keep them from falling.[28] Satan knew his Bible and quoted in accurately. But Satan misused Scripture. With this, Jesus has had enough and calls a halt to the entire ordeal with one more reference to the Torah. "It says: 'Do not put the Lord your God to the test.'"[29] Satan finally gave up and left, while angels ministered to Jesus' soul.

We're reminded of the Lord's Prayer, "Lead us not into temptation, but deliver us from the evil one."[30] These seem to be confusing words. Does Jesus *intentionally* lead us into situations that might cause us to sin? *Temptation* in this context is better translated *testing* which might refer to afflictions, sufferings, and ailments where someone *might* sin. Parenthetically, Job would be a good example of God's testing with no intention of having Job sin. It was Job's wife who sinned by encouraging her husband to curse God. Job remained faithful throughout his afflictions and pain. A paraphrase could be: Lord keep us from sinning when we go through tough times. Such testing is intended to assess the quality of our faith. Just as Israel heard God's words through Moses when tempted in the desert, Jesus quoted the Word of God to withstand temptation.

We'll now turn to how Jesus broke the power of Satan by performing miracles.

---

26. Ibid.

27. Deuteronomy 6: 13. Luke paraphrases this text which in the Torah is "Fear the LORD your God, serve him only . . . " in Luke 4: 8.

28. Psalm 91: 11, 12, paraphrase.

29. Deuteronomy 6: 13, Luke 4: 12 quotes Jesus as saying only part of this verse.

30. Matthew 6: 13.

Miracles

Throughout all the Gospels

All four Gospels record a cross-section of miracles most of which are healings of mind, spirit and body. All such miracles display Jesus' use of divine power to love his neighbor and display his relationship to the One living God who created humanity in his image. We'll briefly get into miracles of *healing, human need, and resurrection.*

First, we find that Matthew, Mark, and Luke all record the familiar miracle of a paralytic let down through a roof so Jesus can heal him.[31] While each apostle records this *healing* in different words, one thought common to all three is that physical healing and spiritual forgiveness may go hand in hand. "Which is easier to say to the paralytic, 'Your sins are forgiven,' or to say, 'Get up, take your mat and walk.'"[32] Jesus then states the purpose of his miracles. "'But that you may know that the Son of Man has authority on earth to forgive sins' . . . He said to the paralytic, 'I tell you, get up, take your mat and go home.'"[33] To the amazement of all, he did. Physical healing and spiritual forgiveness of sins are two sides of the same coin—another example of Hebraic thought which always integrates body, mind, soul, and spirit. Jesus' ministry was to the whole person—body, mind, soul, and spirit.

Arguably the best-known healing miracle from the Tanakh occurs when a little girl and the prophet Elisha trusted God to heal a pagan King Naaman.[34] We also have the healing of the entire nation bitten my poisonous snakes, who, when they looked at a bronze snake erected up on a high pole for all to see, were miraculously healed.[35] The Apostle John looks back on this event in the story of Israel to convince a Jewish leader Nicodemus of the healing and saving power of Jesus on the cross.[36]

Second, we address the only miracle included in all four Gospels –the *feeding of more than five thousand people* including men, women,

---

31. Matthew 9: 2—7; Mark 2: 3—12 and Luke 5: 18—25.

32. Mark 2: 9.

33. Mark 2: 10-11.

34. 2 Kings 5: 1—15. This story has a captive young Israelite girl whose faith suggest to a king's wife that God could heal her husband's leprosy through the prophet Elisha. Elisha told King Naaman to wash himself seven times in the Jordan River who was healed and said, "Now I know that there is no God in all the world except in Israel," v 15.

35. Numbers 21: 4—9.

36. John 3: 1—15.

and children with leftovers. Because the Word became human, Jesus understood hunger from his own temptation. Throughout his ministry, he demonstrated his compassion for the human condition. Recall from the Tanakh the miracle by the prophet Elisha of an endless supply of oil for a woman.[37]

Third, disrupting the natural order of death as the end of life is constitutive of how God breaks its power. *Resurrection* has to be the most dramatic miracle recorded in Scripture. When raising up the daughter of a synagogue's leader[38] or Lazarus,[39] Jesus' conquers sin's ultimate consequence—death.

Jesus demonstrated his love for God with all his heart, mind, body, soul, and spirit through his miracles of healing, feeding, and raising bodies to life. All such miracles implicity or explicitly announced the forgiveness of sins of a holistic gospel.

Transfiguration

Matthew 17:1—13

The Transfiguration portrays how Jesus' story dynamically fulfills the story of Israel. To *transfigure* means to change in appearance. It is not necessarily a religious term. The historic Christ undergoes a vivid change in appearance as a bright light engulfs his entire body. "As he was praying, the appearance of his face changed, and his clothes became as bright as a flash of lightening."[40] The church calendar recalls this event as a summation of Epiphany, the manifestation of God's glory.

Moses represented the Torah and Elijah, the Prophets. The Law and the Prophets were brightly standing next to the transfigured Christ, the Messiah. Impetuous Peter wants to savor the moment. He may have thought how wonderful it was to have all three important persons of his faith and tradition showing up together. It was a photo-op! But Peter

---

37. 2 Kings 4: 1—7, The wife of a prophet's disciple died and creditors demanded payments. She had only one jar of oil. Elisha told her to find as many empty jars she could from her neighbors. Then Elisha told her to start pouring oil from the one she had into all the others. The oil kept flowing until all the jars were filled.

38. Mark 5.

39. John 11.

40. Luke 9: 29. The entire story is included in Luke 9: 28—36; Matthew 17: 1—8 and Mark 9: 2—8.

did not, like we may have not, interpreted the event correctly. He may have been thinking of the Feast of the Tabernacles, *Sukkot*, when Israel constructed booths out in the desert dwelling with God and enjoying his presence. He had every right to think this way looking back. But this event was forward looking. Things were changing.

Now Jesus would be the "booth" in whom Israel could enjoy the presence of God during their journey through life. Jesus was Sukkot. Just as a cloudy mist enveloped all six people, Peter and the disciples heard a voice say, "This is my Son, whom I love, listen to him."[41] When the fog lifted, only Jesus remained. Moses and Elijah had done their work. The Law and the Prophets were in the process of being fulfilled.

The symbolism of the Transfiguration is rich. For from now on, the Torah and the Prophets would be summed up in Jesus—a validation of Jesus' claim in the Sermon on the Mount, not to diminish but fulfill the Law and the Prophets. Jesus is dramatically presented to Peter, James and John, three key future leaders of the church. From now on, Jesus' teaching will imply the goodness of the law and prophetic words of the past along with his new teachings about himself and the kingdom of God.

In a later teaching on the Kingdom of God, Jesus says, "The time is coming when you will long to see the day of the Son of Man, but you will not see it . . . For the Son of Man in his day will be like the lightning, which flashes and lights up the sky from one end to the other."[42]

As the Apostle John said about Jesus in his Gospel written at the end of the first century, "The true light, which enlightens everyone, was coming into the world."[43] Jesus is the Transfiguration's Light of the World who marks a huge turning point in both the story of Israel and the story of Jesus.

The Last Passover

Matthew 26:17—29

While the Transfiguration marks a significant turning point in Jesus' story, the last time Jesus celebrates Passover with his disciples has even greater implications—the ultimate event for the forgiveness of sin. The

---

41. Mark 9: 7.
42. Luke 17: 22—24.
43. John 1: 9.

first Passover occurred in Egypt while the nation was enslaved. God wore down Pharoah until he finally caved in and liberated God's people from slavery. That first Passover involved sacrificing a perfect lamb whose blood was to appear on the door frames of Israel's houses. It was the blood of a perfect lamb which saved the lives of Israel, while death occurred in every Egyptian house. The first Passover became part of an annually celebrated series of festivals and offerings involving the sacrifice of an animal by a priest for the forgiveness of sins. These offerings always involved a priest who had to first perform a sacrifice for his own sins and those of his household prior to performing a blood sacrifice for the sins of the people.

The first covenant of the Mosaic Law involved a *multiple* series of daily and annual blood sacrifices requiring *many* priests, many *different* types of animals [lambs, bulls, and goats] for the forgiveness of Israel's sins.

All of that changed at the Last Passover when Jesus said, "This is my body given for you; do this in remembrance of me . . . This cup is the *new covenant* in my blood poured out for you."[44] [my italics]. In these two monumental sentences the former sacrificial system practiced by Israel for over fifteen-hundred years was consummated in one celebration—the Last Passover. Because of Jesus, there would no longer be any need for *multiple* sacrifices by *many* priests using *many* different animals involving *many* offerings celebrated on *many* different days of the year for the forgiveness of sins and sinners. Jesus replaced the entire historic sacrificial system of Israel by himself in one huge event which became known by the Church as the Lord's Supper, Communion, the Sacrament or Eucharist [*thanksgiving* for redemption through the cross].

The critical term *new covenant* explicitly appears only once in the Tanakh.

> The time is coming declared the Lord
> when I will make a *new covenant* with
> the house of Israel and the house of Judah.
> It will not be like the covenant I made with
> their forefathers . . . This is the covenant I
> will make with the house of Israel . . .

---

44. Luke 22: 19, 20. All three synoptic Gospels quote Jesus as making the connection between bread and his body and wine and his blood of a covenant. Luke explicitly uses *new covenant* to describe the relationship of the cup and the blood of Jesus.

> I will put my laws in their minds and
> write them on their hearts . . . [my italics].
>
> By calling the covenant "new," he made
> The first one obsolete, and what is
> obsolete will soon disappear.⁴⁵

This all-important text from Jeremiah occurred earlier in our discussion of the Story of Israel. The last three lines above are commentary from the author of Hebrews. When the Second Temple was destroyed by Rome in 70 C.E., the Jewish people were unable to maintain the Mosaic sacrificial system. Synagogues replaced the Temple. Judaism doesn't authorize the sacrifice of an animal in a synagogue by a priest for the sins of the community. There has been no celebration of Passover by the Jewish community involving the blood sacrifice of a lamb to this day. No Temple, no sacrifices. Recall that prayer became a substitute for sacrifices. Ironically, the destruction of the second Temple moved repentance of sin away from the slaughter of bulls and towards the person and work of Jesus of Nazareth, the Lamb of God who takes away humanity's sin.

The First Passover in Israel's story is the historic and theological context for the Last Passover in the story of Jesus. The celebration of the necessary and sufficient sacrifice of the human-divine Jesus of Nazareth has been renamed. The amnesia of the Church, however, has removed the kernel of the intrinsic meaning of the needed blood sacrifice for sin and sinners originating with the Mosaic Covenant. The Church forgot that only the husk was no longer needed; or, if you prefer, the Church allowed the baby to go down the drain with the bath water. To fully appreciate what redemption in Christ means, is to remember that part of the Mosaic Covenant requires a blood sacrifice to forgive sin. What was no longer needed from the Mosaic Covenant was the *means* of a blood sacrifice, not its end.

The new covenant offered the once-for-all sacrifice of the historic Jesus for humanity's sins, not only those of Israel. This is one of the blessings of Israel for all the families on earth stated in the Abrahamic Covenant. The historic Jesus of faith, took away the power of sin and specific sins by the once-for-all sacrifice of *his own* blood on a cross.

Jesus never explicitly mentioned crucifixion on a cross at the Last Passover. No author of any Gospel records *cross* in this event. Had you

---

45. Hebrews 8: 8—10a, 13.

and I been there, we may have been just as confused as the apostles by Jesus' cryptic words. As we now turn to the Cross, we also find a lack of recorded understanding of its meaning *at that time* for the forgiveness of sin, sins, and sinners. No one seated at the Last Passover grasped that it would be the bleeding body of Jesus on a cross which explained Jesus' words, "This is my body . . . this is my blood . . . "

The Cross

Matthew 27:32—56

How could a Roman tool of torture and death become the most ubiquitous religious symbol on earth? To fully appreciate the Apostle Paul's words, " . . . we proclaim Christ crucified . . . ,"[46] we must begin with a *non-religious* grasp of the Cross.

The Cross, a Roman death penalty, is the lethal injection in our culture today. The Cross was the ultimate death sentence, *Crucifixion defies life and is designed only for death—slow agonizing death. Jesus' death was life-giving.* These two sentences appear to oppose each other; yet, reminding ourselves of Hebraic thought, they exist in tension as two foci to present the both-and of the Cross. For without the death of Jesus the Christ, no promise of eternal life is possible. This monumental event in the story of Jesus is literally the *crux* [Latin for *cross*] of world history for the salvation of all humanity. There is no greater turning point in *world* history, not merely in a *religious* history. Like other previous events in the story of Jesus, the cross mysteriously and provocatively fulfills aspects of Israel's story.

First, going into the Torah, we have, "If a man guilty of a capital offense is put to death and his body is hung on a tree, you must not leave his body on the tree overnight. Be sure to bury him that same day, because *anyone who is hung on a tree is under God's curse.*"[47] [my italics]. Jewish rejection of their idea of Messiah hanging on a cross is completely rational according to the Torah. From an entirely nonreligious view, there is little about God sacrificing His own son to save human beings that makes sense. On its face it appears cruel in no less a way than the jarring account

---

46. 1 Corinthians 1: 23.

47. Deuteronomy 21: 22—23. Alter, *The First Five Books of Moses*, The Tanakh translates this text as "a hanging person is a curse of God." Alter: . . . for a hanged man is cursed of God," 690.

of Abraham about to sacrifice his son Isaac.[48] There can be no wonder then why the Apostle Paul admits that the cross causes Jews to stumble and Greeks to scoff at its foolishness. The Cross is a completely irrational symbol for salvation. The Apostle Paul calls the cross scandalous.[49]

Second, the words and descriptions of the activities in both Psalm 22 and the Gospel texts about the cross strongly suggest that Psalm 22 is messianic. But such possibility must be tempered with the possibility that its authors may have inserted this statement to make a messianic claim, unintended by David. We have no reason to believe, with proof beyond the shadow of a doubt, that David was predicting the suffering of the Messiah. On the other hand, we have no way to disprove it either. Such an image of a suffering God, the Mighty One, on a cross defies the Davidic Covenant's claim that Mary's son would one day sit at the right hand of God on David's eternal throne. " . . . He will be called the Son of the Most High, and the Lord God will give him the throne of his ancestor David."[50]

However, thinking Hebraically, it's the very contradiction which validates the "My God . . . why have you forsaken me?" statement as a strong possibility of David's prediction, given that other verses in Psalm 22 appear to have no meaning within David's context. David's current situation was about his enemies; not about an execution and therefore unfilled within David's life story. The verse " . . . they divided my clothes among themselves, and for my clothing they cast lots."[51] must refer to some later event which validates it as a messianic prediction. Nothing in the Tanakh later fulfills this reference to clothing. The Apostle John, the only male disciple who witnessed Jesus' crucifixion,[52] explicitly quotes Psalm 22: 18 about dividing garments and casting lots in his Gospel.[53]

This happened that the scripture might be fulfilled. Combined with other texts in Psalm 22 which clearly describe crucifixion [22: 14, 15],

---

48. Genesis 22: 1—19.
49. 1 Corinthians 1: 18—25.
50. Luke 1: 32.
51. Psalm 22: 18.
52. The only direct reference to the presence of a male disciple at the cross is made in John's Gospel. It is a third person reference to himself. "When Jesus saw his mother and the disciple whom he loved standing beside her, he said to his mother, 'Woman, here is your son. Then he said to the disciple, 'Here is your mother.' And from that hour the disciple took her into his own home." John 19: 26-27. All other account of the Cross include, and specifically name, the women who were Jesus' disciples.
53. John 19: 24b,c.

we conclude that Psalm 22 meets the following messianic criteria: 1. Any text about a future person/event in the Tanakh which isn't fulfilled within the Torah, Writings, or Prophets and points to a person and/or event in the future and, 2. Is explicitly quoted in the Younger Testament where only Jesus of Nazareth fulfills a prophetic text.[54] The Cross demonstrates how the Story of Jesus finds roots in Israel's story of sacrifice and suffering. The Cross also demonstrates how the story of Israel is fulfilled in the story of Jesus.

The Resurrection

Matthew 28:1—10

Through the Cross God's forgiving grace offers victory over sin. By the resurrection, God's life-giving power offers victory over death.[55]

The only text in the Younger Testament referring to predictive statements in the Tanakh regarding Jesus' resurrection first occurs in the early preaching[56] of the Church recorded by Luke in Acts referring to Psalm 16: 10. "... because you will not abandon me to the grave nor will you let your Holy One see decay." [Acts 2: 27]. Luke goes on to assure Peter's audience that David is not speaking of himself. "David died and was buried and his tomb is here to this day," [Acts 2: 29b]. Then in Acts 2: 31 records David's words as a prediction of Jesus' resurrection. Psalm 16 without question qualifies as a messianic text introduced with Peter's words, "But God raised him from the dead, freeing him from the agony of death, because it was impossible for death to keep its hold on him." [Acts 2: 24].

> *An empty tomb does not prove the resurrection of Jesus Christ from the dead.*
>
> *An empty tomb merely assures us that Jesus' body was somewhere else, not there.*

---

54. Isaiah 53: 3—12 speaks of a person who clearly fits the description of an execution whose sentence is the result of a perversion of just and whose death includes a vivid theological interpretation of redemption and atonement of sin and sinners. Every Gospel account of the cross fulfills this person's description which is nowhere fulfilled within the Tanakh.

55. Bischoff, *The Human Church*, 77—109.

56. Acts 2: 14—26 records the Apostle Peter's first sermon of the Church.

The mere emptiness of the tomb where Nicodemus and Joseph of Arimathea buried the body of Jesus in the latter's tomb,[57] offers no unique evidence for the resurrection of Jesus Christ. At the time, public opinion suggested that Jesus' disciples would steal his body to validate the prediction of his resurrection. Had they done so, Joseph of Arimathea's tomb would have been empty. *But an empty tomb merely indicates the absence of Jesus' body, not his post-resurrection presence with hundreds of others.* Mary Magdalene assumed[58] that the Roman government's placement of guards anticipated that Jesus' followers would steal his body to "prove" his resurrection. No one who visited the tomb expected it to be empty. The visiting and courageous women, though grieving, would have been satisfied to spice Jesus' body given the decaying heat of the Middle East.

The historic claim of the Church about Jesus' resurrection must go beyond an empty tomb and rests upon a reminder from two angels that Jesus' predicted the raising of his body on the third day after he died. The same women who were shocked standing at the foot of the Cross believed Jesus' resurrection and told the male disciples, who thought "these words were an idle tale, and they did not believe them."[59] The message that catapulted the Church into existence based upon the resurrection of Christ was neither anticipated nor believed by most of the people who followed Jesus during his earthly ministry. Would you and I have believed in Jesus' resurrection at that time?

Jesus' resurrection fulfills the story of Israel predicted by King David. The story of Israel anticipates the resurrection of the Messiah. That said, we now turn our attention to the only credible evidence for Jesus' resurrection—His appearances to and conversations with other human beings.

Appearances

Matthew 28; Mark 16; Luke 24; John 20—21

The post-resurrection appearances of Jesus validate that he rose from the dead. This is why his tomb was empty. No one stole his body. In modern day understanding, he wasn't viewed in a casket, nor was his

---

57. John 19: 38—42. All synoptic Gospel authors mention Jesus' burial.
58. John 20: 2b. Mary Magdalene's assumption was reasonable, though false.
59. Luke 24: 1—12.

body cremated, and he didn't have a funeral or memorial service. None of these events, culturally appropriate or otherwise, occurred for one simple reason—Jesus didn't stay dead. The same eyewitnesses of Jesus' life who recorded his ministry and death also documented his conversations and interactions with hundreds of people.

Jesus physically appeared to his disciples in five events after he rose from the dead.

First, to Mary Magdalene; second, to women who went to spice his body; third, to Simon Peter, fourth, to a husband and wife walking home from Jerusalem after the crucifixion; and fifth, to eleven fearful disciples hiding behind a locked door. All these appearances happened on the day Jesus' resurrection was discovered. The reliability of the Gospel documents validate the Jesus' historic bodily resurrection.

We begin with Mary Magdalene, because Matthew, Mark, Luke, and John mention her by name and record her conversation with Jesus.[60] She knew it was Jesus, not because she saw him, but only when she heard his voice saying her name. Hearing is believing, not just seeing. There were no eyewitnesses of this conversation; we know it occurred because it is recorded by those who heard and believed Mary Magdalene's witness.[61] There was no reason not to believe one of Jesus' most committed followers. No literary evidence exists which proves that Mary Magdalene's eyewitness statement was added later to support an untrue belief. Mary Magdalene was the only human being to witness Jesus' crucifixion and was the first person to whom Jesus appeared. Second only to Jesus' mother, she is unique among all the women mentioned in the Gospels.

Second, Jesus appeared to "the women"[62] on their way back from the tomb to tell the disciples. Matthew records their conversation. "Jesus met them. 'Greetings,[63]' he said. They came to him, clasped his feet and worshiped him. Then Jesus said to them, 'Do not be afraid. Go and tell

---

60. John 20: 10—17.

61. This anticipates the Apostle Paul's much later statement: " . . . faith comes from hearing the message, and the message is heard through the word of Christ." Romans 10: 17. In Mary Magdalene actually heard the resurrected historical Christ speaking to her; we hear God's voice today through Scripture; both methods are the Word of God. Claims at hearing the audible voice of God create too much space for suspicion limited by one person's experience which is not prescriptive for the Church.

62. Matthew 28: 8—10. Matthew doesn't name the women, but they could have been Mary Magdalene, Joanna, Mary the mother of James, and the others with them. Luke does name them in Luke 24: 9, 10.

63. *Rejoice* is a better translation,

my brothers to go to Galilee; there they will see me.'"[64] *Brothers* has several implications in Jesus' vocabulary: biological, any human being, and disciples. Here it's best understood as Jesus' disciples, and not his biological family, who may not have believed in him until after the formation of the Church.[65] The women clasped Jesus' feet as an act of worship but did not receive the same warning not to touch him that Mary Magdalene received. There is no apparent explanation for this difference.

Third, Jesus appeared to Peter—the only recorded one-to-one appearance.[66] The two places in the Young Testament where this appearance is recorded never state Jesus' reason for doing so and record no conversation. Jesus' purpose may have been to begin the process of reconciling their relationship after Peter's three-fold denial. Ultimately, Jesus reconciles their relationship in John 21: 15—19, where three questions about love and Peter's answers prepare him to help lead the church.

Fourth, Jesus appeared to Cleopas and his wife, Mary, on their way home to Emmaus, a village seven miles from Jerusalem.[67] They were two of Jesus' followers and had an interesting conversation with Jesus which Luke records in typical detail. It is during their conversation that they learn of Jesus' appearance to Peter which Jesus might have told them over dinner. Cleopas and Mary located the Eleven and told them that Jesus was alive and that he had appeared to Peter. Here we have the longest recorded post-resurrection conversation anyone had with Jesus. In what may be one of the most humorous interactions Jesus had with anybody, he acts as if he knew nothing about the horrendous events in Jerusalem— one might say he had first-hand knowledge! It's safe to say that Jesus had one of the most bittersweet weekends of his life.

His approach is inductive—leading the information out of his conversation partners. He never tells them who he is. It's all discovery on their part. Only while having a meal together did Mary and Cleopas realize that their dinner guest was the resurrected Jesus of Nazareth when he broke bread and gave it to them and how they felt when he rehearsed

---

64. Ibid.

65. John 20: 17 Note: Jesus first uses *brothers* in his post-resurrection appearances with Mary Magdalene referring to his disciples.

66. Luke 24: 34b, The Apostle Paul mentions the appearance to Peter, which occurs before appearing to the Twelve [which would have been one week after appearing to the Eleven on the first day] in 1 Corinthians 15: 5.

67. Luke 24: 13 and John 19: 25 record Cleopas' wife as the sister of Mary, Jesus' mother.

the Scripture out on the road. Cleopas and Mary were not at the Last Passover, but they may have heard about what Jesus said and did with the bread at that meal. Whether Jesus offered his hosts a private experience of the Eucharist is an open question. The two things that convinced the couple that Jesus was really present with them are the same two things that launched the Church into existence by the power of the Holy Spirit: Word and Sacrament. The essential criteria for an authentic church started in an event where two people heard the Word and broke bread together. Criteria for being the church hasn't changed since.

Fifth, Jesus surprised eleven fearful disciples gathered in a room behind a locked door on the evening of that first day.[68] Jesus didn't knock on the door. No disciple unlocked it to let him in. Jesus simply appeared and, realizing their fear, encouraged them to be at peace. Unlike Mary Magdalene, there is no indication that the disciples recognized who he was by his voice. Rather, it was his wounded hands and side that prompted them to "rejoice when they saw the Lord."[69] In John's account, it was the wounds on Jesus' body that convinced them that it was Jesus.[70] The mysterious nature of Jesus' resurrected [glorified] body echoed the mystery of the human-divine nature of Jesus pre-resurrection body. The incarnate pre-resurrection body of Jesus is stated by John as the "the Word became flesh."[71] The post-resurrection body of Jesus is the incarnate glorified presence of Jesus. Both events are a mystery. How do you explain a human-divine-recently resurrected person who walks through locked doors and asks for something to eat?

In sum, all of the above occurred in less than twenty-four hours spanning the morning through the evening of that first eventful day. The proof of Jesus' resurrection is not determined by where Jesus *wasn't* [the empty tomb]. The proof that God raised Jesus from the dead is determined by where he *was* [with many different people over several weeks].

Two significant events after that first day validate Jesus' resurrection. First, Jesus' encounter with Thomas; second, Jesus' beach-side breakfast meeting with seven of his followers.

68. John 20: 19—23.

69. Ibid.

70. Note on Luke 24: 37: " . . . they thought they were seeing a ghost. Jesus was clearly identifying himself." Luke adds more detail [as always] to suggest that even when they saw the wounds they were still not convinced so Jesus asked for something to eat and they watched him eat a piece of broiled fish. Luke 24: 36—43.

71. John 1: 14.

Thomas has traditionally been given a bad rap by the church as a doubter. One week after Jesus' first appearance, Thomas joined the Eleven who had told him about seeing Jesus that evening of the first day. Thomas wants proof. "Unless I see the mark of the nails in his hands, and put my finger in the mark of the nails, and my hand in his side, I will not believe."[72] As a result of touching Jesus, and being touched by Jesus, Thomas believed.

The third meeting with his disciples finds Jesus on the shores of the Sea of Galilee cooking breakfast. John quotes himself ["That disciple whom Jesus loved"][73] in his Gospel as recognizing Jesus, the one who was giving these seven disciples instructions about where to find fish. A second important part of this post-resurrection encounter involves the restoration of Peter after his denial of Jesus just before the crucifixion. Symbolic of healing their relationship after three denials, Jesus asks Peter three times whether he loves him followed by three commands to love the people of God. In effect, Jesus was making sure that Peter, a future leader in the Church, was truly committed to him as Lord. For the early believers to follow Peter as one of the three church leaders in Jerusalem, they'd need to hear Peter's story of reconciliation with his Savior and Lord.

The post-resurrection appearances of Jesus Christ end with his Ascension back to the Father accompanied by an angelic promise of his return to earth.[74]

The Ascension

Mark 16:19, Luke 24:50—52

The last great event in Jesus' life on earth was the Ascension. Jesus challenged his followers to be his witnesses; that is, the judicial validation that everything that the Gospel was true. Jesus laid out a strategy to proclaim the kingdom beginning in Jerusalem and Judea [a primarily an audience of Greek-speaking Jews], Samaria [a diverse audience of half-breed Jews from the Assyrian Captivity with their own interpretation of Judaism], and to the ends of the earth [a primarily non-Jewish Greek-speaking audience].[75] Matthew, the most Jewish Gospel, records how

72. John 20: 24, 25.
73. John 21: 7a,
74. Acts 1: 9—11.
75. Acts 1: 1—11; Luke 24: 50—53. Mark 16: 19—20.

Jesus commissioned his followers saying, "All authority in heaven and on earth has been given to me. Therefore go and make disciples of all nations, baptizing them in the name of the Father and of the Son and of the Holy Spirit, and teaching them to obey everything I have commanded you. And surely I am with you always, to the very end of the age."[76]

Here we have a break with the Jewish Sh'ma's one God. Jesus speaks of baptizing in the name of a mysterious deity who exists in three forms. The Apostle John gets into an explanation of the Holy Spirit's function in his theological gospel—but not before 90 C.E. This means that the fledgling Jewish church in Jerusalem operated only on the oral tradition handed down from Jesus' words of the so-called Great Commission. Of course, Jews were comfortable with an undocumented word typical of their oral tradition—a tradition which continued throughout the church to this day. It's called preaching from God's Word.

Finally, there is one more crucial evidence for the resurrection—the church, the living body of the Jesus Christ. The gathered community of believers attests to the here-and-now presence of Jesus Christ on earth. The conversations he had with over five hundred people continues as the church hears the proclaimed Word of God. Jesus commended the future of faith of those who could never claim to be eyewitnesses of Jesus' bodily resurrection, yet who would believe. That blessed community is part of the blessed families going back to Abraham's Covenant—the church as the family of God. That blessed community will continue to be blessed as it blesses God's first people—Jewish people.

This concludes the story of Jesus—the completion and fulfillment of the story of Israel.

In this chapter we have focused upon Jesus' life story looking into the following key events: birth, dedication, Passover pilgrimage, baptism, temptation, miracles, Transfiguration, Last Passover, Cross, Resurrection, a number of his post-resurrection appearances and the Ascension—all defining events in Jesus' life.

Given the background of Christian thought and the story of Jesus, we now focus in more detail on Jesus' use of parables as a teaching genre.

---

76. Matthew 28: 18—20.

―――― *Chapter 7* ――――

The Parables of Jesus

IN THE PREVIOUS CHAPTER we analyzed key events in Jesus' life and ministry. In this chapter, we'll analyze Jesus' use of parables in his teaching ministry. We'll discover that his stories are not always original, but rooted in the oral Jewish tradition. One key question will govern our analysis: *What does this parable tell us about Jesus?* While there are many from which to choose, we'll focus on three parables which we believe best represent his ministry: *The Parable of the Hearers, The Parable of the Father of Two Lost Sons* and *The Parable of a Samaritan and an Innkeeper.*

Before discussing the details of these three parables, we'll show that his stories were typically provocative and Hebraic.

Jesus' Edgy Parables

Amy-Jill Levine's states that "we must not 'domesticate Jesus' provocative stories."[1] Levine is a Jewish New Testament scholar teaching at a Protestant graduate school. She asks that we "think less about what they mean and more about what they can 'do' to remind, provoke, refine, confront, disturb . . . and at times indict."[2] Employing a hint of chutzpah, Levine challenges historical Jesus research by claiming the prophylactic value of her book is to not only prevent "the disease of anti-Judaism from infecting the body of his parables, but also to avoid the other less toxic but

---

1. Levine, *Short Stories by Jesus*, 1.
2. Ibid., 4.

equally distressing moves that turn parables into platitudes."³ My usage of *edgy* comes from Levine. "Today (2008), Jesus' words are too familiar . . . too stripped of their initial *edginess* and urgency. Only when heard through first-century Jewish ears can their original edginess and urgency be recovered."⁴ [my italics]. She suggests that God may be thought of as an absent spouse . . . or views Israel as kvetching [complaining] to God for abandoning his part of the covenant.⁵ Levine claims that Christian interpretations of Jesus' parables rarely represent the emotion of their Hebraic counterparts. She scolds the church's disregard for the Jewish origins and context of the stories told by a Jewish Jesus.

Parable by parable, Levine undermines Jesus' nimshals. . Humorously [I think], she regrets that the bad guy in the good Samaritan parable is a Levite; for she herself is a Levite. Identifying the Samaritan as good and the Levite as interested in ritual purity rather than human need creates space for a xenophobic view of Jews.⁶ Levine rejects that the Pharisee is wrong for how he prays compared to the tax collector who prays righteously in Luke 18: 19—24. ""The message of the parable then becomes that it is better to be a repentant tax collector than a sanctimonious Pharisee . . . "⁷ She's concerned about stereotypes, rather than viewing the Temple as the holiest place in Judaism where both Pharisee and tax collector may pray as they desire. We prefer Jesus' nimshal: *All who exalt themselves will be humbled, but all who* humble *themselves will be exalted.*⁸ [my italics]. Rather than this parable being a rigid comparison of Jews and Gentiles or the Temple as [bad Judaism]⁹, as Levine suggests, it is a comparison of *values, not persons.* Amy-Jill Levine's cultural insights help vaporize the imposition of historic church-driven anti-Jewish stereotypes. My issue with her method is that when convenient she's always quick to point out how Christian scholars miss the culture behind a given parable without crediting those who don't. That said, few other biblical scholars, Jewish or Christian, have Levine's expertise to admonish the church for its neglect of the Hebraic thought behind Jesus' parables.

3. Ibid., 18.
4. Levine, *The Misunderstood Jew*, 7.
5. Ibid., 13.
6. Levine, *Short Stories by Jesus*, 74.
7. Ibid., 170.
8. Luke 18: 14. Jesus' interpretation is better than Levine's emphasis on something he doesn't do.
9. Levine, 170.

Jesus' Parables are Hebraic

"The dependency of the New Testament parables on Jewish tradition cannot be questioned."[10] Ruben Zimmerman rightfully challenges the traditional assumptions behind the historic scholarship from the nineteenth century which focused more on social location than exegesis. That is, he releases parable exegesis from the anti-Semitic context of traditional nineteenth-century German research in favor of his "new distinction of Jesus 'remembered.'"[11] His robust method reappraises historic, traditional, literary, and hermeneutical approaches concluding that the extraordinary positions Jesus took in his parables affirm "a plurality of interpretations that is established by the texts themselves,"[12] rather than the message-blurring imposition of an excessive emphasis about "what's behind" the text.[13] Zimmerman exposes the errors achieved by methods which prefer only a historical analysis of Jesus' parables, rather than allowing the texts to speak for themselves. When allowed to do so, the texts portray Jesus as a narrator of stories which convey the memory of the historic Christ. Such an approach views Jesus' parables through a Hebraic lens. "The parable narrator is himself the 'parable of God.'"[14] Zimmerman's analysis gives evidence that Jesus' parables tell us something about himself; that is, that he embodies the story of God. *Jesus* is the parable in his stories.

Brad Young has remarried literary analysis and historic context. He deals with actual texts and establishes its Hebraic context and similarity with historic rabbinic storytelling. In his book, *Jesus and His Jewish Parables*, Young gets into the intimate relationship between "the parables of Jesus and the religious heritage, culture . . . and social concerns of the Jewish people during the Second Temple Period."[15] Referencing his mentor and Hebrew scholar, David Flusser, Young credits him for linking illustrative expressions from agadic instruction with Jesus' parables.[16] That is, he emphasizes the rabbinic parabolic method

---

10. Zimmerman, , "How to Understand the Parables of Jesus: A Paradigm Shift in Parable Exegesis," *Acta Theological*, June 2009, 158.

11. Ibid.

12. Ibid.

13. Ibid., 159.

14. Ibid., 163.

15. Young, *Jesus and His Jewish Parables*, 3.

16. Ibid., 34.

which draws from word pictures to convey a particular nimshal. Jesus used this method to connect with a Second Temple audience. David B. Gowler goes so far as to say that rabbis believed that God created the parable form to study the Torah.[17]

Francois Viljoan divides Jesus' audiences into outsiders and insiders whom he calls curiosity seekers and truth seekers, respectively. Jesus conceals the mysteries of the kingdom of God from the curiosity-seekers and reveals those mysteries to the truth seekers.[18] Viljoan courageously delves into the apparently self-contradictory text from Isaiah 6: 9—10 quoted in Mark 4: 11—12. God calls his prophet Isaiah into ministry with these words:

> "Go and say to these people, 'Surely you hear, but you do not comprehend . . . you see, but fail to know. This people is hardening its ears . . . lest it hear with its ears, ...so that it will repent and be healed.'"[19]

Mark quotes Jesus as saying:

> To you has been given the mysteries of the kingdom of God, but to those outside everything comes in parables, in order that seeing they may see and not perceive, and hearing they may hear and not understand, lest they should turn and it should be forgiven them.[20]

Do both Isaiah and Jesus *not* want their hearers to repent? Is this like Jonah's dismay that the people of Nineveh actually heeded his words and repented? Or, is there something else going on here? Robert Alter explains this awkward text as a "preemptive justification of the Prophet's failure . . . "[21] When God called Ezekiel, He nuanced the same idea, saying:

> Whether they hear or refuse to hear (for they are a rebellious house), they shall know that there has been a prophet among them.[22]

---

17. Gowler, *What They Are Saying About the Parables*, 84.
18. Viljoan, "Why Jesus Spoke in Parables," *In die Skriflig/In Luce Verbi,* November 2019.
19. Isaiah 6: 9—10, Tanakh.
20. Mark 4: 11- 12, *The New Greek-English Interlinear New Testament*.
21. Alter, *The Prophets*, 642.
22. Ezekiel 2: 5.

Alter radically contends that merely knowing that you've heard from a prophet outweighs one's response to the message.

Michael Vlach analyzes five places in the New Testament which reference Isaiah's warning.[23] He addresses each text[24] within its own context, and unfortunately concludes that it's talking about a monolithic national rejection of Jesus as Messiah.[25] In the same breath he acknowledges that some Jews actually did believe that Jesus was the Messiah. For example, all of Jesus' original disciples were Jews. A member of the Sanhedrin, Nicodemus, eventually believed and took the risk of touching Jesus' crucified body. The Apostle Paul was a Jewish Roman citizen and a Pharisee from the tribe of Benjamin. His encounter with Jesus changed not only his life, but also the spread of the Gospel into the first century world. Regrettably, Vlach maintains Dispensationalism's mantras about Israel which can't divorce itself from the misguided notion that all texts quoting Isaiah indicate a national rejection of Jesus. The New Testament nowhere supports that the *entire nation* of Israel rejected Jesus as the Messiah leading to a conspiracy to kill him.

Vlach also proposes that Isaiah's words are messianic; but Jesus never quoted Isaiah when claiming to be the Messiah. When Jesus spoke of fulfilling the Law and the Prophets, he had the Sermon on the Mount in mind. None of the New Testament authors use this Isaiah text to validate that Jesus was the messiah. Rather, Isaiah's mention in the Gospels and by Paul in his letters verify Israel's rebellion and hardheartedness—a continuation from its historical struggle to obey God's commands. It is clear from the Gospels and elsewhere in the New Testament that there were in fact insiders and outsiders, those who believed and those who did not. Insiders emerged from God-seeking Gentile communities and many outsiders were Jewish.

Brad H. Young launches his robust analysis of Jesus' stories by saying, "The reality of God is revealed in the word-pictures of a parable. Jesus and the rabbis of old taught about God using concrete illustrations that reach the heart through imagination. They challenged the mind on the highest intellectual level using simple stories that made

---

23. Vlach, "The Significance of the Five Quotations of Isaiah 6: 9—10 in the New Testament," *Christian World View and Theology* July, 2017.

24. Ibid., Matthew 13: 14—15, Mark 4: 11—12, Luke 8: 10, John 12: 40 and Acts 28: 26 –27.

25. Ibid.

common sense . . . "[26] He continues, "Parables are a shadow of the substance."[27] Jesus' parables were incarnate words. Just as Jesus himself was the Word made flesh [John 1: 14], his parables were ordinary stories that contained divine truth. Just as Jesus, the Storyteller, was one person with two natures [*human* and *divine*], his parables were *hidden* truth *revealed* in words. *Jesus was a living parable of God.* He literally embodied God. His finite parables contained infinitely divine truth. We agree with Young's definition of a parable as shadow [hidden] of the substance [revealed]. Jesus walked this earth as the reality of God hidden in a human body. Jesus' birth story was his first parable. The subsequent key events of Jesus' entire earthly existence may be thought of as one different but related nimshal after another.

One-third of the recorded sayings of Jesus in the Synoptic Gospels are in parables."[28] Young is patient with historical criticism research. "The historical and critical method is a starting point."[29] But to best grasp the purposes of Jesus' parables is to consult the *actual texts* as well as *what's behind the texts*. Young's journey past the starting point and exegesis includes historical rabbinic parables which "describe the relationship between God and men . . . The unknown God is revealed in what is known by human experiences of life."[30]

No better comprehensive resource on the parables of Jesus exists than *Stories With Intent* by Klyne Snodgrass. "Jesus' parables are among the best known and most influential stories in the world."[31] Snodgrass sifts through virtually all other scholarly research to provide the intent of each parable. He identifies the chaff of much research which has neglected the kernel of resolution contained in each story. He lobbies for a nimshal which resolves conflict in any story. However, he states, " . . . a parable is not merely a story . . . [but] in its broadest sense refers to an expanded analogy."[32] He claims that his research transcends merely viewing a parable as allegory. "That is, people have read into the parables elements

---

26. Young, *The Parables: Jewish Tradition and Christian Interpretation*, Grand Rapids:Baker, 2012, 3, and Warren Wiersbe, *Windows on the Parables*, 15.

27. Young, *The Parables*, 3.

28. Ibid., 7.

29. Ibid.

30. Ibid., 11.

31. Snodgrass, *Stories With Intent*, 1.

32. Ibid., 2.

of the church's theology that had little to do with Jesus' intent."[33] Failure to invoke formational Hebraic thinking when interpreting parables creates space for informational-only Greek thought. However, possibly from his evangelical posture, Snodgrass misses the opportunity to validate his appeal for a more Hebraic view of Jesus' parables by failing to cite Amy-Jill Levine's as a resource even if he takes exception with her analysis.

Snodgrass contends that learning involves more than direct information. "People set their defenses against direct communication and learn to conform its message to the channels of their understanding of reality. Indirect communication finds a way in a back window and confronts what one thinks is reality. Parables are indirect communication."[34] Klyne Snodgrass urges that we allow Jesus' parables to change our lifestyles by discovering Jesus' intent—which begs this question—*What is Jesus saying about himself in this story?*

We now consider the following three key parables: *The Parable of the Hearers, The Parable of the Father of Two Lost Sons,* and *The Parable of a Samaritan and an Innkeeper.*

Three Key Parables

The Parable of The Hearers

Luke 8:5—8

> A sower went out to sow seed; and as he sowed, some fell on the path and was trampled, and the birds of the air ate it up. Some fell on the rock, and as it grew up, it withered for lack of moisture. Some fell among the thorns, and thorns grew with it and choked it. Some fell on good soil, and when it grew, it produced a hundredfold.[35]

"The traditional name, *Parable of the Sower*, focuses attention on the farmer. The whole story, however, revolves around four types of *soil* and preparation for that *soil*, and its title should reflect the essence of the message."[36] Brad Young focuses on the audience [Are the hearers insiders or outsiders?], local culture [How would the hearers have understood

---

33. Ibid., 4.
34. Ibid., 8.
35. Luke 8: 4—8a.
36. Young, *The Parables*, 251.

it?], language [How does linguistic structure support the message?], and Jewish background, [Is it linked with historic rabbinic stories?]. Finally, What does the *Parable of the Hearers* tell us about Jesus?

Let's begin at the end. What is the message of this parable which is renamed for its emphasis on *soil* rather than a sower or seed? A proposed nimshal: "The love of Jesus the master teacher emerges from his challenge for each person to receive the word with a good heart ... who ... will produce much fruit."[37] Working backwards, how do we get to the nimshal from the mashal? Are the hearers insiders or outsiders, or both? Yes. "When a great crowd gathered and people from town after town came to him ... "[38] At first glance, it appears that outsiders comprise the audience. But then Luke records, "Then his *disciples* asked him what this parable meant."[39] [my italics]. The question of audience is complicated further by the multiple interpretations of the apparently-contradictory text, "looking they may not perceive, and listening they may not understand."[40] Jesus defines insider and outsider—outsiders will get the message in parables, but Jesus will explain the mysteries of the kingdom to his disciples, the insiders. But even these handpicked insiders don't get it, so in the case of this particular parable, Jesus does something he rarely does—he interprets it for his followers. This makes sense early in his ministry so that the just-called disciples understand future stories about the kingdom of God.

How would the hearers have understood it? Would the agricultural context have heightened the likelihood that the hearers would listen? Yes. "The images of farming in first-century Israel are foreign to the modern world and sometimes word-pictures from another culture will create very wrong interpretations ... Farming the land of Israel was a very special and esteemed calling ... The farmer's greatest concern is the condition of the soil ... Soil preparation is essential for a bountiful harvest."[41] Jesus' mashal would have immediately gotten the attention of farmers in his audience.

How does the linguistic structure of the parable support its message? Young proposes an answer which involves Hebrew parallelism.[42]

37. Ibid., 276.
38. Luke 8: 4a.
39. Ibid., 8: 9.
40. Recall Isaiah 6: 9—10 quoted five times in the New Testament.
41. Young, *The Parables*, 259-60.
42. Ibid., 256.

The idea here is to build the story to a climax. We have the one positive action of sowing related to the parable's three negative consequences. It's like building steps to a staircase. "The climax is reached after the threesome of negative elements that have undermined the positive action have run their course."[43] None of the three negatives would have been foreign to Jesus' audience of skilled farmers. They would have experienced each of the three negatives when planting a crop. Every farmer would know that proper soil preparation as well as good soil are required for a fruitful harvest.[44] Hebrew parallelism created a drama leading to the climax of a unique, but not impossible, harvest.

Finally, *what might this parable tell us about Jesus?* Young states in general that, "When the importance of discipleship in the kingdom is fully appreciated, the Jewish worldview that study of the Torah will give life becomes closely related to the parables of Jesus."[45] *The Parable of the Hearers* represented in the types of soil tells us that Jesus was most concerned about developing followers receptive to the Word of God. Jesus needed informed disciples to help him build the kingdom of God.

Lois Tverberg identifies four types of hearers who sit in the presence of the rabbis: the sponge, the funnel, the strainer, and the sieve. "The sponge," which soaks up everything. "The funnel," which takes in at this end, and lets out at the other. "The strainer," which lets out wine and retains the dregs, and "The sieve," which removes the chaff and retains the flour.[46] Note that even though "the sponge" in modern thinking is often admired, sponges soak up everything, including what needs to be discarded. That is, they retain the chaff and lack the discernment to see the kernel. Could Jesus have had the following Talmudic parable in mind?

> Quick to learn and quick to lose
> His gain is cancelled by his loss.
> Slow to learn and slow to lose.
> His loss is cancelled by his gain.
> Quick to learn and slow to lose
> this is a good portion.
> Slow to learn and quick to lose
> this is an evil portion.[47]

---

43. Ibid.
44. Ibid.
45. Ibid., 261.
46. Tverberg, *Sitting at the Feet of Rabbi Jesus*, 35 quoting Mishnah *Avot* 5: 15.
47. Young, *The Parables*, 265, quoting *Abot* 5: 15.

THE PARABLES OF JESUS

Finally, we need to show that our name-change and approach agrees with the interpretation Jesus offers for this parable. Does our assertion that soil and its preparation constitute the nimshal hold water? Jesus' interpretation is in Luke 8: 11—15:

> Now the parable is this: The seed is the word of God. The ones on the path are those who have heard; then the devil comes and takes away the word from their hearts, so that they may not believe and be saved. The ones on the rock are those who, when they hear the word, receive it with joy. But these have no root; they believe only for a while and in a time of testing fall away. As for what fell among the thorns, these are the ones who hear; but as they go their way; they are choked by the cares and riches and pleasures of life, and their fruit does not mature. But as for that in the good soil, these are the ones who, when they hear the word, hold it fast in an honest and good heart, and bear fruit with patient endurance.

First, note that Jesus says nothing about a sower; second, he uses a simile to tell the hearer that the seed is the word of God. At this point Jesus applies the story to life. He's now talking about how real people may respond to God's word. The "birds of the air" represent the work of the devil to actually take away God's word from people. The "withering plant without moisture" represents how hearers may fall away from faith when times get tough. The "thorns" represent how people disregard the word and opt for the pleasures confined to the material world. Finally, compared to a path, rocks, and thorns, Jesus first uses *soil*, good soil, which produces a bountiful harvest of fruit. In each of the above scenarios, Jesus speaks to the spiritual condition and preparation of each person to receive and retain the word of God leading to a mature spiritual life. *Heart* is the key word in his interpretation. *Heart* in Hebraic thought is the center of the person's entire being involving body, mind, soul, and spirit. Good soil is comprised of those who love the Lord their God with all their heart. Our title change derives from Jesus' interpretation.

In sum, we note that *The Parable of the Hearers* challenges traditional names and interpretations, identifies the audience, tells a story to which that audience may relate and, identifies one clear nimshal,—Jesus wants ordinary people hear and study the word of God.

Next, we get into the parable of the so-called prodigal son.

The Parable of The Father of Two Lost Sons[48]

Luke 15: 11—32 [paraphrased]

"There was a man who had two sons. The younger son asked for his land inheritance and the father divided the property between the two sons. The younger son left home and squandered all his property to find himself destitute since a famine had occurred throughout the country. He ended up with a job feeding pigs and would have been happy to eat what he fed them since no one offered him any food. Finally, he came to his senses and discovered that his father's servants were living better then he; so he rehearsed a repentant speech and went home to his father. His father saw him coming and ran out to meet him and hugged him compassionately. The son admitted his sin to his father and said he was no longer worthy to be called his father's son. But his father clothed him and had a huge celebratory dinner for the return of his son.

The older son heard the celebration and when he was told about the part, he got angry and jealous and refused to join in. He explained how hard he worked for many years and yet never received a party with his friends. But his father said, "Son, you are always with me, and all that is mine is yours. But we had to celebrate and rejoice, because this brother of yours was dead and has come to life; he was lost and has been found."[49]

This parable is traditionally known as *The Parable of the Lost Son*,[50] *The Parable of the Prodigal and His Brother*,[51] or simply the *Parable of the Prodigal Son*. These titles do not accurately describe the story. For example, what defines *lostness* or *prodigal*? None of commonly-used titles say anything about the father, as if he weren't important. What is the correct meaning of *prodigal* as it refers to a family member, in this case, a son? *Prodigal* may be either a noun or an adjective having to do with being wasteful of money or resources.[52] Is only one of the sons lost because he spent money wastefully? In what way was the elder son lost? Two sons were lost in this parable because they fell out of a loving relationship with

---

48. Young, *The Parables*, 110.
49. Luke 15: 11—32, paraphrased.
50. NIV heading for Luke 15: 11—32.
51. NRSV heading for Luke 15: 11—32.
52. *The American Heritage Dictionary*, Wm. Morris, ed., *Prodigal*, as an adjective, means "recklessly wasteful," .,
Boston: Houghton Mifflin, 1969, 1044.

their father for different reasons. It was a father's compassion for each of his sons which restored their relationship as sons.

We find that Young's title steers clear of the above errors by *not* using *prodigal*, by using *father* and including the *lostness* of both sons. How would first-century Second Temple Jewish people have heard this story? Levine maintains that hearers would have considered this parable an intriguing story about healing and reconciliation within a family. An ensuing conflict between younger and elder sibling meant that hearers must identify with the younger. "But those first century listeners were in for a surprise when the younger son turns out . . . to be an irresponsible, self-indulgent, and probably indulged child . . . "[53] While she's closed to the possibility that Jesus uses this story to convey his redeeming love for outcasts, her cultural interpretation is a welcomed addition to other views which "view the parables through the eyes of the church's beliefs about Jesus rather than first century Jewish beliefs about God."[54] Jewish beliefs historically included a compassionate God for sinners who return to him. Young finds no scriptural support for Barth's insistence that the younger son represents Jesus who brings sin to a forgiving father as an example of the atoning death of Christ.[55] Clearly, the church's belief in the atoning work of Jesus is the gospel's message. Brad Young certainly believes that the gospel is the central message of Christianity. He doesn't limit the thrust of this story to a one-for-one representation of characters symbolizing doctrine.

Brad Young verifies the Hebraic roots for this parable by its use of Semitic language and vocabulary. "The Semitic atmosphere created by the story is directly linked with language."[56] He makes special note of the visceral nature of Hebraic thought. " . . . Semitic languages love idioms using terms for the body . . . 'fill his belly' . . . 'bread' . . . refers to all the physical needs of the body . . . "[57] The phrase *came to his senses* would have been understood by a Second Temple audience as code for *teshuvah* [returning to God]. The use of *senses* is visceral vocabulary involving all bodily ways to discern insight into one's experiences. *Senses* goes right to the heart of the matter. A truly repentant young son uses all his senses to discern his mistakes and comes home to his father. This parable is a

53. Levine, *Short Stories by Jesus*, 47.
54. Young, *The Parables*, 132.
55. Ibid.
56. Ibid., 142.
57. Ibid., 147.

good example of the essential characteristic of the Hebrew language—its visceral origins.

David B. Gowler weighs in on *came to his senses* using Albrecht Duerer's *The Prodigal Among the Pigs* woodcut. "Duerer captures the prodigal's utter destitution . . . the moment when the prodigal 'came to himself' . . . as true repentance . . . "[58] Gowler goes on to connect such a moment as getting touch in with the image of God implanted in all human beings. The concept of the invisible image of God as the basis for human dignity is a huge idea in Hebraic thought.

Amy-Jill Levine roots this parable in its oral tradition to challenge a traditionally misinformed interpretation that the father represents a benevolent God, unlike the wrathful one in the Old Testament. This distortion about God goes back to the oldest heresy in the church which used Gnostic thought to split God into two different persons—the angry one in Genesis to Malachi; the nice one in Matthew to Revelation. She assures her readers that God didn't undergo a personality change during the four hundred years between the Old and New Testaments. Jesus never challenged Judaism's concept of God whose kingdom spans all history from the beginning. Levine states, "Rabbinic literature . . . recounts a parable which opens with a citation from Deuteronomy 4.30,[59] 'You will return to the LORD your God.' It continues:

> 'To what is the matter like? It is like the son of a king who took to evil ways. The king sent a tutor to him who appealed to him, saying, 'Repent, my son.' But the son sent him back to his father [saying], 'How can I have the effrontery to return? I am ashamed to come before you.' Thereupon his father sent back word: 'My son, is a son ever ashamed to return to his father? And is it not to your father that you will be returning?'"[60]

The Tanakh and its Talmudic commentary consistently portray God as a loving and compassionate father forming the basis for Jesus' concept of God maintained by every New Testament author.

---

58. Gowler, "What can Renaissance art and Howard Thurman tell us about the prodigal son?" *National Catholic Reporter*, July 8, 2023.

59. The context for this text is God telling Moses about a time when Israel will feel abandoned, but must not forget all that God has done for them as a loving and merciful God. The father-son story that follows fits well with the blessings that accompany coming back home to one's father.

60. Levine, *Short Stories by Jesus*, 57-8, quoting *Deuteronomy Rabbah* 2.24.

Levine's main interpretation of this parable focuses on "finding the lost, of reclaiming children, of reassessing the meaning of family [as] not only good news, but better news."[61] She goes to great lengths to debunk attempts to impose anti-Semitic stereotypes, especially the son's involvement with pigs. "First, the son ate no ham hocks or pigs' knuckles . . . the issue is not Jewish xenophobia or purity. The problem was starvation.[62] Finally, Amy Levine flavors her assessment of this parable with a picture of the father who welcomes his distraught son—one who needn't be ashamed of his past—but rather one who can always return to his father no matter what the situation. "For the rabbis, the challenge is not in seeing God's love in a new way; the challenge–an inevitable challenge in every religious system–is to get the wayward to return."[63]

Lois Tverberg reflects on the Mideastern ritual meal of reconciliation called the *sulha* to explain why a compassionate father would want both of his sons at table. The *sulha* is a "festive meal to mark reconciliation between father and son."[64] Jesus' constantly upset the religious applecart of his day by eating the sulha with sinners. In so doing, Jesus lived his life as a parable. The Lord's Table is a *sulha* where sinners are reconciled to God through Jesus Christ who is both *on* the table as body and blood and *at* the table as host. Every celebration of the Eucharist is another occasion where Jesus is having a meal with sinners.

Both Gary Inrig and David Henson season this parable with spicy interpretations supporting Jesus as a storyteller who is far from domesticated. Inrig pokes at any form of religious self-righteousness which is "content to leave sinners in the pigpen."[65] If this sounds too provocative, Inrig allows for a Jesus who would have eaten with the younger son along with the pigs. All questions about Jesus' relationship with sinners are addressed in his metaphor about sheep and goats in Matthew 25 where he equates himself with the very sinners he came to save.

Once we see a non-religious Jesus, we find a Gospel which dispels pious stereotypes of the Savior. "Here is a God who . . . runs to the filthy."[66] Henson takes *provocative* to another level. "What if . . . God . . . comes to

---

61. Levine, "What the Prodigal Son story doesn't mean," *Christian Century*. Its-baggage.
62. Ibid.
63. Ibid.
64. Tverberg, *Sitting at the Feet of Rabbi Jesus*, 147.
65. Inrig, *The Parables: Understanding What Jesus Meant*, 23.
66. Ibid., 28.

us in the disguise of those we despise?"⁶⁷ He's suggesting that God is not the compassionate father, but the prodigal son. "But what if God is not the father in this story? What if God is the God who comes to us in the disguise of those we despise . . . those who hate us and killed us, rejected us and abandoned us . . . And if God comes to us as this, how do we respond? . . . In this parable, Jesus is asking us whether we will entertain angels even if the angels look to us like demons."⁶⁸ Given Inrig's insight with support from Matthew 25, we find merit in Henson's move making us the father who accepts the Other however he appears. He suggests that Jesus is asking his hearers to overcome prejudice and religious oppression to embrace others whoever they may be. Jesus *is* the prodigal. Would *we* run out to embrace one who ate with pigs?

To complete our analysis of Jesus' parables, we now turn our attention to the so-called Parable of the Good Samaritan.

The Parable of a Samaritan and an Innkeeper

Luke 10: 30—35

> "A man going down from Jerusalem to Jericho was robbed, beaten, and left for dead. A bypassing priest and Levite on their way to Jerusalem came by but avoided the wounded man. Then a Samaritan came by and compassionately bandaged his wounds, brought him to an inn and took care of him. The next day he paid all expenses to the innkeeper for the man's food and lodging."⁶⁹

We rename the parable after the two protagonists: *a* certain Samaritan and *an* innkeeper. Our use of an indefinite article is intentional. The Samaritan and the innkeeper could have been *any* Samaritan and *any* innkeeper. Levine is right to decry the term *good Samaritan,* a term which nowhere appears in the story. "To label the Samaritan, any Samaritan, a 'good Samaritan' should be, in today's climate, seen as offensive . . . tantamount to saying 'He's a good Muslim.'"⁷⁰ The word *good* doesn't appear

---

67. Henson, "God is the Prodigal Son: Reinventing Christianity's Most Beloved Parable," *Patheos*, March 7, 2023.

68. Ibid.

69. Luke 10: 30—35, paraphrased.

70. Levine, *Short Stories by Jesus*, 74.

in the Greek as a description for the Samaritan, In fact, no adjectives accompany any one of the five actors in this story. They are simply ordinary people. Gary Inrig suspects that Jesus' audience would have considered *good Samaritan* an oxymoron. He catches Jesus' edginess to make one of the two heroes in the story a despised Samaritan. The Lord deliberately and carefully shocks his audience.

Ana Marta Gonzalez heralds the humanity of the innkeeper who's just doing his job as an unsung hero in the parable. "To look after the wounded man the Samaritan enlisted the help of the innkeeper. How would he have managed without him? He [the innkeeper] . . . did most of the work, acting in his professional capacity."[71] A Samaritan innkeeper took a risk by lodging a Jewish man. Jews rarely went through Samaria going up to Jerusalem and typically traveled on the east side of the Jordan River. In fact Luke records the lack of hospitality by Samaritans toward Jews when the disciples complain to Jesus that they've been rejected and want to destroy a village [Luke 9: 51—56]. Jesus rebukes his followers[72] and then tells them the above parable.

Ironically, two "church" leaders find their religious duties more important than caring for another human being. Brad Young states, "The priest and the Levite continue the action of the robbers; the robbers abandoned him to die and they pass by in like manner."[73] We must never forget that Jesus' greatest conflicts were with Second Temple elders and teachers of the law. Gonzalez speaks to this issue of professional vs ordinariness when applying faith to living. She talks about "the fusion between a priestly soul and a lay mentality."[74] Consistent with a Hebraic worldview, for her, *all* of life is sacred and *all* work is to be sanctified. A Samaritan's immediate care combined with an innkeeper's room and board were sacramental; that is, ordinary work with deeper spiritual implications.

Where is Jesus in this parable? From his metaphor of the last judgment about sheep and goats, Jesus identifies himself with one left for dead in the ditch. " . . . I was sick and you took care of me . . . ."[75] Even more than showing us *how to* love the poor, Jesus claimed *to be* the poor. *Jesus* was that dying man. Jesus urged the lawyer to do what he already

71. Gonzalez, "Reflections on the Good Samaritan," *Scripta Theologica.*
72. Young, *The Parables*, 109.
73. Ibid., 197.
74. Gonzalez, "Reflections on the Good Samaritan."
75. Matthew 25: 36

knew from the Writings[76]—to feed one's enemy. Loving one's enemy originates in Hebraic thought.

Klyne Snodgrass' candidate for a nimshal is this: "We conclude then that this parable is intended to show that love does not allow limits on the definition of neighbor."[77] He addresses the self-justifying lawyer's misguided question: Who is my neighbor? Luke tells us nothing about the half-dead man, nor that the Samaritan needs to know anything about him prior to anointing him with healing oil. The lawyer's "neighbor" is the one he is passing by at any given moment. As for all his questions in this story, the lawyer had all the right answers and recognized mercy in others. But will this lawyer grasp the story enough to obey Jesus' "Go and do likewise."[78] Luke never tells us.

In this chapter we've investigated three parables which represent a cross-section of Jesus teaching ministry. First, *The Parable of the Hearer* emphasized the spiritual preparation to hear of God's Word. Second, *The Parable of a Father of Two Lost Sons* stressed that all lost sinners need the reconciling compassion and love of God. Finally, The *Parable of a Samaritan and an Innkeeper* urges disciples to abandon any religion which doesn't risk being a neighbor by caring for others without regard to cultural, ethnic, or religious background.

Based upon the intent and nimshals of Jesus' parables, we now turn our attention to the provocative stories Jesus told to convey the kingdom of God.

---

76. Proverbs 25: 21, NIV note: Exodus 23: 4—5 speaks of caring for your enemy's ox or donkey when in trouble. In the Sermon on the Mount [Matthew 5: 44] Jesus called this loving your enemy. In this often-misunderstood sermon, Jesus challenges his audience with ["you have heard it said] misinterpretation of Leviticus 19: 18 which does not include "hating your enemies." His Jewish audience heard it from their misguided religious teachers, not the Tanakh.

77. Snodgrass, *Stories With Intent*, 357.

78. Luke 10: 37.

Chapter 8

The Kingdom of God in Jesus' Parables

IN THE PREVIOUS CHAPTER we discussed three key parables Jesus used to convey who he was. In this chapter, we'll get into how the kingdom of Heaven [Matthew's term] and the kingdom of God show up in Jesus' stories. We've selected three parables which explicitly use *kingdom*, identifying which of Jesus' parables have roots in either the Tanakh, the Talmud, or other rabbinic literature. We'll also explore three parables which focus on the kingdom value of grace.

We begin our study with the familiar parables of the mustard seed and yeast.

Three Explicit Kingdom of God Parables

The Parables of the Mustard Seed and Yeast

Luke 13: 18—21

> What is the kingdom of God like? What shall I compare it to? It is like a mustard seed, which a man took and planted in his garden. It grew and became a tree, and the birds of the air perched in its branches. It is like yeast that a woman took and mixed in with three measures of flour until all of it was leavened.

Like these two short stories, most of Jesus' parables on the kingdom are extended similes.

"What is the kingdom of God *like*?" Jesus compares the kingdom of God to a mustard seed and a disproportionately tiny amount of yeast [leaven] stirred in with three measures of flour [about one bushel]. The smallest of seeds becomes a tree large enough to house birds.

Klyne Snodgrass builds a case for the transformation of the miniscule to greatness as a characteristic of the kingdom. "The Mustard Seed similitude urges, possibly warns, that no one should be put off by what appears unimpressive. Like the tiny mustard seed which grows to a large plant, so the kingdom is present, even if hidden, unnoticed, or ignored, and its full revelation with its benefits will come."[1] Snodgrass speaks eschatologically about God's final consummation of history, the conclusion of the kingdom of God which first appeared in Israel's story, was enhanced during Jesus' ministry, and will be fulfilled in the future.

Jesus' ministry was consistently misunderstood by his own followers. They missed the point of *transformation from insignificance into importance*. The essence of Jesus' ministry was the kingdom of God. We agree with Snodgrass who observes in both parables a strong christological implication: "Jesus' word and work . . . [announce] . . . that the kingdom of God has made its entrance."[2] It is a kingdom which is near, at hand and, within any disciple. Or, in David Flusser's more succinct statement: "the most important innovation by Jesus was that he identified the messianic age with the rabbinic kingdom of heaven;"[3] thus, claiming to be Messiah who will plant a future kingdom of heaven at the end of history. Jesus speaks about fulfilling the historic and present kingdom of heaven on earth from Israel's story. The development of the kingdom of heaven is "not a sudden transformation . . . but a gradual process of growth"[4] as implied in both parables.

"Both parables work together to illustrate the common theme of the evolutionary growth of the kingdom.[5] Brad Young's analysis resonates with other sources leading to this possible nimshal: *The kingdom of heaven grows gradually from the small and apparently unimportant into a*

---

1. Snodgrass, *Stories With Intent*, 225.
2. Ibid., 228.
3. Flusser, *The Sage from Galilee*, 95.
4. Young, *Jesus and His Jewish Parables*, 190.
5. Ibid., 206.

large and significant organism. We now turn our attention to *The Parable of the Owner and Workers in a Vineyard.*

The Parable of the Owner and Workers in a Vineyard

Matthew 20: 1—15 [paraphrased]

For the kingdom of heaven is like a landowner who went out early in the morning to hire laborers for his vineyard. The daily wage was one denarius. Throughout the day, at nine o'clock, noon, and three in the afternoon, he went out and hired more workers. At five o'clock he found others standing around and asked why they were not working and they said that no one had hired them. So he hired them as well. When evening came, the owner had his manager pay all the workers beginning with the last hired going to the first hired. Those hired at five o'clock got one denarius. When the first hired heard about this they complained to the owner that they should receive more, for they had worked longer in the scorching heat of the day. But the owner replied, "Friend, I'm being fair to you, did you not agree to work for one denarius? Take your money and go home. It's my money and I can pay my help as I choose. Are you jealous that I'm generous?

There's no missing the point of this story. Jesus states the nimshal for this parable: "So the last will be first, and the first will be last."[6] For the workers, fairness is at stake; for the owner, envy and generosity are the concerns. Here's an edgy Jesus turning cultural values on their head to assure his audience that his kingdom at times may appear irrational. The workers have a point. The earliest hires worked longer under worse conditions than the last hired. The owner sees it differently. For him what's at stake is who decides and how payment should be made. The parable doesn't mention worker quality. Could the last hired have gathered more grapes in one hour than the first hired did during the whole day? Did the workers hired at noon produce less damaged fruit than those hired at nine o'clock? All questions related to comparison have nothing to do with this story.

Productivity may justify the apparent injustice of the wages, not the amount of hours worked. To say how long one worked is to say nothing about that worker's effectiveness or efficiency. But the question remains:

6. Matthew 20: 16.

Is this parable about a king or his laborers, or both? Torah-based halakhic law requires paying workers on a daily basis, especially if they are poor.[7] However, no king is obligated to debate with his workers the fairness of wages. That is, the worker was assessed against criteria established by the king, not logic. Klyne Snodgrass concentrates on the owner and after his typically thorough analysis, states the following nimshal: "God in his sovereignty will judge as he sees fit."[8]

There is little to recommend Levine's summary which reduces the story to seek out those in need by opening one's hand to the poor. If she takes the risk of involving God in this parable, it is merely that he "makes his sun rise on the just and the unjust."[9] She does, however, link Jesus' parable with rabbinic literature: "Moses our teacher served Israel one hundred and twenty years and Samuel only fifty-two. Nevertheless, both are equal before the omnipresent."[10]

Brad Young mentions God's grace by entitling it, "*The Fair Employer: Jewish Grace in Jesus' Parables* [which] illustrates the divine character in concrete images of money, labor, management, and most especially the wealthy landowner."[11] [author's italics]. He surfaces the obscurity of *fair* by comparing God's notion of fairness with that of accepted practice. Ethical behavior is rooted in worship. "The motive of love, which emerges from a deep awe and reverence for God, should be the guiding principle of moral action and spiritual life."[12] No separation exists among worship, belief, and obedience which co-exist in Judaism. To think Hebraically is to retain apparent contradiction and paradox. Levine's interpretation is essentially ethical and Snodgrass' is theological. When rightly understood, neither ethics nor theological can be separated. Ethics requires a basis; theology is effete without concrete action. Jesus' teaching of a mutuality of grace and obedience resident in a sovereign God is what we should take from this parable.

The next parable, *The Parable of the Merciful Lord and His Unforgiving Servant*, speaks of God's grace and forgiveness.

---

7. Deuteronomy 24: 14—15.
8. Snodgrass, *Stories with Intent*, 379.
9. Levine, *Short Stories of Jesus*, 218.
10. Ibid.
11. Young, *The Parables*, 69.
12. Ibid., 74.

The Parable of the Merciful Lord and His Unforgiving Servant

Matthew 18: 23—34 [paraphrased]

> The kingdom of heaven may be compared to a king who wished to settle accounts with his slaves. One owed ten thousand talents and could not pay. His lord ordered him, his household and possessions to be sold to pay the debt. The slave begged for mercy and the lord forgave him the debt. That same slave came upon a fellow slave who owed him a hundred denarii, seized him by the throat and demanded immediate payment. The fellow slave pleaded for mercy, but the slave threw him into prison until he paid what he owed. When other slaves saw all this, they were distressed and reported it all to their lord. The lord confronted the unforgiving slave about why he didn't extend the same mercy he had received and had him tortured until he paid the entire debt.

Peter asks Jesus a question which seeks to limit forgiveness. ""Lord, how many times must I forgive my brother when he sins against me? Up to seven times?"[13] Jesus responds by telling him that forgiveness has no limit. Peter heard about forgiveness throughout Jesus' ministry and now seeks to apply it to his own life as a disciple. Job credits God who forgives three times. "God does all these things [forgives specific sins] to a man—twice, even three times . . . "[14] Peter has taken one verse from the Writings out of context for the purpose of self-justification. Can you see the surprise on Peter's face when Jesus chides him for putting any number on it at all which is to say that forgiving should become second nature.[15] Jesus tells the story whose nimshal is: "This is how my Father will treat each of you unless you forgive your brother from your heart."[16] Let's get into the story.

Brad Young focuses on *debt* and *debtors* which are the same words Jesus used when teaching his followers how to pray recorded in Matthew 6: 12. He connects *The Lord's Prayer* and this parable both of which endorse forgiveness as an essential quality for a disciple. Even in today's financial parlance, a lending institution may use *debt forgiveness* to wipe out what is owed. Jesus often used money to illustrate the qualities of

---

13. Matthew 18: 21.

14. Job 33: 29.

15. Ryan, "What is the Significance of Seventy-Times Seven in Forgiveness," Jesus' use of "seventy times seven" is a counterpoint to the Torah's [Genesis 4: 24] story about the number of times one might seek revenge for a wrong.

16. Matthew 18: 35.

heaven's kingdom. Young states how a Semitic audience would have understood *debt* as *sin*. "Often a debt is metaphorically related to interpersonal relationships on a moral and ethical level . . . [meaning] . . . release from monetary debt and forgiveness for an injury or wrong."[17] When the church says the Lord's Prayer substituting *sin* and *sinners* for *debt* and *debtors,* it is speaking Hebraically. To forgive is to be loving. This parable has its ultimate roots in the extension of the Torah's *Shema* . . . . love God by loving your neighbor. Treat your neighbor as you would want to treated . . . forgive as you would want to be forgiven. From Hillel's interpretation . . . do not fail to forgive just as you would not want someone to fail to forgive you. Young says "one must be merciful in the same way God shows mercy."[18]

This story is about the Gospel. Derived from Israel's Day of Atonement, the annual clearing of the slate of sin in one's life, we see that Jesus is the only one who could forgive sinners when considering the utter magnitude of all the wrongs of all people for all time. There is nothing about the destitute slave which obligates the king to clear his debt. It is only the heartfelt compassion of a forgiving king who has the power and ability to do so. Just as that same slave knew the king's mercy, he, too, had the power to be forgiving. "Only the king can forgive the debt, and he forgives it by paying it himself."[19] That is the Gospel. The compassion of this king is the actualized grace of God in the person of Jesus Christ on a cross. The tragedy in this mini-drama is that a forgiven slave just didn't get it. Everybody knew how wrong it was not to be forgiving having been forgiven.

"This parable, which only appears in Matthew, . . . [is one of] . . . the most revealing and compelling of all Jesus' parables . . . [revealing] . . . both the nature of parables and the essence of Jesus' kingdom message."[20] Klyne Snodgrass identifies the themes of grace and responsibility in this story, yet excludes *grace* from his title.

He includes the following paraphrased parable from the Oral Tradition which speaks of a God who forgives all misdeeds from previous generations. Here's a midrash on Psalm 79:8, "Remember not against us the iniquities of our forefathers:"

---

17. Young, *The Parables*, 122.
18. Ibid., 129.
19. Ibid., 95.
20. Snodgrass, *Stories with Intent*, 61.

> A money-lender said to a borrower who kept reminding him of how much he owed from years ago, "Why do you remind me of a debt so long ago, I have long since forgotten about it." So is the Sovereign of the Universe. Men sin before Him, and He, seeing that they do not repent, forgives them sin after sin, and when they come and remind Him of the debt they contracted previously, He says to them, "Do not remind yourselves of former sins."[21]

This story from Israel's Oral Tradition takes forgiveness to another level by comparing God to a creditor who graciously surprises even the most responsible sinner of his wrongs. Better statements of God's unconditional forgiveness do not exist.

Can a king be both gracious and judgmental? Can God? Any fair reading of the Tanakh or the Younger Testament consistently portrays God who grace as well judgment. It is the same Creator who makes it rain to help a farmer and at the same time call off a baseball game [to use a trivial example]. Most apparently theological contradictions may be resolved by thinking elliptically; that is, by rejecting Hellenism's *either-or* and accepting the *both-and* from Jewish thought. Often reticent to theologize about parables, Snodgrass does so here by pointing out that it is "wrong to read this parable as an allegory of modern economic circumstances ... the theology of the parable, which is rooted in a *required* compassion and mercy, must be applied in all circumstances."[22] [author's italics].

Just as these three parables convey Jesus' theme of the kingdom of God, we now take look at three parables which focus upon the important kingdom value of grace – *The King and His Son's Wedding Reception, The Bridesmaids and the Bridegroom, and The Investments.*

A common theme unites these three parables: God wants us to have the good things we lose when we reject his grace.

In each analysis of the following three parables, we'll avoid the temptation to allegorize by linking persons in the stories with some outside referent. Rather, we'll consider the scholarship of several sources to determine a nimshal which supports our common theme.

The objective will be to determine one key thought which addresses both God's desire for us and how our behavior may lead to losing His best for us.

---

21. *Exod. Rab.* 31: 1.
22. Snodgrass, *Stories with Intent*, 76.

The Kingdom Value of Grace in Jesus' Parables

The Parable of a King and His Son's Wedding Reception

Matthew 22: 2—13 [paraphrased]

> The kingdom of heaven may be compared to a king who gave a wedding reception for his son. He sent his slaves out to call those who were invited, but they would not come. He invited them again to tell them the banquet was ready, but they still would not come. They made light of it . . . one went to his farm, another to his business and others mistreated and killed the slaves. The king was so angry he sent his army out to destroy the murderers and burned their city. The king decided the first people he invited were not worthy, so he sent his slaves to the main streets of the cities to invite anyone to come, the good and the bad to fill the wedding hall with guests. Looking over the crowd, the king saw a man without a wedding robe and said, "Friend, why aren't you wearing a wedding robe?" The man was speechless. The king then asked his attendees to bind the man's hands and feet and throw him into the outer darkness where there will be weeping and grinding of teeth.

Jesus is an extremist when it comes to telling stories. Why would not wearing a wedding robe be a reason to throw an invited guest into Hell? After all, this man was part of that common crowd of good and bad who were invited when the snobbery of the initially welcomed guests displayed itself in lame excuses for not coming. The king considered him worthy to attend the wedding banquet. Suffice it to say even those who answer the call may not earn a seat at the dinner table. "Many are called, few are chosen."[23]

Jesus' edginess begins at the beginning of the mini-drama. Prior to his harsh judgment on one person, a king's anger resulted in murder of invited guests [elected ones] and burning their city after they killed the king's messengers. Who are these "chosen or elected" persons?

We reject any suggestion that *all Jews* are lumped into this undefined category of initially invited guests. Flusser states: "It seems to me that the designation 'the elect ones' is derived from a dualistic worldview that does not fit the theology of Jesus."[24] Flusser's disciple Brad Young weighs

---

23. Matthew 22: 14. Might this be a possible nimshal for the story? God's grace invites everyone to life, but only those who come receive it.

24. Flusser, *The Sage from Galilee*, 128n30.

in: "This is not a parable about Christianity and Judaism but an urgent message for all people to accept God's gracious invitation and to remain faithful to his call."[25] Once we reject the historic attitudes of the church[26] toward the Jewish people, some of which stem from a misinterpretation of this parable, we can discover its true intent and meaning.

Snodgrass reiterates Bonhoeffer's notion of cheap and costly grace.[27] " . . . unlimited grace of the kingdom always brings with it unlimited demand."[28] Cheap grace deludes the initially-invited guests who think that they'll be able to come even if they disrespect the king. They believe that their self-righteousness will get them into the kingdom. Cheap grace accepts the invitation, but disrespects the groom. Snodgrass reinforces costly grace with his comment that the Matthew 22: 14 proverb about being called but not chosen demonstrates the need to understand the Hebraic thought of divine grace *and* human responsibility.[29]

Finally, Young includes rabbinic support for Jesus' parable. "In the Jerusalem Talmud, the story is told about the village tax collector Bar Maayan . . . *The Tax Collector's Dinner for the Needy:*

> But when Bar Maayan, the village tax collector died, The whole whole town took time off to mourn him . . . Now what was the meritorious deed which Bar Maayan had done? He never did a meritorious deed in his life. But one time he made a banquet for the councilors of his town but they did not come. He said, "Let the poor come and eat the food, so that it does not go to waste."[30]

Jesus consistently elevated the least likely candidates into prominence as examples of his expansive grace and inclusive mercy. We see that Jesus adds the element of judgment which includes the severe consequence of losing God's intended privileges of a seat at a wedding banquet table . . . "for the marriage of the Lamb has come, and his Bride has made herself

---

25. Young, *The Parables*, 175.

26. Ibid., 184, Note: "John A. T. Robinson thought that the first sending was directed toward the Jews and the second to the Gentiles. This assumption is anachronistic . . . Allegorizing the parable in this way divorces the parable from its historic setting . . . "

27. Bonhoeffer, *Discipleship*, 43ff.

28. Snodgrass, *Stories with Intent*, 320.

29. Ibid., 321.

30. Young, *The Parables*, 180-181, from *y. Sanh.* 23c ch 6, halakah (English trans. J. Neusner, *The Talmud of the Land of Israel Sanhedrin and Makkot* [Chicago: University of Chicago Press, 1984] 181.

ready; to her it has been granted to be clothed with fine linen, bright and pure—for the fine linen is the righteous deeds of the saints"[31]

The second parable in this trilogy of stories about losing what God wants us to have is *The Parable of the Bridesmaids and the Bridegroom*.

The Parable of the Bridesmaids and the Bridegroom

Matthew 25: 1—12 [paraphrased]

> The kingdom of heaven may be compared to ten maidens who took their lamps to meet the bridegroom. Five were wise and took oil with them; five, foolish taking no oil with them. While sleeping, waiting for the bridegroom, there was a cry, "Come out to meet the bridegroom." All the maidens got up and trimmed their lamps. The foolish asked the wise to give them oil when their lamps went out. The wise didn't do so thinking there wouldn't be enough for their lamps. So they told the foolish maidens to buy their own. But the bridegroom came while the foolish maidens were away. So only the wise maidens attended the marriage banquet. The door was locked shut. When the foolish maidens returned, they begged the Lord to let them in. He said, "I don't even know you."

Like the last parable, this story is about doing what's necessary to attend a wedding reception. Imagine a bridesmaid needing to leave the procession up a church aisle because she forgot her flowers and had to backtrack to the narthex to get them and then find her place in line. That's what happened when half of the bridesmaids had to go into the village to restore their lamps which burned out during the procession.[32] They returned too late to attend the party. Totally embarrassing for everyone!

Klyne Snodgrass notes that " . . . the bride is never mentioned, as is true of all other Synoptic texts mentioning a bridegroom or wedding festivities . . . "[33] He states, "The most important thing is that the

---

31. Revelation 19: 7b—8.

32. The lamps are a rag drenched in olive oil at the end of a long pole which needed restoring every fifteen
minutes requiring lots of oil along the way. Trimming meant cutting off the charred end of a rag to add more oil
NIV note on Matthew 25: 1ff.

33. Snodgrass, *Stories with Intent*, 512.

bridegroom's appearance is a sign for the festivities to begin."[34] All involved must be ready on cue. Five of the bride's friends were not and they lost their place at the wedding table.

Only Matthew records this parable which many scholars neglect when assessing Jesus' teaching ministry about the kingdom. David Flusser says little more about it than that it is a beautiful parable which represents Jesus' skill as a storyteller.[35] Young references Flusser's thought related to the story as an example of a "wise and the foolish" motif which frequently occurs in the Gospels.[36]

Brad Young warns against positioning the kingdom of heaven as only a future event. "Can the kingdom be both present and future?"[37] He says yes. Reviewing earlier parables of the mustard seed and yeast points out the gradual process of a present kingdom's growth. There is no reason to opt for an *either-or* approach to the kingdom when we have the elliptical *both-and* of Hebraic thought helping us see the partially present kingdom [already, but not yet] waiting its future complete fruition in the messianic age.

Finally, *The Parable of Investments* completes the trilogy of mini-dramas which warn against losing what God really wants us to have.

The Parable of Investments

Matthew 25: 14—28 [paraphrased]

> For it [the kingdom of heaven] will be like a man who went on a journey and entrusted his three servants with his money giving five talents to one; two to another; and one to yet another. The servant with the five talents doubled his money; the servant with the two talents doubled his money as well; but the last servant with one talent buried his and only had that one talent when the man returned. The master applauded the investments of the first two servants and awarded them each the joy of the master. The master scolded the last servant, told him he was lazy and said, "You should have invested my money with the bankers so that at my return I would have interest. The master took the talent from him and gave it to the servant with ten talents.

---

34. Ibid., 513.
35. Ibid., 505.
36. Young, *Jesus and His Jewish Parables*, 35.
37. Ibid., 190.

In his first analysis of this parable in 1989, Brad Young compared Matthew's and Luke's version of this story citing Matthew's as the most Jewish which "more accurately reflects the better sources for the text."[38] Over ten years later, he focuses on the theme of stewardship. "The underlying theme of the parable of the Talents . . . is stewardship. What will the steward do with his master's goods?"[39]

Young challenges a traditional interpretation centering only on the so-called end times and return of the Son of Man to earth. Rather than pitting practice against doctrine, he employs the *both-and* motif inherent in Jesus' holistic use of stories to communicate responsible daily living in the kingdom of God. "As a Jewish teacher in the first century, Jesus combined apocalyptic thinking with practical living. The practical message of the parables should never be eclipsed by an overemphasis on the coming of the Son of Man . . . Even if the context in the Gospel of Matthew highlights the theme of preparedness for the end times, the parable's deeper message teaches the disciple to recognize God's gifts, to be a responsible caretaker of his gracious endowment, and to serve God faithfully."[40] Rather than using this parable to advance the return of Jesus Christ, Young urges Jesus followers to live responsibly toward others here and now. The sheep-goats metaphor about judgment at the end of time in the last section of Matthew 25 mentions nothing about belief, but about ethical living toward the marginalized where Jesus equates himself with the homeless, thirsty, hungry and incarcerated.[41] Belief is evidenced by action. At the same time, parables have a theological basis which supports the nimshal of action.

Jesus tapped into the culture of his day to gain a hearing about the kingdom using this mini-drama about investment. "The actual setting of the parable is found in dramatic events from the everyday life of the people . . . Big money and the high risk of investing capture the interest of the audience."[42] But it is also Jesus' Jewishness which effectively reaches his audience. Young prefaces a similar rabbinic parable, *Love and Fear of the King's Servant*[43], by pointing out in a sermon regarding

38. Young, *Jesus and His Jewish Parables*, 168.
39. Young, *The Parables*, 82.
40. Ibid., 84.
41. Matthew 25: 40. "And the King will answer them, "Truly, I say to you as you did to one of the least of my brethren, you did it unto me.'"
42. Young, *The Parables*, 88.
43. Ibid., 89 quoted from *Yalkut Shimeoni*, vol. 1, Remez 837.

the Sh'ma that loving God doubles your reward both in this life and the next, while being afraid of God stifles God's blessing.

While he stresses the here-and-now, Young addresses the theological basis for the parable. "The theological foundation of Jesus' parable embraces the Jewish worldview of God and his creation. The world belongs to God . . . [therefore] . . . each person must recognize God's sovereignty by giving thanks to him whenever one benefits from God's world in any way. This pervasive Jewish understanding of the world is found in the practice of giving thanks."[44] Young's mention of God's sovereignty thrusts this story right into a portrayal of the kingdom of God with its emphasis on productive and obedient living in a daily relationship with the Creator.

Klyne Snodgrass finds no need for a nimshal "because the reality depicted is allowed to shine through in the telling of the story and because of the context in which it appears."[45] So in a way the mashal *is* the nimshal. Snodgrass takes a stronger position than Young regarding eschatology in favor of stewardship. While endorsing Flusser's thesis that the parable is really derived from rabbinic stories which emphasize how human beings would behave if they believed God was not present, Snodgrass states, "The stewardship themes are important, but they derive their significance within the context of Jesus' teaching about the kingdom and the future."[46]

God wants us to live the good life in relationship with him. The three above parables have focused upon what we lose when rejecting God's grace.

Next, we'll get into several short stories beginning with how Jesus used harvesting and fishing to convey the kingdom of God.

The Kingdom of God in Jesus' Short Stories

The Parable of Growth

Mark 4: 26—29 [paraphrased]

> The kingdom of God is as if someone would scatter seed on the ground and would sleep and rise night and day while the seeds sprout and grow. The earth then produces of itself, first the

---

44. Ibid., 93
45. Snodgrass, *Stories with Intent*, 519.
46. Ibid., 534.

stalk, then the head, then the full grain in the head. But when the grain is ripe, he goes in with a sickle, because the grain is ready to harvest.

The nimshal of this parable speaks of the kingdom of God as a process, not only a future once-for-all event. It is a synergy of human and divine activity because it requires the mysterious phenomenon between planting and harvesting. The planter sleeps and gets up night and day having nothing at all to do with its becoming visible out of the soil. It is a progressive series of growth stages resulting in a second intervention of human activity involving a metal tool and cutting motions of a planter turned harvester. The planter must decide when to cut the plant [when it's ripe]. If harvested too soon the plant possesses undeveloped fruit; if too late, it may rot on the stalk. In either case, the fruit is damaged and ill-prepared for consumption.

Snodgrass advocates a present, not futuristic view of this growth process "which is like a *whole process* narrated by the parable."[47] [author's italics]. He divides the human activity involved first in the planting and secondly in the harvesting pairing the parable with that of the mustard seed—a small beginning resulting in a larger harvest even though it does not "provide the key to . . . [this parable's] . . . interpretation."[48]

The *Parable of Growth* anticipates the Apostle Paul's comparison of spiritual growth with the Fruit of the Holy Spirit. The invisible mysterious activity of the Spirit accounts for the growth of joy, patience or longsuffering within the believer.[49] Such personal growth depends on an intimate relationship with Christ.

Finally, "the parable illustrates the proper attitudes toward the kingdom and its eschatological harvest—it will come when God's time is ripe . . . because God is the one at work . . . "[50] The following story is a nuanced version of *The Parable of Growth*.

The Parables of the Wheat and Weeds

Matthew 13: 24—29 [paraphrased]

---

47. Snodgrass, *Stories with Intent*, 184 quoting Jones, *Studying the Parables*, 106.
48. Ibid., 185.
49. Galatians 5: 22-23.
50. Snodgrass, *Stories with Intent*, 190.

> The kingdom of heaven may be compared to someone who sowed good seed in his field. But when everyone was asleep an enemy sowed weeds among the wheat and left. When the plants came up and bore grain, the weeds appeared as well. The slaves asked their master about how the weeds got in with the wheat to which he replied, "An enemy has done this." The slaves asked if they should pull up the weeds to which the master replied, "No, for in gathering the weeds you would uproot the wheat . . . at harvest time I'll tell the reapers to collect the weeds first to be burned, then gather the wheat and put it into my barn.

Snodgrass is the only scholar who thoroughly analyzes *The Parable of the Wheaton and Weeds*. He notes several parallels from *Early Jewish Writing*: " 'From the spring of light stem the generations of truth, and from the source of darkness the generations of deceit, God does not punish sinners immediately but allows time for repentance . . . ' "[51] " 'For the evil about which you ask me has been sown, but the harvest of it has not yet come, Behold the days are coming and it will happen when the time of the world has ripened and the harvest of the seed of the evil ones and the good ones has come . . . ' "[52] From *Later Jewish Writings,* " 'A heave offering is valid even if given from the worse of two kinds of produce that are not diverse 'save only when tares are given instead of wheat . . . ' "[53]

The nimshal may be that both good and evil exist during the time when the kingdom of heaven is present. Noting this parable's agricultural theme, Snodgrass states that this narrative along with the parables of a Sower "are the most revealing about the nature of the kingdom."[54] For example, it is present despite the existence of evil. The concept of purity is absent from Jesus' definition of the kingdom evidenced by the fact that Jesus does not purify either individuals not communities, Jewish or otherwise. He doesn't fix the Samaritan woman's relationships with men or promises that healed people won't get sick again. Jesus feeds many people with no guarantee that will never again be hungry. He succinctly says, 'The kingdom of God is near, repent, and believe the good news?' "[55] Jesus' spiritual presence is the only criterion for the kingdom of God.

---

51. Ibid., 192, 1QS 3: 19– 23 and Philo, Leg. 3.106.
52. Ibid., 193, *4 Ezra* 4: 28—32, *2 Bar.* 70: 2.
53. Ibid., 194, *m. Terumot* 2.6.
54. Ibid., 197.
55. Mark 1: 15.

Employing Hebraic thinking, Klyne Snodgrass states that "The Bible always leaves us dealing with tension. We cannot be tolerant of evil, but the destruction of evil is not our task. We must stop being evil, and we must stop evil from destroying, but how can we stop evil without becoming evil in the process. That may well be *the* human question."[56] [author's italics].

The Net and the Fish

Matthew 13: 47—48 [paraphrased]

> [The kingdom of God] . . . is like a fishnet which caught every kind of fish. When it was full, the fishermen put the good into baskets and threw out the bad.

Is this parable about a net or the fisherman? Is it about a present kingdom or the eschatological kingdom? What similarities and differences might it have with the *Parable of the Wheat and Weeds* which employs the familiar good and bad motif? These questions have historically surrounded this short narrative.

Brad Young suggests that though it alludes to the future, its emphasis lies with the conflict of a present kingdom on earth with the forces of evil. "The kingdom is bursting forth . . . like leaven in the dough or like a tiny mustard seed which grows and grows . . . in the dynamic ministry of Jesus and his followers as men respond to the call of total obedience."[57]

As he has stated before, Snodgrass finds this short parable emblematic of a whole process of an emerging kingdom as opposed to one which occurs in a single event. Suggestions for how to interpret the parable vary from "the ministry of the church, . . . Jesus' ongoing relationship with a wide variety of people, . . . [and], a story which reflects the mixed character of Matthew's church . . . "[58]

Wide support for this story derives from both the Elder Testament texts and rabbinic literature where " . . . the net and fishing imagery has a long Old Testament history of representing hardship, captivity, and judgment from God."[59] The prophets speak of God as judging the nations by

---

56. Snodgrass, *Stories with Intent*, 215.
57. Young, *Jesus and His Jewish Parables*, 221.
58. Snodgrass, *Stories with Intent*, 487.
59. Ibid., 488.

gathering the wicked in his net and trawl and by throwing his net over Pharoah.[60] Jesus adds the hope of a positive place for the righteous.

Reminding the reader that the kingdom of heaven is a whole process of gathering and separation, Klyne Snodgrass concludes his analysis with the following statement: "We ... need to recover a healthy understanding of judgment, which undeniably was a central feature of Jesus' message with regard to Israel and as part of his kingdom preaching ... We should never forget that without judgment, there is no need for salvation."[61]

We've just reviewed a few short of parables whose theme is the kingdom of heaven. They span a wide variety of illustrations from agriculture, labor, and finance. We've saved the following familiar parable on treasure and pearls for last. It will serve as a summary of the entire chapter which has been a focus on how Jesus used stories and parables to convey the kingdom of God.

The Parables of Joy in the Kingdom

Matthew 13: 44—46 [paraphrased]

> "The kingdom of heaven is like treasure hidden in a field, someone found and hid; then in his joy he goes and sells all that he has and buys that field. It is also like a merchant in search of fine pearls who finds an expensive pearl and bought it after selling all that he had.

Brad Young asserts that the twin mini-dramas of the treasure and pearl include complementary aspects of the cost of discipleship and the value of the kingdom.[62] On behalf of all his friends, Peter reminded Jesus about the high price they've paid to become disciples "Look, we have left everything and followed you ... "[63] to which Jesus responded, "And everyone who has left houses ... will receive a hundredfold and ... inherit eternal life."[64]

---

60. Habakkuk 1: 14—17 and Ezekiel 32: 3.
61. Snodgrass, *Stories with Intent*, 492.
62. Young, *Jesus and His Jewish Parables*, 213.
63. Matthew 19: 27,
64. Ibid., 19: 29. Earlier, Matthew quotes Jesus, "But strive first for the kingdom of God and his righteousness, and all these things will be added to you as well." Matthew 6: 33.

Young entitles this short story, *The Find,* and suggests that anyone may attain the kingdom's benefits in this life by being willing to sacrifice anything.[65] Recall our earlier study of the positive rabbinic view of the yoke of the kingdom. Hebraically, the changed life derives from bearing the "yoke of the kingdom . . . Such devotion to God and God's revelation in the Torah was not without sacrifices."[66] The yoke of the kingdom for the rabbis is "The Torah . . . the pearl of great price. It contained . . . the Kingdom of God within itself. By studying and serving the Torah . . . [and] . . . practicing it and fulfilling its laws, the Israelite . . . took upon himself the glad yoke of the kingdom . . . "[67]

The treasure's joy doesn't occur until one takes the huge step of faith of selling everything and trusting that God will provide for any material need to live. The Writings anticipate this story. " . . . store up my commandments within you turning your ear to wisdom . . . and if you search for it as hidden treasure, then you will understand the fear of the Lord and find the knowledge of God."[68] The hidden joy of the kingdom is knowing God.

Klyne Snodgrass notes how the Early Jewish Writings anticipate this parable. "Wealth and wages make life sweet, but better than either is finding a treasure."[69] He maintains the theme about any cost being worth it to find a treasure. Echoing the joy in finding a treasure, Snodgrass continues his theme of the kingdom of God as a whole process, not a one-time event. "The kingdom of heaven is like the case of a man who finds a treasure, covers it, and because of joy, sells all, and purchases the field. The kingdom encompasses all these aspects."[70] Snodgrass concludes his comparative analysis of these twin parables homiletically with "The gospel we proclaim must deserve and explain the label 'treasure,' and our lives must express the ultimate value found in Christ."[71]

Amy-Jill Levine virtually challenges every allegorical, commodification, and homiletical interpretation within biblical scholarship. "A healthier way of reading the parable begins with de-allegorizing both the merchant and the pearl, persists by recognizing the exaggerated

---

65. Young, *The Parables*, 201.
66. Ibid., 206.
67. Ibid., 210, quoting Montifore, *Rabbinic Literature and Gospel Teaching*, 254.
68. Proverbs 2: 1—5.
69. *Sir* 40: 18. , 236.
70. Snodgrass, *Stories with Intent*, 242.
71. Ibid., 247.

absurdity of the merchant's actions, and addresses how the parable raises questions of surprise, identity, and ultimate concern."[72] She focuses on the merchant in the second story.

"'The kingdom of heaven is like a merchant . . .' not fine pearls, or even the best pearl. It's about a person, the merchant."[73] How does she arrive at this conclusion? She starts with the audience. How would Jesus' audience thought of merchants? Were they held in high respect for their business acumen leading to wealth? Overall, Levine casts a negative shadow over any person whose livelihood rests on selling or buying. "Merchants receive dismissive treatment in the Septuagint."[74] They set prices too high, sell people into slavery, and cannot be trusted. So when Jesus inserts a merchant into his story about costly pearls, he's getting the attention of his audience by proposing a radically joyous outcome to one typically regarded with suspicion . . . yet another example of edginess. The least likely individual becomes the protagonist to communicate the joyous value of living by kingdom values. We agree. Jesus consistently did this throughout his ministry. Recall the story about a mustard seed.

Levine's interpretation turns on the re-invention and transformation of the merchant. For having found the pearl of great price, having sold everything, he's out of business. That is, he in no longer a merchant. He's changed his identity. He's a different person. Levine extends her initial challenge and builds upon the idea of a transformed merchant referring to four specific misinterpretations.

First, she dismisses the *Gospel of Thomas* for its *Gnostic flavor* where a special pearl symbolizes the special elitist knowledge for salvation. Its allegorical interpretation is a misreading. Second, Levine rejects any interpretation of the Christian value of *sacrificial charity* possibly implied by selling all his possessions and giving to the poor. She adds that "The parable cannot mean anything related to economics."[75] Third, she separates the two parables even though they are stated together. Most people can relate to the logic finding, burying, and buying to get what you don't need to obtain what you want. It's logical for the most part to do so. The second parable contains no such logic. The first story speaks of joy without explaining it; the merchant displays no joy in the second

---

72. Levine, *Short Stories of Jesus*, 129.
73. Ibid.
74. Ibid., 131.
75. Ibid., 141.

parable. All attempts to focus on economics are dismissed by Levine. So then what *is* her interpretation?

Fourth, she sees a certain detachment in the second parable regarding, not the pearl, but the merchant. To repeat, after selling all that he has, merchant is no longer a merchant. He's a changed man who has reinvented himself—possibly one could say he's *found himself*. The merchant is detached from his previous life for something better, he's found the best pearl. Levine goes so far as to call the whole process the essence of Christian spirituality.[76] Levine, a non-Christian Jewish scholar, has provided a Christian interpretation of these two short stories creating space for the joy of following Jesus. Jewish fishermen literally dropped their nets and found joy in following Jesus as transformed members of the kingdom of heaven.

To summarize: in Parts One and Two, we've explored a Hebraic and Christian view of the kingdom of God communicated through parables. We've stated that only by looking at the Bible through a Jewish mode of thought can any reader accurately interpret Scripture. Then, we've demonstrated where possible how Christian thought is rooted in Hebraic thinking. The best example of this is recognizing the Jewishness of Jesus as a storyteller.

In Part Three, "Distortion," we'll discuss the synagogue and church as embodiments of God's kingdom. We'll get into the sad history of how God's kingdom was severed as Christians departed from their Hebraic roots.

We begin our analysis of the synagogue in the next chapter.

76. Ibid., 145

— PART THREE —
Distortion

— Chapter 9 —

The Synagogue

Part Three, "Distortion," includes a look at the synagogue, the church, and a parting of the church from its Hebraic roots. In this chapter, we'll begin an analysis of the synagogue, by addressing its etymology [definition], origin, history, purpose, and liturgy.

The Etymology of Synagogue

The Hebrew for synagogue may be translated as *"beit k'nesset* ["house of assembly"], *bet-ha-tefillah* ["house of prayer"], and *bet-ha-midrash* ["house of study"].[1] It is a gathering place for worship, a place to pray, and a place to study. We will trace its evolution from the Tabernacle and Temple. Deriving *synagogue* from word pictures, Jeff A. Benner defines it as an "appointed place for an event."[2] The synagogue is a gathering of Jewish worshippers for a solemn time of communal readings, prayer, and a homily from the Torah.

Mary Wright nuances *synagogue* as "an entrance into the experience of worship through a door."[3] The physical building offers a way into the Presence of the *Shekinah* going back to Moses and the Tabernacle. The synagogue's doors open so the bride of the Sabbath may enter.

---

1. Editors of Britannica, "Synagogue: Definition and Fact."
2. Benner, *Ancient Hebrew Lexicon*, 207.
3. Wright, *Hear God's Heart*, "Hebrew Letters and Meaning."

Yiddish for synagogue is *shul*. In Greek it is *sunagogue* or *ekklesia*; the former connoting a building, the latter, an assembly. A synagogue is "a democratic institution established as a community of Jews who seek God through prayer and sacred studies."[4] This definition focuses upon Torah study where Torah it is not only the Five Books of Moses, but also an overall statement of instruction. During first-century Second Temple Judaism, the Pharisees urged all Jews to study the Torah individually and communally. Given this brief overview of the word, we now turn our attention to the synagogue's origin, history, and purpose.

The Origin, History, and Purpose of the Synagogue

"The Jewish synagogue is one of the oldest surviving religious institutions."[5] Most scholars believe the synagogue started during the Babylonian Captivity. The purpose of the fledging synagogue as an informal gathering offered a place to worship, pray, and study by which Judaism began. Robert Drews credits the exile of the southern kingdom, Judah, as the event which launched "the beginning of Judaism in Mesopotamia."[6]

At his own initiative, Moses pitched a small tent where "Hashem would speak to him face to face, as a man speaks with his fellow."[7] The people never entered his tent, where God spoke to him. Functioning as a priest, Moses took what he heard as the word of God and shared it with the people. This informal tent anticipated the detailed design and construction of the Tabernacle where God also appeared only to Moses while the people stood by at the door. God's Presence appeared as cloud through which He spoke to only one person, Moses. This one-to-one correspondence established Moses' leadership and authority as a mouthpiece for Yahweh.

Parenthetically, the LORD seemed perfectly content with the mobile Tabernacle. Speaking to Nathan, King David's prophet, God said, "I

---

4. *Encyclopedia Britannica*, https://britannica.com/topic/synagogue.

5. Smith, "The Ancient Synagogue, The Early Church and Singing," JSTOR.

6. Drews, "The Babylonian Captivity and Its Consequences," *Judaism, Christianity, and Islam to the Beginnings of Modern Civilization*.

7. Exodus 33: 7—11, Note: "Since God announced to Moses that His Presence would not reside among them, God's prophet set up his Tent in isolation, where God would speak to him. However, Moses remained available to any Jew who sought the word of God."

have not dwelt in a house from the day I brought Israel up out of Egypt to this day. I have moved from one tent site to another, from one dwelling place to another. Wherever I have moved with all the Israelites, did I ever say to any of their leaders whom I commanded to shepherd my people, 'Why have you not built for me a house of cedar?'"[8]

God requested only a Tabernacle for which he gave very detailed specifications. Moses initiated oversaw the construction of the Tabernacle and Solomon built the first Temple which was destroyed by the Babylonian army. Ezra managed the construction of the second temple. Herod exquisitely remodeled Ezra's second Temple and it was destroyed by the Roman army in 70 C.E. The Tabernacle was never destroyed. As the first and only structure never destroyed, we view the Tabernacle as the model for where God's people eventually worshipped, prayed, and studied the Torah. The Talmud reports that the Shekinah may be found in acts of public prayer. "Where ten are gathered for prayer, there the Shekinah rests."[9] Just as the Shekinah cloud hovered over the Tabernacle, it also rested upon worshippers in the synagogue where the people were publicly reading and hearing the word of God from the Law and the Prophets.

Intermediary priests were no longer needed to offer multiple sacrifices on multiple sacred days as in the days of the Tabernacle and the Temples. "The priesthood, a hereditary institution dating back to the time of Moses, became defunct."[10] After the destruction of the second Temple, no sacrifices for the forgiveness of sin could be offered. "Jewish prayer ... occurred ... as a substitute for sacrifice ... as Hosea said, 'The offerings of our lips instead of bulls.'"[11] Communal confessional prayer for forgiveness of sin replaced the blood of lambs and goats. Rabbis challenged the people to continue study on their own individually or possibly in small groups, a tradition continued in synagogues to this day. "As the synagogue became increasingly organized, "The so-called 'democracy of the synagogue,' ... strongly encouraged each layperson to be a virtuoso in Torah ... in which the rabbi—though learned as a scholar-teacher—was considered a layperson ... "[12] From the small and often-overlooked tent of Moses, to the public Tabernacle to the first

8. I Chronicles 17: 5, 6.
9. *Sanhedrin*, 39a.
10. Wilson, *Exploring Our Hebrew Heritage*, 258.
11. Rich, "Jewish Liturgy," Judaism 101.
12. Ibid.

and second Temples, the longest lasting house of worship for the Jewish people evolved into the synagogue.

Given this brief summary of the origin, history and purpose of the synagogue, we now get into the synagogue's liturgy.

The Liturgy of the Synagogue

Liturgy is what people *do* when worshipping God; literally, it is "the common work of the people."[13] It is active participation as a community. Without a temple during the Babylonian Captivity, the Jewish people lamented not only the loss of a spirit of worship, but also grieved over the absence of a place to worship.

> By the rivers of Babylon—there we sat down
> and there we wept as we remembered Zion.
> On the willow there we hung our harps.
> For there our captors asked us for songs.
> And our tormentors asked for mirth, saying,
> "Sing us one of the songs of Zion."
> How could we sing the LORD's song in a foreign land.[14]

Without a Tabernacle or a Temple, Israel maintained its worship "in a foreign land" by creating the synagogue. It is likely that the Israelites met in homes. With no ability to perform sacrifices, Torah study and prayer formed the basis for worship. One could read and study the Torah and prayer behind closed doors. Some of the Jewish captives caved into the pagan worship of Babylonian gods; however, the Jews in Babylon also remade themselves and their world view and looked back to their Mosaic origins in an effort to revive their original religion. Hearing the word, studying the Torah, and praying formed the backbone of Jewish liturgy in fledgling synagogues while the nation was imprisoned in Babylon.

What constituted the liturgy in the informal synagogue? Observing the Sabbath was especially important. "Praiseworthy is the man who . . . guards the Sabbath . . . " [Isaiah 56: 2, NRSV], which would have been the time people met *as* a synagogue. That is, the community of people *was* the synagogue in the absence of any physical structure. The essence of a revived Judaism without a temple in Babylon greatly

---

13. Ciferni O.Praem, "The Work of the Hour", *FDLC*, 2.
14. Psalm 137: 1—4.

influenced the close community of the Jews not only then, but also to the present day.

Synagogues and the construction of the Second Temple allowed by Cyrus, the king of Persia, moved religious restoration forward. The nation could now experience both the intimacy of synagogue as well as their Mosaic inheritance in the temple.

The synagogue offered congregants the "study of the Law... prayers and hymns, in which all joined as individuals...;[worship]... was in its nature personal and individualistic."[15] Rabbis proclaimed and taught the Tanakh in a new way speaking about the context of a reading as well as its practical application to living the good life. Liturgy was a drama of worshiping and engaging God.

Prayer

Prayer transforms us. Answered prayer is not the bottom line. What *should* change is *us*, not a certain situation, although both may occur. Prayer requires a certain mindset called *kavanah*, translated as *intent*. Contributing to kavanah was also location, time of day, music standing or sitting which enhanced one's ability to pray effectively—"All my limbs will say, 'HASHEM,' who is like you?"[16] Note the visceral reference to the body going back to the origin of the Hebrew language.

Language enhances praying. Even if one doesn't speak Hebrew, knowing Hebrew vocabulary enriches this vital practice. For example, *commandment* in English compared to Hebrew *mikvah* illustrates the difference between feeling burdened to obey God compared to sensing the joy of a covenant relationship with God. Recall the earlier discussion of the *yoke of the commandments* as entrance into the kingdom of God

A *Berakah* (blessing) is a special kind of prayer that is very common in Judaism. While praying, we bless God. But how can we bless the God who continually blesses us? "Bless the LORD, O my soul, and forget not all His benefits [Psalm 103: 2, RSV]. Hebrew helps here; for to bless God is to marvel at how extravagantly God blesses us. Praying *Baruch ata Adonai Eloheinu* may be translated, 'LORD, our God, we wonder at all your blessings.'"[17] [author's italics].

---

15. Peters, *The Religion of the Hebrews*, 387.
16. Psalm 35:10.
17. *Mishkan Tefillah: A Reform Siddur*, Elyse D. Frishman, ed., "Mei-Ein Sh'Moneh

"Prayer must move us beyond ourselves . . . prayer should reflect *our* values and ideals. God is not made in our image; we are in God's."[18]

Praying in the synagogue's liturgy is accompanied by other important acts of worship. "The Mishnah lists five actions which it says cannot be performed without the presence of a quorum (minyan) of ten adult males: The recitation of the *Shema*, the recitation of the *Tefillah [Amidah]*, the priestly blessing, a reading from the Torah, and the reading from the Prophets,"[19] [author's italics], called the *Haftorah*.

Prayers offered during synagogue worship varies with the time of a service [morning or evening]. However the following prayers occur in both services: The *Sh'ma, Tefillah, Shemoneh Esrei,* and the *Aleinu*.

The Sh'ma [Shema]

The *Shema* is the essence of all Jewish prayer. It is Judaism's oldest fixed prayer. *Hear*, the translation of *Shema* into English, signals the initiative of God speaking to us before we speak to Him. This prayer not only contains content, but also a method of praying. Before we say anything to God, we first listen to Him. To hear is to obey. Hebraic prayer does what God has spoken after speaking with Him. It is not only an affective devotional exercise of inspiration, but also a call to obedience. Psalm 95: 7b, states, " . . . even today, if you heed his call . . . " *Heed* and *call* accurately replace *hear* and *voice* in most English translations, respectively. *Hear* and *heed* express action in Hebraic thought.

"While prayer invites us to beseech God, we must also be open to what God wants from us . . . [and] . . . over the course of praying many voices are heard . . . *the Shema and Its Blessings* . . . "[20] [author's italics]. The *Shema* is one of those "many voices."

Sh'ma Yisrael, Adonai Eloheinu, Adonai Echad!
Hear, O Israel, the LORD our God, the LORD is One!

Esrei," 103.
  18. Ibid., ix.
  19.
  20. *Mishkan T'filah*, ix.

THE SYNAGOGUE

Tefillah [Amidah]

The English for *Tefillah* ["prayer'"] may be nuanced as "the state of being swept away in thought or meditation, a speech with authority, a whisper, and intercession on behalf of another."[21] Two other Hebrew words pertain to prayer: *Amidah* refers to posture when praying ["stand"], and *Shemoneh Esrei* refers to the number of prayer blessings, ["eighteen"]. Essentially, all three titles interrelate and together form one of the most important rabbinic prayers. In fact, "the Mishnah refers to the *Shemoneh Esreh* as simply ha-tefillah, 'the Prayer.'"[22] King David prayed three times a day. "As for me, I shall call unto God, and HASHEM will save me. Evening, morning, and noon, I supplicate and moan; He has heard my voice." [Psalm 55: 17, 18]. The Talmud comments on this text by urging every Jew, including women, slaves, and children to recite the prayer three times a day.[23]

Amidah

This *Amidah* prayer is the core of every Jewish worship service in three distinct sections—blessings, requests, and statements of gratitude.

Rabbi Dr. Karen Reiss Medwed discusses how prayer might change regarding when it is offered. For example, "the blessings are very different whether one is saying the *Amidah* on Shabbat or on a weekday."[24] Her succinct list and name for each benediction [blessing] of the Amidah is helpful. A cross-section of praise, petition, and thanksgiving blessings include:

> *Avot* (Ancestors): an acknowledgment of God as Author of history and destiny.
>
> *G'vurot* (Divine Might): an acknowledgment of God as Redeemer and Author of life.
>
> *K'dushat Ha-Sheim* (Divine Holiness): acknowledging God as the source of holiness.

The following are intermediate blessings and reflect the mood of the day:

21. Benner, *Ancient Hebrew Lexicon*, 197, 221, 362, 473.
22. Wilson, *Our Father Abraham*, 66.
23. *Berakhot* 3:3; 4:1.
24. Rabbi Medwed, "Prayers and Practices of the Amidah."

T'shuvah (Repentance): a prayer for the strength to repent and return to God.

S'lihah (Forgiveness): a prayer for forgiveness of sin.

R'fu-ah (Healing): a prayer for healing from illness.

David (King David): a prayer that the messiah come speedily and within our time.

Avodah (The Temple): a prayer that our worship equals that of ancient Jerusalem.

Hoda-ah (Thanksgiving): gratitude to thank God for who we are and all we have.[25]

Note how the specificity of Hebraic concrete thought permeates the above blessings as the flow of benedictions. It begins with praising God for Who He is and how He acts, then to confession and repentance concluding with thanksgiving.

Shemoneh Esrei [18]

The *Amidah* and *Shemoneh Esrei* differ in that the former refers to standing when praying; the latter, indicates the number of blessings. Standing while praying is required since taking steps are taken throughout the prayer.

Taking three steps forward symbolizes Moses approaching God having passed through the 'darkness,' the 'cloud,' and the 'mist.'[26] After Moses passed through the noise of thunder and the flames, "The people stood from afar and Moses approached the thick cloud where God was."[27] Because prayer replaces the sacrifices as the priest would perform ascending a ramp to the altar and after doing so descend, three steps are taken forward, then backward. "At the conclusion of the *Shemoneh Esrei,* one takes three steps backward in a bowing posture, as a slave takes leave of his master . . . [28]

---

25. Ibid.
26. *Mechilta,* Yitro.
27. Exodus 20: 15a, 18.
28. *Darkei Moshe,* OC 123; OC 123:1, Talmud.

Aleinu

The *Aleinu* prayer praises the Master of all and then *"Ours is the responsibility* to praise the God of all, the greatness of the Creator, who has set us apart from the other families of the earth, giving us destiny unique among the nations . . . We bend the knee and bow, acknowledging the supreme Sovereign, the Holy One of Blessing."[29] [author's emphasis].

Tension exists with this prayer in that on the one hand God is praised as Master of all, but on the other hand this God has *set us apart from the other families of earth*. Is God the Master of all, or is it only the Jews who need to praise Him? The key word is *all, in that all* people will call upon God's name, every knee will bow, all will accept the yoke of your kingship. Note the use of *yoke of your kingship* associated with the kingdom of God. The prophet Isaiah forecasts the hope represented at the end of the *Aleinu*: " . . . that to Me every knee shall bow and every tongue swear."[30] "And it is said, 'A-donai will be king over the whole Earth, on that day, God will be One, and his name One.'"[31]

We've just completed a rapid journey through the key Jewish prayers and now turn our attention to another main category of synagogue liturgy—the priestly blessings.

Priestly Blessing [Birkat Kohanim]

"May the LORD bless you and safeguard you. May the LORD illuminate His countenance for you and be gracious to you. May the LORD lift his countenance to you and establish peace for you."[32] The three blessings relate to protecting one's blessings of prosperity [Rashi], offering perception into the Torah's wisdom [Sforno], and a reminder that prosperity without peace is worthless [Sifra].[33] Historically, rabbinic scholarship identifies the *Birkat Kohanim* with "the blessing recited by Aaron at the conclusion of the first public service after the consecration of the

---

29. Mishkan T'filah, 284. Note, "*Aleinu*, one of our oldest prayers, was composed to introduce the sound of the shofar on Rosh HaShana, announcing God's ultimate and universal rule. By the fourteenth century, this prayer joined the final . . . kaddish as a concluding note of hope for every service." *Lawrence A. Hoffman*.

30. Isaiah 45: 23. This text is the basis for the Hebraic statement by the Apostle Paul in Philippians 2: 10.

31. Zechariah 14: 9.

32. Numbers 6: 24—26.

33. Note on Numbers 6: 24—26.

wilderness Tabernacle."³⁴ "The Priestly Blessing is one of the most spiritually uplifting moments in Jewish life felt as a 'divine hug.'"³⁵

Scripture Readings

Congregants hear both the Torah and Haftorah as an important segment of synagogue liturgy; the former being the first five books of Moses, the latter, a reading from the Prophets. Ezra read the Scripture publicly after the completion of the Temple as the nation was rebuilding Jerusalem in the fifth century BCE.

> "Then all the people gathered together as one in the plaza before the Water Gate. Ezra brought the Torah before the congregation—Men, women and those who could listen with understanding—He read it in front of the common men and women. He read it from a tower . . . the ears of the people were attentive . . . others and the Levites helped the people understand the reading."³⁶

Note the use of *common men and women*. Public reading from the Jewish Bible is not only intended for the teachers of the law, elders, or scholars; but also for the ordinary people. Note how the phrase—*others and the Levites helped the people understand the reading*. Rabbis offered a brief homily/commentary to apply the reading to the lives of the Jewish people.

"The origins of the haftarah reading are somewhat vague, and several theories have been suggested . . . the most common is that in 168 BCE . . . under the rule of Seleucid . . . [of Chanukah infamy], the Jews were forbidden to read from the Torah . . . so the sages instituted that a section of the Prophets be read instead."³⁷ The Torah and Haftarah are selected as complements to one another on a similar theme. For example, the Torah reading for the first day of Rosh Hashanah is from Genesis 21, the story about a mother and son—Hagar and Ishmael. 1 Samuel 1: 1—2: 10 tells the story of another mother and son, Hannah and Samuel. Both are birth stories. The readings for the first day of

---

34. Leviticus 9: 21-22.
35. Silberberg, "The Priestly Blessing."
36. Nehemiah 8: 1—8.
37. Rabbi Davidson, "When and Why We Started Reading the Haftarah."

Succos are Numbers 29: 12—16 and Zechariah 14: 1—21 both of which talk about the major holy convocation of *Succos*.[38]

The Shabbat service concludes with two prayers: The *Kaddish* [a prayer of remembrance for the dead] and the *Kiddush* [a prayer that sanctifies God's name]. We treat these prayers separate from the above types of prayers for their significance related to the loss of a loved one and categorically as a benediction for the Shabbat service.

The Kaddish [Mourner's Prayer]

While commonly read during funerals and Jahrzeits, the Kaddish never mentions the deceased:

> Magnified and sanctified be His great Name in the world which he hath created according to His will. May He establish His Kingdom during your life and during your days, and during the life of Israel.[39]

The Kaddish is a prayer of restoration. Judaism views a person's death as event which diminishes "God's radiance . . . when the Kaddish is recited, it restores this radiance and brings additional glory to God's name in the world."[40] The Kaddish is the prayer of hope which all loved ones of the deceased need at the time of death. At the same time, all congregants, whether at a funeral or toward the end of the Shabbat service, also benefit from the reminder that at the time of the Messiah all suffering will end.

Kiddush [Benediction]

Kiddush is a Jewish benediction and prayer typically recited over a cup of wine on the eve and morning of the Sabbath. It acknowledges the sanctity of the holy day. It may be performed at home or in the synagogue. *Kiddush* translates as 'sanctification.' It's a mitzvah which declares Shabbat, the seventh day of the week, separate and holy.

The Kiddush originates from the time of the Talmud (200—500 CE) . . . Kiddush worked its way into Shabbat service at the synagogue during

---

38. "Torah Readings, Maftir, and Haftaros," Tanakh, x.

39. Fr. Siluoan Thompson, "First-Century Christian Synagogue Liturgy," SILUAON (2007).

40. Editors of *Chabad*, "What is Kaddish?"

the Middle Ages.[41] This benediction is especially convenient for travelers to hear in a home where "the head of the household typically recites the *Kiddush* and pours some wine for everyone in attendance."[42]

Baruch atah Adonai, Eloheinu Melech ha olam borei p'ri gafen. Blessed are you, Lord our God, Ruler of the Universe, who creates the fruit of the vine.

In this chapter we've derived *synagogue* from its original languages, discussed its origin, history and purpose; and its liturgy. In the next chapter, we'll use a similar model to analyze the church giving special attention to how it derives from the synagogue.

---

41. Gordon-Bennett, "Discover Everything About Kiddush," *Learn Religions*, February 10, 2019.

42. Ibid.

― *Chapter 10* ―

The Church

IN THE PREVIOUS CHAPTER we discussed the etymology, origin, history, and liturgy of the synagogue. In this chapter we'll cover the origin, history, and liturgy of the church emphasizing how the church evolved in three phases. First, we'll discuss how the church appeared to be a sect of Judaism in Jerusalem. Second, we'll demonstrate how the spread of the gospel into the known world created a new demographic for the church—a mixture of Jewish people and God-fearing Gentiles. Third, we'll get into the sad and final stage of the church which devolved into a Gentile community suffering from theological amnesia over its Hebraic roots.

The primary takeaway of this chapter is that a *theologically-biblically-normative Christian church as the new humanity remembers its Jewish roots and worships the Crucified-Risen Jesus Christ, the Messiah.* "It seems fairly obvious that Christians, as a sect within first-century Judaism, worshipped essentially as other first-century Jews did. And we are justified in expecting to find in historical Christian worship some vestiges of earlier Jewish liturgy."[1] Implicit in a mutual sharing of a view of both Jewish synagogue community and the evolving Christian community is that "God is not only in the Temple; God is where the *congregation* is."[2] [author's italics].

---

1. Thompson, "First-century Christian synagogue liturgy." SILOUAN. Note, the author hereafter
referenced as Silouan.

2. Ibid.

Etymology

The essential meaning of *church* is Hebraic as noted by the author of Hebrews who urges Christians "to meet together . . . ."³ [the Greek word used here is *episunagoge*]. We've already noted the Hebrew *biet K'nesset*, house of assembly, as one of the three expressions used for synagogue. At its core, the Christian church has evolved as a house of assembly comprised of persons who, despite differences of ethnicity and culture, worship Jesus of Nazareth, the Messiah, as Lord of the Universe. Like the synagogue its purpose is to build a community through "teaching, sharing meals, prayer, worship, and caring for one another's needs."⁴

Church does not appear in any English translation of the Old Testament. The Greek used in the Septuagint [LXX] is *ekklesia* . . . derived from two Hebrew words *kahal* and *edah* . . . generally translated as assembly."⁵ The church may be considered an assembly of persons gathered in worship. The Hebrew word for *gather* is denoted by a pictograph shepherd's staff⁶ who calls his flock to gather around him. Finally, Latin for church is *ecclesia*.

Just Hebrew-Greek-Latin collaborate to mean church, any tradition of the Christian assembly, be it Catholic, Orthodox, or Protestant needs to realize the etymological roots for gathering its people together for worship and community.

Having briefly discussed word origins for Christian congregations, we now turn our attention to the theological issues and the demographical evolution of the Christian congregation as the gospel spread from "Jerusalem, Judea, Samaria, and to the ends of the earth."⁷ Our method will be to show how theological issues provided the basis for three phases of the church resulting in a Jerusalem congregation of only Jewish people, the church outside of Jerusalem, the Jewish-Gentile congregation [Samaria was a region created by mixed marriages from the Assyrian deportation], and finally, the unfortunately final phase, a Gentile-only church, essentially comprised of non-Jewish people detached both demographically and theologically from the church's Hebraic origins.

---

3. Hebrews 10: 25a, *The New Greek-English Interlinear New Testament*.
4. Acts 2: 42–47a.
5. Parsons, "Defining the Church," *Hebrew for Christians*.
6. Benner, *Ancient Hebrew Lexicon*, 246.
7. Acts 1: 8b.

Origin, History, and Liturgy

The theological basis for the church is the Trinity, the unique community of love among the Father, the Son, and the Holy Spirit. *Trinity* appears nowhere in the New Testament. However, there is textual evidence of plural pronouns, conversations between the Father and the Son, the function of the Holy Spirit to exalt Christ, not himself, and the familiar reference to Creation even from the Torah, "Let us make Man, after Our likeness . . . male and female He created them."[8] Jewish exegete Robert Alter makes no comment on the use of *us* in Genesis 1: 26. Christian scholars derive the concept of a triune Godhead from the familial relationship among three different deities mentioned throughout Scripture.

God the Father may be considered as the First Person of the Trinity; God the Son, the Second Person of the Trinity and God the Holy Spirit, the Third Person of the Trinity. The mystery of a three-in-one Godhead may be termed a Tri-Unity from which *Trinity* is derived.

There is no reason to believe that the original church, which met in synagogues and homes, which had its start on a Jewish Feast Day [Pentecost], and which quoted the Tanakh to explain its existence, departed from its Hebraic roots. To be sure, non-negotiables like the divinity of Jesus of Nazareth and the Trinity were significant theological differences between Judaism and Christianity. The Passover celebration [the Seder Meal] certainly doesn't speak of Jesus' crucified body fulfilling the sacrificial system of Moses. Clearly, Jesus' statement that He and His Father are One contradicts the Shema's claim for the Oneness of God. The early Christian community maintained a tension between its derivation from Hebraic roots and theological disagreements.

Prior to getting into the three phases of the evolving early church, it's important to discuss the early community's generic characteristics. To do this, we'll briefly discuss what might be called a Church Manifesto:

> "They devoted themselves to the apostles' teaching and to the fellowship, to the breaking of bread and to prayer. Everyone was filled with awe, and many wonders and signs were done by the apostles. All the believers were together and had everything

---

8. Genesis 1: 26—27c. This appears to contradict the Hebraic Shema, the Lord our God is One. But even In the Torah on the one hand we have the plural "us" and then the singular "He" which leaves the plurality of a Godhead an open question, at least in this text. Later New Testament texts assign Creation to the Son, the Word, from John 1 and Colossians 1. A note from the Tanakh on this text accounts for the plural that God "took counsel with the ministering angels." (Midrash).

in common. Selling their possessions and goods, they gave to anyone as he had need. Every day they continued to meet together in the temple courts. They broke bread in their homes and ate together with glad and sincere hearts, praising God and enjoying the favor of all people. And the Lord added to their number daily those who were being saved."[9]

The key terms in this succinct description are *teaching, fellowship, breaking bread, prayer, wonders and signs, selling,* and *praising.*

Devotion to hearing the *teaching* of the Scriptures was the first characteristic of this blueprint for the church. They had experienced a great moving of the Holy Spirit, but their first focus was not upon internal experience, but reading, studying, and hearing the word of God taught by apostles, elders and teachers, just like in the synagogue.

The first Christians gathered together in worship and *fellowship* to develop a community of love among themselves as a model within their pagan culture that one God and His Son, the crucified-risen Jesus, was the Messiah. Gatherings occurred in their homes, not always in the Temple or synagogue. Breaking bread was not a celebration of the Eucharist, but ordinary eating meals together which deepened relationships among the believers.

The church celebrated the Eucharist during the earliest days of the church, However, the first explicit documenting of *breaking bread as a liturgical event* among members of the church occurs in Acts 20: 7a during Paul's third missionary journey about twenty years after Pentecost, "On the first day of the week we came together to break bread." Clearly, this is an act of worship, not dinner in a home. Following this event, the next explicit mention we have of breaking bread and drinking wine occurs in Paul's instruction[10] to the Corinthian church in about 55CE. Not before about 90CE did the Apostle John go into great theological detail quoting Jesus' words about eating His flesh and drinking His blood."[11] While elements of Hebraic liturgy were retained in the church, the day of worship shifted from Saturday, the Sabbath to Sunday, the first day of the week. Camilla Klein states, "The central observance was the Eucharist, celebrated every Sunday from at least the end of the first

---

9. Acts 2: 42—47.

10. I Corinthians 10: 16; 11: 23, 26. Here Paul uses the radical expressions "participate in the blood and body of Christ," speaking of the unity of the church as one body and its identity with Christ's sufferings for the world.

11. John 6: 32—59. The Hebraic roots of the Lord's Supper go back to Moses and manna [Exodus 16: 31] in the desert and the bread of the Presence [Exodus 25: 30] on a table in the Tabernacle.

THE CHURCH 175

century."[12] That said, "At the end of the Sabbath comes the observance called *Havdalah*, in which candles are lit on Saturday evening. Liturgical Christianity still retains [today] this traditional service of prayer at the kindling of the evening light, known in English as Vespers."[13] The church drew much of its liturgy from the synagogue.

To show the liturgical acts of the church have Hebraic roots, we now briefly scan the historical background of the Lord's Supper, or what came to be called the Eucharist [derived from the Greek for "thanksgiving"]. We'll reference the following key persons/events from history which foreshadow the Lord's Supper[14]: Melchizedek, Passover, *Todah* sacrifice, John the Baptizer's use of Lamb of God, Jesus' statement about eating his flesh and drinking his blood,[15] and at the Lord's Supper, "This is my body ... this is my blood of the new covenant."[16]

The Lord's Supper goes back to Genesis where the Torah records that a mysterious king named *Melchizedek* offered a blessing of bread and wine to Abraham. This king of Salem was a priest and is said to foreshadow Christ.[17] Jesus identified himself with the *Passover* lamb sacrificed by the Israelites on their way out of Egypt. They ate the flesh of the lamb and smeared its blood on their doorposts to preserve their lives as the angel of death came over Egypt.[18] From the Torah we discover what was called the *Todah* [Hebrew for *thanksgiving*] offering by anyone who received a blessing from God. The sacrifice included meat, bread and wine.[19] The *Todah* sacrifice may be considered as foreshadowing the Eucharist. The prophet John the Baptizer announced repentance and forgiveness through Jesus of Nazareth, the *lamb of God* who was able to take away the sins of the world.[20] John the Baptizer summarizes all former sacrifices for removing sin with this radical claim the divine-human being, Jesus, is the Lamb of God.

Finally, given the above background, we analyze two of Jesus' statements referencing *bread and wine*. Jesus said, "Very truly, I tell you,

---

12. Camilla Klein, "The Surprising History of Sunday Worship," Christian Educators Academy, https://christianeducatorsacademy/the-surprising-history-of-sunday-worship.
13. Thompson, "First-century Christian synagogue liturgy."
14. Mauricio-Perez, "The Eucharist Throughout History," *Denver Catholic*.
15. John 6: 53—55.
16. Luke 22: 19, 20.
17. Hebrews 7: 3.
18. Exodus 12: 5—8.
19. Leviticus 7: 11—15.
20. John 1: 29.

unless you eat the flesh of the Son of Man and drink his blood, you have no life in you . . . for my flesh is true food and my blood is true drink."[21] When Jesus' followers heard this outlandish claim, many deserted him. On the more familiar occasion of the Last Passover, while breaking a loaf of bread and giving thanks for a cup of wine, Jesus said, "Take, eat; this is my body . . . Drink from it, all of you; for this is my blood of the covenant, which is poured out for many for the forgiveness of sins."[22]

Praying permeated the life of the early church. It would take the rest of this book to number and comment upon all the references to prayer in that first community of believers. Jesus spoke of praying in the Sermon on the Mount [Matthew 5: 33] and throughout the Gospels, Paul prayed for the church that God would give them the Spirit of wisdom [Ephesians 1: 17], James urged the church to pray with faith [James 5: 13], and Peter reminded Christians that God heard their prayers [1 Peter 3:12]. Clearly, the Tanakh is filled with references to prayer by both the leaders and Israel's gathered tribes.

At is inception, the church experienced *signs and wonders*, and miracles, performed by the apostles to encouraged the faith of the disciples and to demonstrate God's power to onlookers. Miracles occurred among the Israelites, the most graphic of which is the parting of the Red Sea allowing the nation to escape Pharoah's pursuing army. Jesus, of course, performed miracles throughout his ministry. He fed thousands. He raised a synagogue leader's daughter from the dead as well as his dear friend Lazarus. As practicing Jews who believed in Jesus, Peter and John went to Temple to pray at three in the afternoon and said to a crippled man that they had no money, but told him "what I have I give to you. In the name of Jesus Christ of Nazareth, walk."[23] Those who witnessed this miracle of hearing were awe-struck.

The early Christians believed in private ownership, yet freely shared them with anyone in need—within or outside the church. The church took selfishness with one's money and possessions seriously. Note the Ananias and Sapphira story about keeping back money while making it appear that they were giving it all. Their sin was lying, as well as violating Malachi's mandate to bring "all the tithes into the storage house, and let it be sustenance in my Temple."[24] They both died on the

21. John 6: 53.
22. Matthew 26c—28.
23. Acts 3: 6.
24. Malachi 3: 10.

spot. Generosity was a key element of the first Christians. That is, they sought the kingdom of God trusting Jesus' words that "all these things will be given to you as well."[25] Seeking Jesus' kingdom of value of generosity held the promise of God's provision.

Finally, the early church was a community characterized by *praise*. The pictograph for the Hebrew *praise* is a man with raised hands looking at a great sight like a shining star and the shepherd staff. This suggests the idea of movement toward a certain direction as a shepherd would use his staff to guide his flock. Literally, the root for praise may be given as "To cause the shining of one by praising or giving thanks to another . . . ."[26]

Synagogue worship included songs of praise to One God. The church simply maintained this practice by worshipping Jesus as Lord and Savior. From its inception singing complemented speaking as vital elements of Spirit-filled praise. Over time hymns were written. Some would suggest that Philippians 2: 5—11 is derived from a hymn offering praise to God for his humility and Lordship. Paul encouraged the members of the church in Colosse to "Let the word of Christ dwell in you richly . . . as you sing psalms, hymns, and spiritual songs with gratitude in your hearts."[27] Of course, the major difference was that Christians worshiped and praised Jesus the Christ as the divine-human Lord and Savior of humanity. The Jewish community confined their praise to an invisible One God without human form.

Below is graphic comparison of both liturgies[28]:

Synagogue	*Church*
Synagogue Service	Liturgy of the Word
Profession of faith	Creeds
Prayer of eighteen blessings	Prayers of intercession
Readings (Law, prophets)	Readings (Gospel, apostolic writings)
Sermon	Sermon
Priestly blessing	Benediction

25. Matthew 6: 33b.
26. Benner, *Ancient Hebrew Lexicon*, 102—103.
27. Colossians 3: 16.
28. Thompson, "First-century Christian synagogue liturgy," *SILUAON*. [paraphrased].

We now consider three phases of the church's evolution regarding the theological, cultural, and ethnic issues faced by the Jerusalem Jewish church in Jerusalem, the Jewish—Gentile church outside Jerusalem and the Gentile church from the Apostle Paul's ministry throughout the first century.

The Jewish Church: Acts 2—8, 33CE—49CE

What might be considered an *initial* phase of the church starts with Pentecost up to the ministry of Philip through whom the first Gentile, an African from Ethiopia, came to faith. This interval of approximately sixteen years included the major events of the arrival of the Holy Spirit Jesus promised, the first sermons of the church, the scattering of Jewish believers out of Jerusalem, the first recorded conversion of a Gentile, and the dramatic conversion of a Pharisee named Saul who was murdering his own people because they believed in Jesus as the Messiah.

As a result of Peter's first sermon, the Jerusalem congregation of Jewish believers grew from the original twelve eye-witnesses of Jesus' ministry to over three thousand believers. Peter explained the fulfillment of prophecy given to the prophets that God would send His Holy Spirit focusing upon Messiah Jesus' resurrection. People responded with this question: "Men and brethren, what shall we do?"[29] They knew they had to *do* something. Peter answered "Repent, and be baptized every one of you in the name of Jesus Christ for the remission of sins, and you shall receive the gift of the Holy Ghost."[30] Peter's sermon paraphrased Jesus' first words, "The time has come, the kingdom of God is near. Repent and believe the good news."[31]

Peter's second sermon spoke in more detail about how Jesus fulfilled the covenants given to Abraham and Moses. Both of the church's early sermons referenced the Hebraic roots of this new religion, considered a sect of Judaism. Both sermons proclaimed a new covenant [first mentioned in the Tanakh by the prophet Jeremiah] about which Jesus spoke at the first Eucharist which celebrates the sacrificial blood of the divine-human Jesus of Nazareth, the Christ, for the forgiveness of sin.

---

29. Acts 2: 37.
30. Acts 2: 38.
31. Mark 1: 15.

THE CHURCH

The impact of Peter's two sermons landed Peter and John before the Jewish religious establishment who tried to muzzle Peter's preaching. The Sanhedrin didn't know what to do about the early signs and wonders of the healing of a cripple by the Holy Spirit through Peter. This confrontation by Jewish leaders represents the first event of how the radical gospel message of Jesus' death and resurrection launched a major split within Judaism. At this time, the Jerusalem community of believing Jews represented a sect of Judaism[32] which either attracted Jews to Jesus or hardened their hearts against him. No middle ground existed. There was no denying that this new message called for a change in both faith and action. Persecution of the first believers included jail time, beatings, and the death of Stephen, a deacon and the first martyr of the church. His death marked the beginning of a mass exodus of Jews from Jerusalem into Judea and Samaria,[33] a fulfillment of Jesus' earlier words about taking the gospel out of Jerusalem. Stephen's sermon detailed Israel's story showing how it anticipated the story of Jesus and how Jesus fulfilled the Law and the Prophets.

The initial conversion of Gentiles to the faith occurred when the deacon Philip proclaimed the gospel in Samaria.[34] The significance of Philip's mission into Samaria amazed Peter and John who realized that the half-breed Jews resulting from the Assyrian deportation were becoming believers. As leaders in the Jerusalem church, Peter and John prayed over the Samaritan believers so that they could receive the Holy Spirit. It was important that the Jerusalem church validate the conversion of non-Jews. This meant that ethnicity had nothing to do with faith in Jesus as the Messiah leading to membership in the newly-established church.

Philip is best known for the conversion of an African from Ethiopia. The nameless Ethiopian official was the first documented Gentile to name Jesus as his Lord.[35] The stage was set for what would become a radical shift in demographics and ethnicity of the church—all of which Jesus predicted\ when speaking of the spread of the Gospel to Samaria and the rest of the world.Believers were now persons living *outside* Jerusalem with ethnic, cultural, and theological differences with Jerusalem Jews. Philip's evangelism established a precedent on as the

---

32. Rabbi Zaslow, *Jesus: First-Century Rabbi*, 48.
33. Acts 8: 1.
34. Acts 8: 5.
35. Acts 8: 26—39.

church transitioned from a purely Jewish congregation in Jerusalem to a Jewish-Gentile church outside of Jerusalem.

The Jewish-Gentile Church: Acts 9—21, 49CE—57CE

As the gospel spread beyond Jerusalem and Judea, Gentiles became Jesus followers in Samaria primarily through the missionary efforts of the Apostle Philip. The church gradually became a Jewish-Gentile community beyond Jerusalem, Judea, and Samaria as Jesus had predicted just prior to His ascension, "Therefore go and make disciples of all nations . . . "[36] This phase of the church lasted about eight years beginning with Paul's conversion lasting through the final days of his journeys of planting and teaching new churches going as far west as Rome.

Recall our earlier assertion: A biblically theologically *normative* church is characterized by members who never forget their Hebraic roots while worshiping Jesus as the Christ, the Lord and Savior of the world. We name such a congregation as a *Jewish—Gentile* church.

A Pharisee named Saul was dramatically converted by seeing a blinding light and hearing God's voice. ""Saul, Saul, why are you persecuting Me . . . I am Jesus whom you are persecuting, but get up and enter the city, and it will be told to you what you must do?"[37] That city was Damascus where Saul was taught Jesus' teaching and began to preach the gospel claiming that Jesus was the Son of God. Saul continued his ministry in Jerusalem as Jewish Jesus followers gradually accepted him as a genuine believer. Saul, whose name was later changed to Paul, is the one person in church history who had the greatest influence on the numerical growth and theological development of the church. His bold ministry was a key transition of the church from a Jewish-only community to the normative Jewish-Gentile church. His conversion had a direct influence upon Peter who struggled with the idea of non-Jews in the church.

The Apostle Peter experienced a dramatic encounter with the Holy Spirit in a trance which convinced him that Gentiles as well as Jews could become authentic members of the growing church. A key person in Peter's life in his transition toward accepting Greeks into the church was a Gentile—a Roman centurion God-fearer named Cornelius. Cornelius' conversion to belief in Jesus motivated Peter to say in his third recorded

---

36. Matthew 28: 19a.
37. Acts 9: 4b—6.

sermon "I most certainly understand now that God is not one to show partiality; preaching peace through Jesus Christ, who is Lord of all"[38]

Peter returned to Jerusalem excited about this important ethnic change in the church and told the leaders to which they responded, "Well then, God has granted to the Gentiles also the repentance that leads to life."[39] Peter's change of heart toward Gentiles is significant given his strong leadership in an all-Jewish church. Things continued to move rapidly regarding the spread of the gospel into the regions beyond Jerusalem, Judea, Galilee and Samaria.

Meanwhile, the Apostle Paul was commissioned as a missionary at a Jewish-Gentile church in Antioch. Partnering with a fellow disciple, Barnabas, they told Jesus' story as the fulfillment of Israel's story. Continuing his travels westward, Paul proclaimed the good news of Jesus leading to persecution by disbelieving Jews and returned to Antioch sharing with the church, " . . . how God has opened a door of faith to the Gentiles."[40]

But entry of Gentiles into the church began what would become a gradual parting of the ways between the Jewish community and the church. The conflict centered on circumcision, the identifying sign that a man was a Jew as commanded by Abraham, the first Jew. The tension is reasonable. For centuries the defining mark of being Jewish was circumcision going back to the covenant God made with Abraham. Why wouldn't Jews be confused? Could circumcised Jews also be members of this new sect of Jesus followers? Would worshiping Jesus replace circumcision? Would non-Jews need to become circumcised to believe that this carpenter's son was Messiah?

The fledgling Jewish-only Jerusalem church had to make a decision. How might the Jewish history and culture of the church be maintained while encouraging non-Jewish people to come to faith. James and other leaders decided that only a minimal expectation regarding their Hebraic traditions should be required of Gentile believers so as not to lay an unnecessary burden on them. In what may be considered the First Council of the Church, the following four stipulations mandated that Gentile believers . . . 1. Abstain from things sacrificed to idols . . . 2. Not eat blood . . . 3. Not eat meat from a strangled animal, and 4. Refrain from fornication.[41] Note that circumcision was not mentioned. But formerly critical

38. Acts 10:34, 36b.
39. Acts 11: 18b.
40. Acts 14: 27b.
41. Acts 15: 20, 29.

traditions don't die easily. Circumcision would continue to be a source of conflict throughout the growth of the first-century church.

The Apostle Paul with other disciples traveled westward from Antioch during three trips where he preached Jesus in both synagogues and in the open air seeing many Jews and Gentiles become Christians.[42] In Acts 13 –20 Luke records the details of each journey where Paul planted new congregations of Jews and Gentiles keeping in touch with many through letters we have in what eventually became the New [Younger] Testament.

For example, *Galatians* is one of Paul's letter to a region of churches where circumcision continued to be a divisive issue. Jewish believers violated the First Council's liberties prompting Paul to write "I am astonished that you are so quickly deserting the one who called you by the grace of Christ and are turning to a different gospel—which is really no gospel at all."[43] In a letters to the church in Corinth, Paul addressed division, baptism, Greek wisdom, fornication, and other matters of immorality. To the church in Ephesus, the Apostle Paul talked about marriage, family, and spiritual warfare. *Colossians* contains one of the most robust Christologies in all the New Testament; the second coming of Jesus Christ is the dominant theme of the Thessalonian correspondence. Paul wrote letters specifying church structure and leadership in what are known as the Pastoral Epistles: first and second *Timothy* and *Titus*. AS the first-century spread throughout the world, Paul's letters established what would become the core teachings of the Christian church. Yet, other Jewish converts added to the corpus of Christianity.

The early letter by James might be considered the "Proverbs" of the New Testament where he makes practical suggestions applying faith to daily life. The Jewishness of the letter would indicate an audience of Jewish believers in churches scattered around the world. Peter's letters address holy living and dealing with suffering; Jude talks about doctrinal heresy and apostasy. No one knows who wrote *Hebrews* whose name suggests that the author wrote primarily to Jewish believers who were tempted to substitute traditional Jewish rituals for faith in Jesus Christ. The author attempts to show the superiority of Jesus to any patron saint from the historic tradition including Moses and Aaron. As you can see by the relationship between dates of writing and theme, no hard and fast

---

42. *Christian* was first used to name Jesus followers in Antioch, possibly in a pejorative way [Acts 11: 26].

43. Galatians 1: 6—7a.

boundary exists to accurately categorize a given church as only Jewish, only Jewish-Gentile, or only Gentile. Overlap of audience and theme exists for each phase of the evolving church as seen in a diverse series of letters written by the early apostles.

The takeaway from this section of the chapter is simple: *The only biblically-theologically-culturally sound congregation of Christians is what we've defined as a Jewish—Gentile church.*

The Gentile Church; Acts 22—28, 57CE to Present

As the influence of Hebraic thought waned with the increased influx of Gentiles, a *Gentile-only* church emerged. This *doesn't* mean that there were no Jews in the church. It *does* mean the Hebraic-historical roots of the church were all but forgotten. As we'll later observe, a future Gentile-only church would have a harmful impact not only on the church, but also upon the surrounding culture influenced by the church. A Gentile church would become an incubator for theological anti-Judaism and racial anti-Semitism.

Paul's letter to the church in Philippi serves as a transition to this Gentile-only phase of the church. Philippi was a Roman military colony which meant that all of its citizens were also citizens of Rome. It had no synagogue and was primarily a military town for Roman soldiers. The letter contains no quotes from the Tanakh. "Philippians contains no Old Testament references."[44] Essentially, one can see why the church in Philippi serves as an example of an abnormal church in that it forgot its Jewishness. While Paul had many good things to say to this church; sadly, it represents the first failure of a Gentile-only congregation to recall its Hebraic roots. As a non-Hebraic congregation, the church at Philippi serves as a sad precedent for a Christian church which would to the present-day suffer from a memory-loss of its Jewishness.

We now consider Paul's unique letter to the church in Rome written around 57AD. Like the Philippian church, the Christian community in Rome was primarily Gentile with a minority of Jewish members. Yet Paul makes repeated references to the Jewish history of the church [Romans 4:1, "Abraham, our forefather . . . ;" Romans 1: 16, " . . . to the Jew first, and also to the Greeks . . . ;"] and his poignant recollection of his own Jewish roots as a Pharisee from the tribe of Benjamin. Paul's lament for

---

44. Introduction, "Characteristics," Philippians, NIV, 1802.

his Jewish brothers and sisters in Romans 9—11 includes the cryptic statement about the salvation of the Jews [Romans 11: 26a, "And so all Israel will be saved . . . "]. This statement merits its own further research and analysis far beyond the scope of this book. Romans is a relatively early letter to a church. Yet, Paul ends it with a most poignant lament and sadness over Jewish disbelief with hope that someday and in some way his fellow Jews would come to faith in Jesus as Messiah.

The Apostle John wrote his Gospel, three brief letters, and letters to seven churches recorded in Revelation during the late first century when Gentiles dominated the churches. His objectives included combatting heresies, primarily the Hellenistic concepts in Gnosticism. While speculative and hypothetical, had such churches retained their Hebraic inheritance, they would have not been duped by Gnostic thought which demeaned the physical and favored the spiritual. John's programmatic warning included this statement regarding how to tell a true spirit from a false spirit: "Dear friends, do not believe every spirit, but test the spirits to see whether they are from God . . . Every spirit that acknowledges that Jesus Christ has come in the flesh is from God . . . "[45] This text is the most explicit attack on Gnosticism in Scripture. Beyond his Gospel and short letters, the Apostle John recorded seven brief summaries of letters to churches

John referred to seven churches in much the same way Paul wrote to his churches—commending what he could followed by rebuke or advice related to doctrine or lifestyle. There's good reason to believe that each of the seven churches were Gentile-only congregations as we've defined them with minimal, if any, Jewish persons and certainly an absence of Hebraic thinking. Certainly the nature of the problems in each church have to do with Greek thinking, not issues of traditional; Jewish rituals. By the end of the first century, the churches were comprised of and led by Gentiles. Our text is Revelation 2: 1—3: 22.

The Apostle John's first addresses the church the Apostle Paul planted in Ephesus [Revelation 2: 6] plagued by a gnostic group called the Nicolaitans named after "Nicolas, a proselyte from Antioch."[46] He was a twice-converted person; first, from paganism to Judaism, then second from Judaism to Christianity. " . . . Nicolas taught a doctrine of compromise . . . with a stomach for occultism, Judaism, and Christianity . . . intermingling all these belief systems."[47] He was religious, but

45. 1 John 4: 1a, 2b.
46. Acts 6: 5.
47. Renner Ministries, "Who were the Nicolaitans, And What Was Their Doctrine

not a Jesus follower. We can assume that his followers were vocal and active members of the Ephesian church. This was a cancer within the fellowship, not an outside influence. Had the church retained its Hebraic roots, it would have discerned how this "religion" violated the Law of God. This wouldn't be the first church to suffer implosion within its ranks. We also note how different from Paul's earlier letter to the church was from John's. The Apostle Paul's letter didn't address any specific heresy but spoke in broad theological and practical categories. The letters in Revelation hone in on specific heresies.

Another sect was named after Balaam, who encouraged the Israelites "to eat things sacrificed to idols, and to commit fornication."[48] They would have recalled Balaam as a hurtful influence to the Jewish community documented in the Torah. Also, more recently, note how Balaam's sin violated the mandates of the Jerusalem Church Council which forbade such meat sacrifices as well as fornication. The Apostle John finds Balaam's false teaching in the Pergamum church.[49] Both sects were tolerated by churches late into the first century in part because they forgot their Hebraic roots, the warnings offered in the Torah, and the tenets of the First Jerusalem Church Council.

Yet another problem occurred in other churches gathered in Smyrna and in Philadelphia. John talks about a synagogue of Satan.[50] This sect denied that Jews who did not accept Jesus as Messiah were no longer the people of God; that you had to convert to Christianity in order to retain your status as a Jewish person. There is no biblical basis for this teaching which we'll address in the next chapter under the heading of replacement theology also known as supercessionism. The new Christian church did not negate the covenants God made to his people documented in the Torah. Even non-believing Jews remained under the covenants. The issue at the time is politically and economically complicated. Suffice it to say that since Satan means accuser, there were Jews in the church who informed the Roman government that believing Gentiles were not really Jews and therefore were atheists subject to Romans law as criminals against the state.[51] The Roman government made exceptions for the Jewish community on the topic of worshiping Caesar.

---

and Deeds?"
    48. Ibid.
    49. Revelation 2: 14.
    50. Revelation 2: 9; 3: 9.
    51. Messiah, "The Synagogue of Satan."

In sum, what began as caring fellowship of Jesus followers at Pentecost in Jerusalem and grew as Jewish-Gentile community ended up as an ab-normal gathering of confused Christians who lost the memory of their Hebraic ancestry. The condition of the church at the turn of the century was dismal, lacked any Jewishness, and ripe for deepened conflict eventually characterized by an evolving separation of Christianity from Judaism.

In this chapter we've endeavored to describe the church from its origin at a Jewish Festival called Pentecost through its three phases as a Jewish-only congregation, a normative gathering of Christians called a Jewish-Gentile church followed by the unfortunate Gentile-only church.

We now turn our attention to a deepening detachment of the church from its Jewish roots leading to theological anti-Judaism and racial anti-Semitism.

——— *Chapter 11* ———

A Parting of the Ways

IN THE LAST CHAPTER, we analyzed the origin, purpose, and history of the Christian church. In this chapter we'll discuss the events, people, and dates which influenced a parting from the church rom the synagogue. Our analysis will include those issues within the Way itself, the entrance of Gentiles into the church, and the exodus of Jewish persons from the church. Overall, we'll consider the timeframe involved from 33CE to about 400CE; that is, from the pristine beginnings of the Jerusalem Jewish congregation, the evolution of the normative church comprised of Jews and Gentiles, and finally the non-Jewish Gentile church where Jewish presence and Hebraic thought had virtually disappeared.

No Jewish or Christian scholar pins down a specific event, person, or date for the separation of Christianity from Judaism.

Overview

"To decide on a date at which the separation took place is no easy task, for there are so many parties to be considered."[1] For example, James Parkes cites the destruction of the Temple in 70CE which the Christian church used "as a gibe, as a proof that their [Jewish] glory had departed."[2] Parkes list several texts from the Gospel of John, written late in the first century, which indicate animosity between Jews and Christians. "All

---

1. Parkes, *The Conflict of the Church and the Synagogue*, 77.
2. Ibid., 82.

this is redolent of the atmosphere which must have existed at the end of the century, when, indeed, confession of Christianity meant expulsion from the synagogue."[3]

After the fall of Jerusalem in 70 C.E., the synagogue recoiled to endure its own identity. The teaching of forgiveness and repentance played a significant part in the separation; for Jews had no place to sacrifice. "Origen tells us that in his day [late second and early third centuries], Jews told him that as they had no altar, no temple, no priest, and therefore no offerings for sacrifices, they felt their sins remained with them, and that they had no means of obtaining pardon.[4] Finally, and as a boundary for our analysis of the parting, Parkes states, "The fourth century marks a decisive moment in the history of both Judaism and Christianity . . . So far as the future was concerned Christianity was a Gentile religion, and . . . The Jew . . . was a 'theological abstraction . . . ' He is a 'monster,' . . . of superhuman cunning . . . unreal . . . a menace . . . it is amazing how this myth of Jewish character could so long have passed muster."[5] This statement, and more examples of anti-Judaism and anti-Jewishness that Parkes gets into, provide a basis for the thick boundary between Judaism and Christianity to this present day. Ironically, Constantine's legalization of Christianity as Rome's state religion coincided with the obliteration of the church's roots in the synagogue and the loss of Hebraic thought from Christian theology.

Given a rapid overview of the gradual separation of the church from the synagogue over the span of four centuries, we now reference the biblical data which documents the subtle nuances of internal conflict which anticipate the departure of Christianity from Judaism.

Early Signs

We begin with an often-overlooked doctrinal concern within the Way regarding the resurrection of Jesus Christ. "While Peter and John were speaking to the people, the priests, the captain of the temple, and the Sadducees came to them much annoyed because they were teaching the people and proclaiming in Jesus there is resurrection of the dead."[6]

---

3. Ibid., 83
4. Ibid., 115. Parkes quotes Origen's *Hom. On Num.*, x, 2; P.G., XII. P. 638.
5. Ibid., 153-158.
6. Acts 4: 1, 2.

This exposed an already-extant *theological disagreement within Judaism* itself, not originating with the Way. The Sanhedrin was composed of two main parties—Pharisees, who did believe in resurrection, and Sadducees, who did not. The latter group imprisoned the early apostles for their teaching about resurrection and healing miracles. It's important to point out that Second Temple Judaism was not some monolithic religion to which all Jewish persons subscribed.

A second event symbolized *internal conflict with the Way* over language and culture—"when the Hellenists complained against the Hebrews because their widows were being neglected in the distribution of food."[7] This second illustration exemplifies the powerful role of culture in an eventual parting of the ways. "The first obvious breaking of threads comes with the Hellenists."[8] A third, far more significant event involved Stephen, the newly-appointed deacon distributor of food, who, like Peter, proclaimed Israel's story culminating in Jesus of Nazareth, the coming Righteous One. The stoning of Stephen, the first martyr of the church, triggered a massive exodus of Jewish believers from Jerusalem into the Mediterranean Basin to escape persecution prompted by Jerusalem's Jewish priestly caste.

As the Gentiles became Jesus followers, internal conflicts ensued. Philip, another deacon became a Jewish missionary to half-breed Jews in Samaria and is present at the conversion of an Ethiopian [Acts 8]. Saul, a serial-killer of Jewish Jesus followers came to faith in Jesus and began preaching the Gospel in Damascus, Syria. Peter and a Roman centurion discussed their visions which changed Peter's mind about the purity of Gentiles as acceptable members of *The Way*. Antioch, a cosmopolitan city with a large population of Jews and Gentiles, became the location for the first recorded Jewish-Gentile church. The expansion of the faith into non-Jewish communities created both theological and cultural conflicts within *The Way*.

---

7. Acts 6: 1, NRSV. Note: "When poor Jews became Christians, they lost Jewish support . . . " This explains, in part, Why the early church "had all things in common." Acts 2: 44b.

8. Dunn, "From the Crucifixion to the End of the First Century," *Partings: How Judaism and Christianity Became Two*, Shanks, ed., 31.

The Jerusalem Council

As we stated earlier, the leaders of the Jerusalem congregation were delighted with this expansion of the church. They also realized the need to deal with issues within the church. Peter, James and John presided over the first Church Council which decided to make matters simple for Gentile believers and stipulate only four tenets for inclusion into *The Way*—"abstain from things polluted by idols, from fornication, from whatever has been strangled, and from blood."[9] Thus a streamlined version of the purity laws and God's covenant with Noah [that is, with all humanity] cannot be considered accidental.[10] The Council decided that a Gentile didn't need to become Jewish to believe in Jesus as Messiah. The genius of this first informal meeting of Jewish leaders removed the issue of one's culture as a stipulation for faith. "'The decision reached by the council must be considered one of the boldest and magnanimous in the annals of church history.'"[11]

Note the absence of any mandate to be circumcised—an intentional omission which would yet prove to become a major conflict within the expansion of Jewish-Gentile congregations.

Other "Gospels"

The Jerusalem Council's genius would soon be challenged by the churches the Apostle Paul planted in Galatia. The issue was the Gospel. Paul stated early in his letter, "I am astonished that you are so quickly ... turning to a different gospel—which is no gospel at all."[12] Specifically, the conflict was over whether Gentiles had to become Jews by being circumcised to be Jesus followers—precisely the idea addressed by the Jerusalem Council. Requiring circumcision was a blatant violation of the Jerusalem Council's decision. It replaced grace with ritual; it substituted religion for faith and obedience. The so-called Galatian Heresy

---

9. Acts 15: 20.

10. "The seven Noachian laws are related to idolatry, blasphemy, cursing, murder, sexual sin, robbery, and eating flesh with the blood of life in it. Marvin R. Wilson, *Our Father Abraham*, (see endnote 11), 49.

11. Longnecker, *New Testament Social Ethics for Today*, 39.

12. Galatians 1: 6-7a.

proved to be a conflict extended into future churches where any form of legalism[13] replaced the liberty of the Holy Spirit.

The Jewish proponents of Galatian legalism were called Judaizers.[14] The Apostle Paul would continue addressing circumcision and its legalistic implications in a later letter to the church in Rome.[15] One of the second-century church patriarchs, Ignatius, coined the term, *Ioudaismos*, (literally, 'Judaizing')" to be contrasted with his term, *Christianismos* from which "Christianity" is derived.[16] Judaizers are not to be confused with those in a Jewish-Gentile congregation, Jewish or not, who sought to retain the Hebraic thought of the Gospel. The term applied only to those Jewish believers who unnecessarily added circumcision which demeaned God's grace for salvation. . .

Throughout his ministry, the Apostle Paul time and time again had to bring a church back to a Gospel rooted in Hebraic thought, the Covenants, the Jewishness of Jesus, and the church as the new humanity of Jews and Gentiles. Note that one of the most powerfully succinct statements of the Gospel comes from the Apostle's pen in 1 Corinthians 1: 18—25 which states,

> For the message about the cross is foolishness to those who are perishing, but to us who are being saved it is the power of God . . . For Jews demanded signs and Greeks desire wisdom, but we proclaim Christ crucified, a stumblingblock to Jews and foolishness to Gentiles, but to those who are the called, both Jews and Greeks, [we proclaim] Christ the power of God and the wisdom

---

13. Ironically, the Torah itself and the Israel's prophets consistently spoke out about what new Jewish believers wrongly advocated to be good Jews. Deuteronomy 10:16 challenges Israel to "circumcise its heart . . . "—an internal, spiritual issue. Jeremiah 31: 31—33 speaks about a day in the future when God will put his "law within them . . . and write it on their hearts. The Prophet Ezekiel talks about God giving Israel a new heart . . . and a new spirit . . . and will remove the heart of stone and give you a heart of flesh . . . and put a new spirit within you. [Ezekiel 36: 26—27]. Legalism negated all of the above mandates given by the Law and the Prophets. It tried to replace the forest of God's Word with trees of ritualism.

14. Judaizers attempted to challenge the Jerusalem Council which dealt with this very issue. Paul discusses the issue in Galatians 2:14ff. Judaizers could have been members of a conservative political party, the Zealots, who considered any identity with Gentiles as harmful to safety guaranteed to Jews by Rome. Reading Acts, "Galatians 2—Who were the Judaizers?" Phillip J. Long, 2011.

15. Romans 2: 25—4: 12.

16. Yoshiko and Lily Young, "Christianity in Antioch: Partings in Roman Syria," Partings, Shank, ed., 106.

of God. For God's foolishness is wiser than human wisdom, and God's weakness is stronger than human strength.

To summarize, we've focused on the first century's Jerusalem Council and its impact upon the theological, spiritual, and cultural concerns related to including non-Jews in *The Way*. We now turn our attention to other types of separation between the synagogue and the church over the next several centuries.

"In the mid-2nd century C.E., Christianity began a gradual process of identity-formation that would lead to the creation of a separate, independent religion from Judaism. Initially, Christians were one of many groups of Jews found throughout the Roman Empire. The 2nd century Jewish community and early church experienced a change in demographics, institutional hierarchy, and Christian dogma."[17]

Demographics

The Roman destruction of Jerusalem and its Temple in 70 C.E. impacted not only the fledgling Jewish church, but also the Jewish community as a whole. Even though rejection of Jesus as Messiah existed from the early years of the church in Jerusalem, the main task of the church was to prove to their unconvinced fellow-countrymen that Jesus was the Messiah using the same Scriptures which both parties believed to be the word of God.[18]

After 70CE, Jewish-Gentile relationships were strained by Rome's suppression. Jewish leaders were less interested in debating Jewish Jesus followers, even though the problem of the Jews was important to the Christians. The tone of discussions between Jews and Jewish Jesus followers changed from dialoguing in good faith for theological answers from the Tanakh, to disputing one another's position leading to outright rejection of Jews. The difference in tone regarding the Apostle Paul's empathy for his Jewish community prior to 70 C.E. and that of the Apostle John's references to Jews in his Gospel during the 90's C.E. represent a shift in attitude between Jewish believers and the Jewish community as a whole.

---

17. Denova, "The Separation of Christianity from Judaism," *World History Encyclopedia*, June 2021, https://worldhistory.com/article/1785/the-separation-of-christianity-from-judaism/

18. Parkes, *The Conflict of the Church and the Synagogue*, lx.

That said, the Gospel of John, when read objectively, doesn't deserve the harsh accusations of anti-Semitism made by mainline Protestant liberalism. . . . "The Gospel of John is not anti-Semitic . . . When read correctly, The Fourth Gospel not only ceases to be a source of religious acrimony; it points the way forward for all seekers of truth to sojourn together, across the boundaries of religious movements, time, and space."[19]

Unlike Jesus of Nazareth, who validated being the Messiah by healing and saving others, Bar Kokhba, a self-proclaimed Messiah, led a revolution against the occupying Roman government in 135 C.E. He persecuted Jewish-Christians which led to pronouncing curses against Jewish Jesus followers and even a curse against Jesus of Nazareth himself. Such curses were documented in the *Birkat-ha-Minim*.[20] The suppression of that revolt led to "what can only be described as 'ethnic cleansing.'"[21] Unlike life in Jerusalem after the first Jewish revolt leading to the destruction of Jerusalem and the Temple in 70CE, "Jewish life in the heartland of central Judea was not crushed until 135 C.E . . . "[22] Jewish people were fighting for their very survival.

The aftermath of the Second Jewish Revolt changed everything in Jerusalem. "Given the exclusion from Jerusalem and the vicinity after 135 C.E. that afflicted all Jews, including Jewish Christians . . . the leaders of the church in Jerusalem were gentiles."[23] This represented a serious conflict given the history of the Jerusalem church as a sect of Judaism, now led by non-Jews. It meant that the Roman government would need to accept gentile leadership of a heretofore Jewish religious community, granting them the same freedoms offered to Jews within the Roman Empire to practice their rituals and customs.

The best evidence we have for this period of conflict involving Rome, the Jewish community, and the Jewish-Gentile community is Justin Martyr's *Dialogue with Trypho* [160C.E.], the former being a Gentile convert from Greek philosophy to Christianity, the latter, a practicing Jew. It is the first documented interfaith discussion between a Jesus follower and a Jewish person outside of the New Testament.

---

19. Anderson, "Anti-Semitism and Religious Violence as Flaws Interpretations of the Gospel of John," *Faculty Publications—George Fox School of Theology*, (2017).

20. Taylor, "Parting in Palestine," *Partings*, 99.

21. Ibid., 87.

22. Ibid., 92.

23. Ibid., 98.

While it deserves a more thorough analysis than we can give it here, suffice it to say this dialogue presents the major points of both Christianity and Judaism such as: circumcision, the Sabbath, the Law of Moses, death as a sign of a failed Messiah, and Christianity's violation of the Sh'ma's claim of only One God. Unfortunately, in his desire to defend the truth of Jesus, Justin can be rightly blamed for beginning the vitriolic rhetoric which would attempt to explain Jewish suffering as God's punishment for rejecting Jesus as their Messiah. Justin Martyr's statements and tone launched an anti-Judaism previously unheard of in the first century. As early as the mid-second century, the die had been cast for what would be an anti-Judaistic apologetic as a way to define Christianity itself.

The church now saw itself as non-Jewish, and even expressed its self-awareness in anti-Jewish terms. "Justin argues with Trypho that the church is a largely Gentile entity (11.7-23), existing separately from 'you Jews' (11.2); that the old law and covenant have become 'obsolete,' and have been 'abrogated' and replaced by a new law and covenant (11.2-4); that the church has now become 'the true spiritual Israel" (11.5); that the Scriptures are no longer 'yours, but ours' (29.2) . . . "[24]

Terrence L. Donaldson states, "We should be cautious about assuming that even in Justin's day 'Christianity' and 'Judaism' represented two separate and distinct entities."[25] He claims that the boundaries in 150 CE are simply not that clear. As time went on and the church evolved into a non-Hebraic religious organization, the rigidity of bolder ecclesial boundaries between the two religions surfaced.

Institutional Hierarchy and Church Fathers

Along with the demographic changes in second-century Jerusalem, Christians distinguished themselves with the election of *bishops* derived from a Roman model of provincial administration. Beyond the specific issue of substituting cultural leadership models for the clear biblical models from the New Testament, to its determent, the church has continued to accommodate local, regional, and national culture throughout its history. The categories going back to the second century are the same; only the degree of those same categories has changed.

---

24. Donaldson, "Supercessionism and Early Church Definition," *JJMJS*, (2016), 7.
25. Ibid.,8.

Recall from Acts 6 the earlier conflict between Greek-speaking Jews and Hebrew-Speaking Jews which created the office of *deacon* to serve food allowing the leaders of the Jerusalem church to study the word of God. In the same vein the church added the following offices of "*apostle* [sent to plant new churches], *prophets* [proclaimers of the word; Peter was the first prophet of the church], *evangelists* [mission to those outside the community [Philip was one of the first *evangelists* taking the Gospel to Samaria and beyond], *pastors* [congregational care including *priestly functions* of representing God to the people and the needs of the people to God], and *teachers* [explain the details of the proclaimed word] . . . [26] [my italics]. The creation of functions, titles, and jobs revolved around *serving the church*. As the church continued to grow and accommodate Gentile cultural values, *serving the church* evolved into the church *serving the status of the offices*. The power of authority often replaced the humility to serve God and others.

For example, the early office of overseer[27] emerged in the church. Paul offered the qualification of a *bishop* as Timothy's mentor.[28] The *office of elder*[29] surfaced during the days of the Way in Jerusalem Paul bade the Ephesian *elders* of the church a poignant farewell address.[30] [my italics]. One of the significant turning points in the second century was the formalization and power attributed to the *bishops* of the church who are simultaneously referred to as the Church Fathers or Patriarchs. *Bishops* were overseers of regional churches modeled upon Roman provincial leadership. Today's *Archbishop* is considered a shepherd of the bishops symbolized by a shepherd's staff.

A higher level of bishop emerged during the second century as the church grew in number requiring extended organizational structure. Terms used for expanded leadership included *Apostolic Fathers, Church*

---

26. Ephesians 4: 11.

27. See note on 1 Timothy 3: 1 from the NIV: "overseer in the Greek culture was the word used of a presiding official in a civic or religious organization . . . The equivalent word with its qualifications and functions from the Jewish background of Christianity is *elder* used interchangeably with *overseer* throughout the New Testament. *Bishop* may also be considered the same as both terms.

28. 1 Timothy 3: 1—7; then, in 3: 8—10, 12, 13, Paul further developed the office of deacon.

29. James may be considered the lead elder in the Jerusalem Jewish church [see Acts 15: 2, 6], even though the term doesn't appear in Luke's history of the church recorded in Acts.

30. Acts 20: 17ff

Fathers, and *Patriarchs of the Church.* One of the key tasks of these scholars and theologians was to develop church doctrine and dogma setting boundaries to distinguish Christianity from Judaism. We'll also note, on the negative side of the ledger, how the early Church Fathers formalized anti-Judaism leading to racial anti-Jewishness within the church. The presence of church fathers wasn't inherently wrong. The theological anti-Judaism that they promulgated was the problem.

We now consider those fathers of the church going back to the first century. Clement [65—100 C.E.] is thought to have had contact with the original church apostles Peter and Barnabas, was held to be a Bishop of Rome, and the author of several influential letters which state "the need for Christians to maintain Jewish purity laws."[31]

Ignatius [85—115 C.E.], the Bishop of Antioch was a student of the Apostle John and the friend of Polycarp [also a student of the Apostle John]. He coined the term *catholic* and became a strong advocate for episcopal supremacy. He assigned a monarchial role to the Bishop—one never found in Scripture—when listing the tasks or job of an overseer. This idea of one powerful person was another accommodation of culture into the church. It violated any Hebraic understanding of church leadership displayed by a Jewish Jesus who washed his followers' feet coming to seek and to save a lost humanity.

It was Governor Pilate, not s religious leader, who put the sign, "Jesus of Nazareth, King of the Jews," on the cross. Jesus never claimed to be the king of the Jews, but a servant who came to seek and to save the lost. Only those who misunderstood Jesus' mission called him a king. The wise astrologers from the east didn't come to worship Jesus as Lord, but to merely pay homage [reverent regard] to a king, like any other king of a nation.

However, the early church fathers took it further by castigating all Jews. In the spirit of the Apostle Paul, "Ignatius castigated the 'Judaizers,'"[32] Ignatius removed all doubt regarding his anti-Jewishness when he said, "'Judaism' is nothing but funeral monuments and tombstones of the dead."[33] The Bishop of Rome also allegorized the relationship of the Jews and Christians postulating that the covenants were really

---

31. Reed and Young, "Christianity in Antioch: Partings in Roman Syria," *Partings,* Shanks, ed., 125.

32. Attridge, "The Christian Movement: 70—312 CE," *Christianity and Rabbinic Judaism,* 158.

33. Ignatius, *To the Philadelphians,* vi, I.

for the Christians, not the Jews launching a growing Catholic Tradition of Jew-hatred unhitched from the Old Testament.

Non-biblical hierarchical structures dominated church leadership by assigning powers to church officials. This may even be considered another form of separation within the church; that is, the establishment of Tradition vs Scriptural Authority. Over time, the biblical moorings of the church were marginalized and eventually neglected. No longer was the Christian community "devoted to the apostles' teaching."[34] Hierarchical power, impersonal organization and a growing "parting of laity from church leaders" symbolized how far apart Christianity had degenerated from its Hebraic roots of concrete intimacy between church leaders and the laity.

Beginning late in the first century, church leaders began documenting the key tenets of the Christian faith as culture knocked on its doors. Further caving into culture led to doctrinal heresy. Greek ideas influenced the church as the church encountered the surrounding culture. The Gnostics were among the earliest group to influence the church in this way.

Gnosticism

In his 90 C.E. letters, the Apostle John was the first Christian theologian to warn the late first-century church about Gnosticism. This Greek philosophy injected a dualism which violated the oneness of God and a holistic Gospel. The Sh'ma laid a sure foundation of God's unique oneness. Gnosticism split God in half speaking of a so-called evil god of the Old Testament and a so-called good God of the New Testament. In a world imbued with spiritualities of all sorts, John established a test for knowing the true Holy Spirit of God. "Beloved, do not believe every spirit, but test the spirits to see whether they are from God . . . By this you know the Spirit of God: every spirit that confesses that *Jesus Christ has come in flesh is from God* . . . "[35] [my italics].

Gnosticism asserted that only spirits were good and that material was evil, which included the human body. The Incarnation, one of Christianity's major tenets, asserts that "The Word became flesh and

---

34. Acts 2: 42.
35. 1 John 4: 1,2.

lived among us . . . ."[36] Many in the first century church, a community which became increasingly Greek, were often unable to discern the difference between and spirits [read demonic] and the Holy Spirit of God. The Apostle John laid down the criterion in his letter based upon the nature of Jesus Christ of *one person* mysteriously characterized by *two natures—divine and human* confirmed by fifth century church council.

Had the church remembered its Hebraic roots, it would have recognized that such a dualism of spirit against flesh was wrong and violated Judaism's view of a good Creator who saw that all His creation was good. The church would have recalled the Torah's injunction that God made human beings in His image [Genesis 1: 27]. That the Gentile church was in full swing by the end of the first century meant that key teachings of the faith rooted in the Tanakh and adopted by the early church were eventually forgotten.

Gnosticism led to the parting of the ways between the church and the synagogue in that basic Hebraic thought was lost by accommodating Greek philosophy. A Gentile church began parting ways theologically from a balanced Jewish-Gentile ecclesiology as the body of Christ before the end of the first century. For example, "in the basic structures of Gnostic teaching the people of Israel and the people of Christ were identified by different Gods and thus were set over against each other across a cosmological divide . . . [and there was] . . . a sharp distinction made between the literal (fleshly) sense of Scripture and its deeper spiritual (Christocentric) meaning (e.g., *Barn.* 10.9)."[37] Scripture asserts that Christ became flesh. Mary gave God a body.

Irenaeus [130—202 CE] was the most prolific opponent of Gnosticism in church history. His tome, *Against Heresies*, is by far the most thorough refutation of Gnosticism ever written. Building upon the Apostle John's use of the Incarnation as a test for spirituality, Irenaeus borrowed the following truths about Jesus Christ: " . . . one God, the Almighty, and one Jesus Christ, the Only-begotten, by whom all things were made . . . [and] . . . this was the Son of God, this the Only-begotten, this the Former of all things, this the true Light who enlighteneth every man, this the Creator of the world, this He that came to His own, this He that became flesh and dwelt among us . . . ."[38] No other better theological statement regarding Gnosticism exists.

36. John 1: 14.
37. Donaldson, *JJMJS*, 14.
38. Irenaeus, *Against Heresies*, Chapter IX, "Refutation of the impious of these

Generally speaking, the church fathers who created and documented sound church doctrine simultaneously proclaimed anti-Judaism and antisemitism within the church. Even Patriarch Irenaeus, who intellectually challenged Gnosticism, spoke of the Jews as Christ-killers stating, "Their synagogues are conventicles of heretics."[39] How one of the church's greatest scholars and theologians could simultaneously be anti-Gnostic and anti-Jewish boggles the mind. Ignatius wrote that "if we continue to live in accordance with Judaism, we admit that we have not received grace" (Magnesians 8: 1).[40] The Epistle of Barnabas (130 C.E.) argued that only Christians properly understood the Hebrew Scriptures, especially the laws of the Torah, while "they" [the Jews] do not (2: 7; 3: 6 . . .) . . . "they" received the covenant but were not worthy, therefore, "we" have received it (14: 1, 4, 5)."[41] Sadly, there are too many sermons to address from the Church Fathers which are either theologically anti-Judaistic or racially anti-Jewish. "Christian literature from 100CE to 150CE was uniformly hostile to Jews and Judaism."[42] The virulent rhetoric against the Jews continued right up to Constantine and beyond, even to this day. As I write this chapter the news is broadcasting anti-Semitic terrorism around the world.

Gnosticism's destructive dualism created what became known as Replacement Theology. The church was falsely considered to have superceded Israel as the community who now deserved the blessings of the covenants. Falsely, the church thought of itself as the New Israel where the covenants no longer applied to the Jews but only to Christians.

Supercessionism/Replacement Theology

Christian doctrine written from the second century on "shows that these authors understand Christianity to be not-Judaism. The texts regularly assert that Christians constitute a new people beside pagans ('Greeks') and Jews, a people that is both old and new, in that it fulfills the prophets of scripture and new in that it replaces the old Israel."[43] Christian com-

---

heretics," 63.

39. Rozzini, "Irenaeus and Israel," *Jerusalem Post* (2013).

40. Cohen, "The Ways That Parted Jews, Christians, and Jewish-Christians ca. 100–150 CE," *Jews and Christians in the First and Second Centuries*.

41. Ibid.

42. Ibid.

43. Ibid.

mentary and doctrine implied or explicitly stated that the Jews were no longer the people of God, or His Covenants, or His promises about their land—all of which were God's punishment of Israel for rejecting Jesus as the Messiah. "Surely at this point the extinction of national Judaism could have been affirmed once and for all."[44]

The church's so-called supercession over Israel is a clear example of Tradition, not biblical mandate. It does, however, have roots in the theological anti-Judaism prevalent in the church during the second century where Bishop Melito of Sardis was first to call the Jewish Bible "the Old Testament." Torah was thought to be outdated; the church was to replace it as the so-called new and improved way—the New Testament. Elder and Young Testament better characterize Scripture's chronology without making it the basis for replacement of Israel by the church.   The Christian view of the story of Israel being fulfilled in the story of Jesus is totally different from a view of supercessionism or replacement of Israel by the church. Completion or fulfillment in no way negates the Covenants. Recall Jesus' claim that he didn't come to "abolish the Law and the Prophets, but to fulfill them."[45]

That said, it is possible to cherry-pick Scripture to make it appear to say what one may want it to say. Take for example, the Apostle Paul's somewhat Gnostic sounding cryptic discussion in Romans 2: 25—29: "For a person is not a Jew who is one outwardly, nor is true circumcision something external and physical . . . " Here we have Paul's concept of a circumcision of the heart rooted in Hebraic thought from both the Torah and The Prophets. He is not favoring the spirit over the body, but comparing a physical ritual with one's inward personal faith. Putting Romans 2: 25—29 in its theological context solves the apparent gnostic implication where Paul is making an argument about the need for pure faith [circumcision of the heart] rather than rituals [circumcision of the body].

Going beyond this early text in Romans, the Apostle Paul's Jewish autobiography moves the needle away from supercessionism even further. There is simply no way to interpret the Apostle Paul's metaphor of the cultivated olive tree as Israel and the grafted-in wild olive branch [Romans 11] as the Gentile church and arrive at a supercessionist view. "For Paul, then, the believing Church will never be separated from its

---

44. Ibid.
45. Matthew 5: 17.

root, Jewish Israel. If the Church thinks that it can be separate and in fact replace Jewish Israel, it has become 'proud' and 'arrogant.'"[46]

God's Covenants given to Abraham, Moses, and David are still valid and in part yet to be fulfilled. Clearly, nothing, certainly not the church, has invalidated the immutability of the Abrahamic Covenant in Genesis 12: 1—3, which contains seven specific promises of God to the first Jewish person, Abraham, the Father of Israel. God's Covenant with Abraham is eternally valid to this moment.

Supercessionism and Replacement Theology vanish as credible with the Apostle Paul's statement that "All Israel will be saved . . . for the gifts and the calling of God are irrevocable."[47] The apparent boundary between Israel and the church is merely temporary as Paul states, "For God has imprisoned all . . . that He might show mercy to all."[48]

It is clear that so bold a boundary between the church and synagogue surely implied the existence of a dysfunctional church [read, a Gentile church]. Christian texts (like Justin's *Dialogue with Trypho the Jew*) emphasize that Christianity is right and Judaism is wrong. There is certainly a parting of the ways here. In contrast, rabbinic texts completely ignore gentile Christians. Here the parting of the ways is expressed through avoidance and neglect. But it is a parting just the same.

We assert that any view of Israel by the church which denies the Jewish people their particularity as the first and continuing people of God is to be rejected out of hand. The Scriptures nowhere demonstrate that the true church saw itself as anti-Jewish sustained by an anti-biblical notion that a new covenant exists for Christians which no longer exists for the Jewish people.

A stated earlier, we've limited our discussion of the parting of the ways up to and including Constantine [4th century C.E.] and his legalization of Christianity. Often misconstrued as a theologian who desired correct teaching, this Roman emperor called the Nicene Council to make peace. Theological rancor between church factions existed during his watch. He urged the church fathers to call a council to resolve their differences by agreeing to disagree. Constantine's desire for national peace superceded any wish he might have had for doctrinal clarity on the person and nature of Jesus Christ.

---

46. McDermott, "Is the Church God's New Israel?" *Patheos*.
47. Romans 11: 25—36.
48. Romans 11: 32.

We now turn our attention to the statements of Christian doctrine contained in both *The Apostles' Creed* and the *Nicene Creed* resulting from several church councils whose authors proclaimed virulent anti-Semitic sermons on Sunday and formulated creedal Christian doctrine during the week.

Creeds & Councils

In and of themselves, doctrinal statements aren't inherently polarizing. We all want to know where someone stands on the issues. Jesus told everyone where he stood on the Law and the Prophets. The Apostle Paul asserted the scandal of Christ crucified and the cross' role in dismantling the hostile wall between Jews and Gentiles. Irenaeus told the world where the church stood on Gnostic philosophy during the late second - early third centuries when he took three years [183—186 C.E.] to write *Against Heresies*. As much as the church creeds are refined statements of Christian teaching, they failed to mention any Hebraic thought, neglected the covenants, and didn't mention Israel's role in global redemption. The creeds were a photo-op of a church family which left Israel out of the picture.

The Apostles' Creed [*Symbolum Apostolorum*] may have originated as far back as 200 CE as derived from Tertullian's and Irenaeus' *Old Roman Creed*.[49] Much of the discussion about the Creed's content and origin centers on baptismal formulae which may have been derived from Paul's admonition to "confess with your lips that Jesus is Lord and believe in your heart that God raised him from the dead . . . "[50] The Apostle Paul's hymn from Philippians 2: 5—11 provides broad theological background for the more specific statements of the Apostles' Creed—"born in human likeness . . . death on a cross . . . God also highly exalted him." Later in his instructions to Timothy, Paul offers a succinct Christological formula which anticipates elements of the Creed: " . . . revealed in the flesh . . . vindicated in spirit . . . taken up in glory."[51] Unnamed patriarchs wrote the creeds with no reference to the first-century sermons and teaching of the early church documented in the New Testament. Arguably, the creeds were not finalized until the second half of the fifth century.[52]

---

49. Thurston, "Apostles' Creed," *The Catholic Encyclopedia*.
50. Romans 10: 9, 10.
51. 1 Timothy 3: 16.
52. Thurston, "Apostles' Creed."

No one would ever get the impression that Christianity originated from Judaism when reading The Apostles' Creed—the oldest and most familiar statement of Christian belief. Nothing in the Apostles' Creed makes the Torah, the Prophets, or the Writings necessary. Nothing in the Apostles' Creed makes the Jewishness of Jesus necessary. The Apostles' Creed, if not "pen to paper" written by the early church fathers was certainly "inspired" by anti-Judaistic thinkers like Ignatius, Justin, Melito, Irenaeus, Tertullian and, worst of all, "the greatest preacher of the Fathers," John Chrysostom. By default and omission, the Apostles' Creed indirectly contributed to the parting of the ways between Christianity and Judaism *by what it didn't say* about the Jewishness of Jesus or the Jewish Jerusalem church. Absent its omissions, The Apostles' Creed is yet a succinct statement of the Christian teaching about God, Jesus Christ, the Holy Spirit, and the church.

The Apostles' Creed

I believe in God the Father Almighty, maker of heaven and earth. And in Jesus Christ his only Son, our Lord; who was conceived by the Holy Spirit, born of the Virgin Mary, suffered under Pontius Pilate, was crucified, dead, and buried; he descended to hell; the third day he rose again from the dead; he ascended into heaven, and sitteth on the right hand of God the Father Almighty; from thence he shall come to judge the quick and the dead. I believe in the Holy Spirit, the holy catholic Church, the communion of saints, the forgiveness of sins, the resurrection of the body, and the life everlasting. Amen.

About one hundred years after The Apostle's Creed was fully documented, Emperor Constantine called The Council of Nicea hoping that it would make peace among the warring factions of the church. Just before the Council, Constantine sent a letter to Arius, a Libyan priest and to Alexander, the Bishop of Alexandria, who opposed each other on the topic of the Trinity, urging them to reconcile their opposing positions for the sake of unity in the church and in the Roman State.[53] By the time Constantine became emperor of the Roman Empire, any memory of a Jewish church was totally gone. The Gentile church at this time was considered a nominal gathering of Christians who were members of the church *only* because they were citizens of the Roman Empire. The bittersweet role

---

53. Baghos, "The Historical Context of the Nicene-Constantinopolitan Creed," Lecture, 2013.

of Constantine was that while he legalized Christianity and stopped the early persecutions of Christians, he weakened the commitment of following Jesus as a disciple. The glue that Constantine had recently chosen to hold his empire together was tearing the church apart.

There is nothing in the Nicene Creed which makes Judaism necessary. Justin Martyr is a clear example of a Christian theologian who contributed to the seminal thoughts considered in the construction of the Nicene Creed. Ironically, Justin was also one of the many theologians who proclaimed vitriolic sermons which demonized the Jews both theologically and racially.

The Nicene Creed

> We believe in one God, the Father almighty, maker of heaven and earth, of all things visible and invisible. And in one Lord Jesus Christ, the only Son of God, begotten from the Father before all ages, God from God, Light from Light, true God from true God, begotten, not created. Through him all things were made. For us and for our salvation he came down from heaven; he became incarnate by the Holy Spirit and the virgin Mary and was made human. He was crucified for us under Pontius Pilate; he suffered and was buried. The third day he rose again, according to the Scriptures. He ascended to heaven and is seated at the right hand of the Father. He will come again with glory to judge the living and the dead. His kingdom will never end. And we believe in the Holy Spirit, the Lord, the giver of life. He proceeds from the Father and the Son, and with the Father and the Son is worshiped and glorified. He spoke through the prophets. We believe one holy catholic apostolic church. We affirm one baptism for the forgiveness of sins. We look forward to the resurrection of the dead, and to life everlasting. Amen.

In sum, the theologians who composed the Nicene Creed were theologically anti-Judaistic and racially anti-Semitic. Over a period of almost 2000 years, the church debated theological and practical issues in about 30 formal Church Councils. The issues included everything from determining the nature of Jesus Christ, deciding the canon, authority, the perpetual virginity of Mary, statues in sanctuaries, the Protestant Reformation, tradition vs. biblical authority, and how the Church should respond to global religions.

The first Church Council in about 50 C.E. involved whether a Jesus follower needed to become Jewish.

No church council after 50 C.E. had anything to do with the Jewish origins, presence or Hebraic thought involving the church.

For the last 1900 years where the Church forgot, avoided, or neglected the Hebraic heritage of Christianity, the church became both a perpetuator and bystander while others marginalized, oppressed, and murdered the Jewish people.

The events of the church's horrible treatment of the Jewish people greatly influenced the myths and legends which resulted in ghettoes, pogroms, the Crusades, the Inquisition of 1492 and other expulsions of Jews from countries around the world.

As I conclude this chapter, the Hamas-Israel War begun on October 7, 2023 continues a militarized-terrorist determination to wipe Israel off the map "from the river to the sea." Today's [June 22, 2025] news is broadcasting war not only between Israel and Iran, but also between the United States and Iran. The far-reaching consequences of the parting of the ways remain to this day.

In the next chapter, on a more constructive note, we'll seek to rediscover a Christianity whose rootedness in the gospel mandates that to love God is to love the Jewish people.

— PART FOUR —
Restitution

Chapter 12

Rediscovering Christianity

IN THE PREVIOUS CHAPTER, after defining and analyzing both the synagogue and the church, we navigated our way through the sad history of a dysfunctional church. We noted how an anti-Judaistic and anti-Semitic church influenced a cultural ethos which oppressed the Jewish people. This chapter is about rediscovering an authentic Christianity which embraces its Hebraic origins and loves the Jewish people.

In part, the Shoah was the church's problem. It stood by voicelessly while Jewish people were shoved to the boundaries of society, oppressed, and ultimately exterminated. Symbolic of its racism, European culture raised the so-called *Jewish Question*. What was questionable about the Jews? What made a question about Jewish people necessary? What made it acceptable to hate people just because of their religion or culture? Why wasn't there a *German Question* or a *French Question*? A full analysis of these questions requires more investigation than we can get into here. Suffice it to say, a healthy Jewish-Gentile church would have challenged any attempt to marginalize the Jewish people. It did not.

"Theologians claimed that the presence of a Jewish minority in society was a problem that needed to be solved . . . Many who supported this belief often expected Jews to . . . abandon their customs, behavior, traditions, and even religion in order to assimilate into society . . . they believed that Jews were a separate 'race,' whose behavior, traits, and character were negative and unchangeable."[1] The parting of the ways created

1. Editors of the Holocaust Encyclopedia, "The Jewish Question," *The Holocaust*

space for theological anti-Judaism and racial anti-Semitism across European culture which climaxed in the Catastrophe.

Our analysis will demonstrate how the parting of the ways undermined three significant aspects of Christianity creating a need for the following: First, to *recover the gospel*, to *restore the church* and, to *reclaim the kingdom of God*.

Recovering the Gospel

The Gospel is Christ crucified and risen– the historic events in the life of Jesus Christ that saved, save today, and continues to save humanity. Humanity's sins were forgiven and death was destroyed during one weekend about 33 C.E. The necessary and sufficient work of Jesus Christ on a cross in an empty tomb proclaimed victory over sin and death, respectively.

Any so-called gospel which excludes the covenants given to Abraham, Moses, David, and Jeremiah's new covenant is not the gospel. "The gospel . . . is declaring the Story of Israel as resolved in the Story of Jesus."[2] Scot McKnight set the gospel message within the context of Israel's history fulfilled in Jesus' life on earth. "Paul's 'gospel' was the Story of Jesus completing Israel's Story . . . The apostolic gospel, the tradition the apostles passed along, can be found in the Gospels of Matthew, Mark, Luke, and John . . . *If you read the gospel, hear the gospel, or preach the gospel, read, listen to, and preach the Gospels.*"[3] [author's italics].

McKnight equates Jesus' message of the forgiveness of sins with the Apostle Paul's summative statement of the gospel: "For I handed on to you as of first importance what I in turn received—that Christ died for our sins in accordance with the scriptures, and that he was buried, and that he was raised on the third day in accordance with the scriptures . . . "[4] That is, Paul preached Jesus' gospel. Was Jesus himself the completion of the Story of Israel? "The question that 1 Corinthians generates for us is this question: Did Jesus preach a gospel that concerned that same Person?"[5] Yes. Later, building upon our previous discussion of Jesus' view of the kingdom of God, we'll get into how Jesus uses *kingdom* to

---

Encyclopedia, The United States Holocaust Museum.

2. McKnight, *The King Jesus Gospel*, 95.
3. Ibid., 96.
4. 1 Corinthians 15: 3—5.
5. McKnight, *The King Jesus Gospel*, 96.

explain how in his own person, he, *Jesus is the gospel*. No need for a Jewish Question, a German Question, or a Church Question exists. Ultimately the only question is Dietrich Bonhoeffer's question: "Who is Jesus Christ for you, today?"[6] Jesus followers must answer this question for themselves; the church must answer this question for itself as it recovers its only message—the gospel.

David Flusser discusses the story of Israel as the context within which the Story of the historical Christ makes sense. Flusser's discussion of Jesus' Jewishness complements McKnight's restoration of the gospel defined as the person of Jesus. Together both theologians, one a Christian scholar and the other a Jewish theologian, provide a balanced gospel. Flusser points out that Jesus only wanted to work among the Jews to confirm the divine truth of the covenants.[7] Flusser's statement is based upon Romans 1:16—"... the gospel ... is the power of God for everyone who believes: first for the Jew, then for the Gentile." No rediscovery of a genuine Christianity can occur without recovering of gospel of Jesus.

In his compelling article, "Reconciling Gospel and Torah: The Catechism," Joseph Ratzinger proposes that the church must accept the mission of Israel to the world based upon the visit of the Magi to the infant Jesus recorded in Matthew 2: 1-12. He writes, "The Magi's coming ... to pay homage to the king of the Jews shows that they seek in Israel, in the messianic star of David, the one who will be king of the nations."[8] That is, Ratzinger links a historic event with theological fact—Judaism's mission to all humanity. He references the Abrahamic Covenant to show an early linkage of Israel with all nations. The king of Israel is the king of the nations.

Furthermore, he says, "The mission of Jesus consists in leading the history of the nations in the community of Abraham, in the story of Israel."[9] Ratzinger's nuance anticipates Scot McKnight's mutuality of both Israel's and Jesus' stories. The former pope references Ephesians 2: 18-22, which validates how the church must find in the Abraham covenant its shared mission of Israel—proclaiming one God for Israel and all nations. A recovered gospel message includes the specific covenants to Israel which begin by proclaiming Israel's mission to the world as the context within which the mission of the church exists.

6. Bonhoeffer, *Letters and Papers from Prison*, 362.
7. Flusser, *The Sage from Galilee*, 53.
8. Ratzinger, "Torah and Gospel," *Catholics for Israel* (2010).
9. Ibid.

Edith Schaeffer was among the first, if not the very first, theologians to assert the Jewishness of the Gospel in her ground-breaking book, *Christianity is Jewish*. She writes about the poignant story of Abraham and Isaac from Genesis 22 where God tells Abraham to sacrifice his son as a burnt offering. The Torah spoke of slaughtering and burning a lamb to receive forgiveness from sins. God was asking Abraham to murder his only son as a ritual sacrifice for sin. Schaeffer writes, "These two had to understand with their intellects as well as to believe that God was going to fulfill His promise that one day the nations would be blessed through their seed,"[10] which seemed about to end.

We find David H. Stern's thoughts useful when he says that Christianity, "no matter how un-Jewish some of its current forms of expression may be, has its roots in Judaism and in the Jewish people."[11] Stern is a Messianic Jewish worshiper. He contends that the gospel must be contextualized for non-Jewish Jesus followers if the church is to proclaim the gospel as the whole counsel of God. Stern claims that his book "will show that the separation between the Church and the Jewish people . . . is completely out of God's will, a terrible mistake, the worst schism in the history of this world."[12] Repairing the tear between Judaism and Christianity must characterize a recovery of the gospel.

Twentieth-century theologian-martyr Dietrich Bonhoeffer read the entire Old Testament twice in a Nazi prison. Reading the Tanakh changed his mind about the Gospel. In an April 30, 1944 letter to his friend and biographer, Eberhard Bethge, Bonhoeffer's said, " . . . we don't read the New Testament nearly enough in the light of the Old."[13]

Specifically, Bonhoeffer changed his mind about *redemption*. Theologically, traditional notions of redemption involved the liberation of an *individual* from bondage, the saving of *one's* soul. He opined, "Does the question of saving one's soul even come up in the Old Testament? Isn't *God's righteousness and kingdom on earth* the center of everything?"[14] [my italics]. He was beginning to think of salvation from a *communal* sense, not reduced to individualistic piety or inner experience. God continually addressed Moses as a priest to and on behalf of the His chosen people, tribal communities and the entire nation of Israel as representatives of

10. Schaeffer, *Christianity Is Jewish*, 45.
11. Stern, *Restoring the Jewishness of the Gospel*, 57.
12. Ibid., 13.
13. Bonhoeffer, *Letters and Papers from Prison*, 367.
14. Ibid., 373.

His kingdom on earth. The reduction of the gospel to individualistic pietism does not represent the whole counsel of God which begins in the Elder Testament. A communal sense of Israel's redemption must precede any notion of being redeemed as an individual. A recovered gospel begins with God's redemption of a community, of Israel which sets the stage for the redemption of another community, the church. The story of Jesus is anticipated in the story of Israel.

The aforementioned scholars root the gospel within its Hebraic context. Yet from the second century C.E. on, the gospel hung out in space as the second story of house without a first floor or foundation. As we've discussed earlier, the early presence of misguided Judaizers and later dominance of non-Hebraic thought injected the poison of other "gospels" into the veins of the church. While the sacrament of the Eucharist was celebrated weekly, the sacrament of the Word to explain and proclaim the gospel was marginalized. Luther's sixteenth-century recovery of the gospel took shape as a proclaimed sacrament of God's Word of salvation by grace through faith. Practicing the sacrament of the Eucharist without the sacrament of the Word is a half-truth. Proclaiming the sacrament of the Word without the Eucharist is sterile.

In the above segment we've attempted to begin a rediscovery of Christianity by recovering the gospel of the Scriptures. A next step toward rediscovering Christianity involves restoring the church to which we now turn our attention.

Restoring the Church

The Apostle Paul defined the church as *one new humanity*.

> For he [Christ] himself is our peace, who has made the two one and has destroyed the barrier, the dividing wall of hostility . . . His purpose was to create in himself *one new humanity* out of the two[15] thus making peace and in this one body to reconcile both of them to God through the cross . . . [16] [my italics].

---

15. The NIV follows the Greek, "out of the two." The NRSV replaces "out of the two" with "in place of," a misleading translation emanating from theological bias rather than correct exegesis. See David B. Woods discussion of this error in his article "Jew-Gentile distinction in the one new man of Ephesians 2: 15," *Conspectus* 2014, Vol. 18, 95—135.

16. Ephesians 2: 14—16a, paraphrased from NIV.

His radical definition of the church is rooted in the Jewish people. Paul states, " . . . remember that at one time you Gentiles by birth . . . were without Christ, being aliens from the commonwealth of Israel, and strangers to the covenants of promise, having no hope and without God in the world."[17] Continuing to address Gentiles in the church, Paul writes, "But now in Christ Jesus you who once were far off have been brought near by the blood of Christ. For he is our peace; in his flesh he has made both groups one . . . that he might create in himself *one new humanity* . . . "[18] [my italics]. Note how he describes that Gentiles as aliens and strangers to Israel are without Christ and God. He states that Gentiles are far off. *Far off* from what or from whom? Or, *near* to what or to whom? If the blood of Christ creates one new humanity, he's speaking about being far off from Christ and being brought near to Christ as the church. This must mean repairing the damage from the historic parting of the ways. It means reconciling with Jewish people.

David Rudolph, the director of Messianic Jewish Studies at The King's University, states, " . . . the Church is at a crossroads in understanding its relationship to Jews and Judaism . . . "[19] He goes on to point out that not heeding Paul's definition of a normative Jewish-Gentile church results in "departures . . . resulting in One New Jew and . . . One New Gentile,"[20] neither of which defines the church based upon Ephesians 2. He advocates a "vision for the Church in which Jewish and Gentile believers affirm each other in their respective callings and where interdependence and mutual blessing are highly valued."[21] RK Soulen resonates with Rudolph's thesis. "The church of Jesus Christ is a sphere of mutual blessing between Jew and Gentile where the distinction between them is not erased, but recreated in a promissory way . . . as the foretaste of messianic peace . . . "[22] It is his hope and vision for the church that each group maintain its identity as followers of Jesus. Practically speaking, this means not lording over each other one's own identity or

---

17. Ephesians 2: 13—15b.

18. Ibid.

19. Rudolph, "One New Man, Hebrew Roots, Replacement Theology," Lecture at The King's University, September, 2013.

20. Ibid.

21. Ibid.

22. Rudolph and J. Willitts, eds., "The standard canonical narrative and the problem of supercessionism," *Introduction to Messianic Judaism: its ecclesial context and biblical foundations*, 282—291.

religious culture. He believes that Jewish followers of Yeshua are called to maintain their Jewish biblical heritage and that Gentile followers of Yeshua are called to unity with their Jewish brothers and sisters.

That said, non-biblical aspects of each culture must be abandoned and clearly not retained simply because of one's cultural identity. However, when required, the normative Jewish-Gentile church must be counter-cultural as one new humanity of Jews and Gentiles both of whom reject anti-biblical cultural values. This radical relationship has been found difficult and essentially left untried. For the sake of the church and the survival of the Jewish people, what is difficult must be tried, since all else has failed.

Arguably, Bonhoeffer's theological-anthropological ecclesiology of the cross offers the broadest latitude for the church. His concept of the church dismantles the ecclesial distortions extant during the parting of the ways. Echoing the Apostle Paul, Bonhoeffer calls the church "the body of Christ . . . this means that we are now 'with Christ' and 'in Christ.' And that 'Christ is in us.'"[23] This is an anthropological statement supporting the church as one humanity in Christ. In such a radical community, the physical bodies of both Jews and Gentiles have the chance to be reconciled in community with one another.

"The church is one; it is the body of Christ. At the same time it is the multiplicity and community of its members . . . "[24] His theology of the church negates Greek influence and originates in "the temple of the Old Testament . . . a shadow of the body of Christ . . . the living temple of God and of the new humanity."[25]

"Christ exists *as* the church"[26] [my italics]. This programmatic statement appears in Dietrich Bonhoeffer' first dissertation, *Sanctorum Communio*. Bonhoeffer *doesn't* say that Christ is *in* the Church. That would mean something *outside* of Christ would be *in* the church—an inherent contradiction. All definitions, characteristics and functions related to the church must be simultaneously true of Jesus Christ. A restored church equates Christ and the church. It eliminates those elements seeking to invade the congregation which are non-Christian, even if culturally relevant.

---

23. Bonhoeffer, *Discipleship*, 216.
24. Ibid., 220.
25. Ibid., 224.
26. Bischoff, *Evangelicalism Is Dead*, 23.

The church resides within a culture without needing to accommodate that cultural values of that culture. In Nazi Germany, the church accommodated its surrounding racist culture. Christ is the only one relevant to the church; not culture. At its best a restored church carefully discerns it surrounding culture to determine which of its aspects are not be accommodated within the body of Christ. The " . . . danger of confusing the church with some wishful image of pious community . . . "[27] threatens the heart of church-community. The Jewish-Gentile church isn't perfect. It is comprised of forgiven sinners in whom sin still resides. Forgiveness is the issue.

Bonhoeffer stresses the theological implications of participation. "Christian community is not an ideal we have to realize, but rather a reality created by God in Christ in which we may participate."[28] He echoes the sacramental words which consecrate the Eucharistic body and blood of Christ. " . . . the cup that we bless, is it not a participation in the blood of Christ . . . and the bread, a participation in the body of Christ . . . "[29] How does a church participate in the body and blood of Jesus Christ since worship is not a spectator sport?

Bonhoeffer speaks of the crucified Christ as the vicarious representative for humanity as the "human being for others."[30] While in no way denying Christ's deity, "Bonhoeffer calls Jesus Christ the best example of what it means to be human."[31] His theology of the non-religious church is characterized by this statement: "To speak non-religiously of the church is to view it as a community of recovering sinners."[32] A restored church must proclaim a recovered gospel. A restored church must participate in the body and blood of Christ by taking his place in the world as a vicarious representative for others. Such restoration echoes a Hebraic view of hearing; that is, the church must take leaps of action in concrete deeds of love.

Bonhoeffer speaks of three types of service which flow from the punctured and lacerated flesh of Christ: listening, deeds of love, and bearing one another's burdens. Jesus *listened, acted in love* and *bore the sins of the world* on the cross. He heard accusations and rants and asked his

27. Bonhoeffer, *Life Together*, 34.
28. Ibid., 38.
29. 1 Corinthians 10: 16, NIV, substituting *participation* for *koinonia*.
30. Bischoff, *The Human Church*, 93.
31. Ibid.
32. Ibid., 110.

abandoning father to forgive them. He laid down his life for the world he loved. He bore every past, present, and future sin of every human being who ever lived, was living then, and who would ever live. Once the church realizes what Christ did for it, it too must serve others by similarly listening, loving, and bearing as empowered by the Holy Spirit.

In sum, hopefully and prayerfully, a church separated from its Hebraic roots may yet admit, confess, and repent of its sins against God's first people. Such a church will offer an antidote to the theological and anthropological sins of historic Christianity. We've attempted to demonstrate how a parting of the ways may become a joining of the ways in a restored church, a Jewish-Gentile community, as one new humanity.

Having discussed how the gospel may be recovered and the church restored, we now discuss ways to reclaim the Kingdom of God.

Reclaiming the Kingdom of God

A recovered gospel and a restored church prepare the way to reclaim the kingdom of God. To demonstrate that Jesus preached himself as the saving story, the completion of Israel's story, Scot McKnight explores "Jesus' favorite term: kingdom."[33]

He begins his analysis with a Hebraic view of the kingdom of God from Psalm 72 which " . . . brings into words the hopes of Israel for a king and his kingdom."[34] McKnight stays with his overarching theme: *The Story of Israel is completed in the Story of Jesus and the Story of Jesus is anticipated in the Story of Israel.*

Parenthetically, we must keep in mind that while this statement regarding Judaism's fulfillment in Jesus is Christian, it is not Jewish. Judaism doesn't claim that it requires any completion in Jesus as a person or in Christianity as a religion.] Theological disagreement can never be a reason not to love another. A healthy between persons requires respect for the other's boundaries.

The occasion for this Davidic psalm, the coronation of his son King Solomon, includes such kingdom language as "Endow the *king* with your justice . . . May he *rule* from sea to sea . . . May all *kings* bow down to him . . . "[35] [my italics]. David validates his son's kingdom

---

33. McKnight, *The King Jesus Gospel*, 109.
34. Ibid., 110.
35. Ibid., 111.

echoing words from the Abrahamic Covenant—"Then all nations will be blessed through him, and they will call him blessed."[36] In the Torah, *him* referred to Abraham; in this psalm, it refers to Solomon. Here we find Scriptural continuity for the kingdom of God begun with God's promise to Abraham and continued in the Davidic Covenant. God's promise about Solomon's kingdom emerges from the Davidic Covenant and anticipates the eternal kingdom of Christ.

McKnight gets into themes which cohere with Jesus' concept of the kingdom of God—*present, a new society, a radically new citizenship, about God, and Jesus is its center.*[37] [my italics]. Recall that Jesus' first words recorded in Mark 1 were, "Repent, the kingdom is near. believe the good news."

McKnight asserts that the kingdom of God was *present*; it " . . . was breaking into history."[38] While acknowledging the eschatological aspects of a future messianic age, he quotes Jesus' initial words—" . . . the kingdom of God *has come near* . . . "[39] [author's italics]. Jesus' arrival inserts into present time the one Hebraic sovereign God who rules the universe. He complements *has come near* with " . . . the kingdom of God *has come upon you* . . . "[40] [author's italics]. A kingdom which has *come near* and *upon us* speaks of its timing. But what does this kingdom look like? How might we recognize the kingdom?

McKnight's goes on to discuss the kingdom as a *new society with a new definition of its citizenship.* The kingdom of God is a radically new Spirit-filled society whose citizens are not self-righteous, but forgiven sinners. Supported by the Sermon on the Mount, Jesus redefines membership in this new society . . . spiritually speaking . . . the poor, hungry, mourning and insulted. Jesus begins his ministry with the manifesto which derives from Isaiah 61[41] about the physically poor, ill, and oppressed. Jesus' gospel and his kingdom are Hebraic. It is a holistic community derived from the Shema . . . .loving God and loving the neighbor with all one's heart, soul, spirit and resources.

---

36. Ibid.
37. Ibid., 112—114.
38. Ibid.
39. Ibid., Mark 1: 15.
40. Ibid., Matthew 12:28.
41. This text anticipates Jesus' reading in his synagogue which we earlier labeled his Manifesto at the outset of his Ministry quoted verbatim in Luke 4.

Jesus makes it clear to John the Baptizer's disciples that *he is the center of this new community* comprised of the blind who now see, the lame who now walk, the deaf who now hear, and the dead brought back to life. Jesus shows us what the kingdom looks like when the Spirit of God breaks into history. Jesus is the One who ushers in the Holy Spirit. Just as Jesus is the gospel, he is also the kingdom of God without whom there can be no kingdom.

> He is the image of the invisible God,
> the firstborn of all creation; for in him
> all the things in heaven and on earth
> were created, whether thrones or dominions
> or rulers or powers—all things have been
> created through him and for him. He himself
> is before all things, and in him all things
> hold together. He is the head of the body,
> the church; he is the beginning, the firstborn
> from the dead, so that he might come to have
> first place in everything. For in him all the
> fullness of God was please to dwell, and through
> him God was pleased to reconcile to himself all
> things, whether on earth or in heaven, by making
> peace through the blood of his cross.[42]

To summarize McKnight's themes of the kingdom: Jesus is central to a radically new society as one new humanity where God presently rules over his kingdom.

In this chapter we've called for a whole-sale rediscovery of Christianity. To that end, we've addressed the need to *recover the gospel*, to *restore the church*, and to *reclaim the kingdom of God*, one result of which is an intentional love for the first people of God, the Jewish people, to which we now turn our attention.

---

42. Colossians 1: 15—20.

─── *Chapter 13* ───

Loving Jewish People

IN THE LAST CHAPTER we proposed a rediscovery of Christianity by recovering the gospel, restoring the church, and reclaiming the Kingdom of God.

In this chapter we will discuss loving the Jewish people from both a *theological* and *spiritual* perspective. We'll interact with Scripture and conversation partners from both the Jewish and Christian communities who promote love for the Jewish people.

Loving Jewish People Theologically

"You can't love God without loving the Jewish people."
[Corrie ten Boom].[1]

Jesus endorsed the Shema and the two greatest commandments recorded in the Tanakh and the Younger Testament. "Love the LORD your God with all your heart, and with all your soul, and with all your might". .[and] . . . "you shall love your neighbor as yourself."[2] For over two thousand years, Jews and Christians have been neighbors. Sadly, theological differences have been allowed to damage personal relationship between

---

1. ten Boom, A Dutch Christian saved Jews as part of the Dutch resistance. She survived Ravensbrueck and told her story in *The Hiding Place*. In 1967 she was honored as a Righteous Among the Nations by Yad Vashem.
2. Deuteronomy 6: 4—5 and Leviticus 19: 18b; Mark 12: 29—31.

these two neighbors. To disagree theologically doesn't mean you can't be friends. Iron sharpens iron.

Christians believe that Jesus is the Messiah. Jews do not. Christians believe that God can become visible as a human being. Jews believe God is invisible and should never be represented by any visible image. Christians believe in the mystery of one God in relationship as Father, Son, and Holy Spirit—the Trinity. Jews believe that God is One.

Is it necessary to demean another who may hold differing beliefs? Scripture doesn't justify hate because of differing beliefs. Even if Christians saw the Jews as an enemy, Jesus commanded love for one's enemies in his Sermon on the Mount. The relational wounds between Christians and Jews can be healed when the church applies what it believes about Jesus' sacrificial love for all humanity.

Christians believe that the prophet Isaiah was talking about Jesus's atoning death when he said:

> Surely he has borne our infirmities and carried our diseases; yet we accounted him stricken, struck down by God . . . afflicted. But he was wounded for our transgressions, crushed for our iniquities; upon him was the punishment that made us whole and by his bruises we are healed.[3]

A Christian cannot claim the healing of Jesus' suffering and death on the cross and simultaneously feel justified in not loving Jewish people whose Torah tells the church that all people are created in God's image—the theological basis for the value and dignity of all persons. There is no person who has ever existed, lives today, or who will exist in the future who has not been created in the image of God. Christianity learned this from the Torah.

There is no human being who ever lived, who lives now, or who will ever live for whom Jesus did not die. Salvation for all human beings is available because Jesus "was wounded for our transgressions . . . that made us whole." When the church gives up denying its own sin against the Jewish people, it will be restored because it has recovered the gospel of God proclaimed by the prophet Isaiah and echoed by the Apostle Paul when he talked about the fellowship of Christ's sufferings[4] as a participation in the body and blood of Jesus.[5] Theological disagreements

---

3. Isaiah 53: 5, 6.
4. Philippians 3: 10.
5. 1 Corinthians 10: 16.

between Christians and Jews do not make hatred between Christians Jews necessary. All have sinned and come short of God's glory. The death of Jesus Christ for the sins and sinners of the world added to the fact that all people are created in God's image is the robust theological basis for the worth and salvation of all humanity. Jews believe only in the Torah. Christianty's addition of the Younger Testament includes the person and work of Jesus on the cross for salvation.

Marvin R. Wilson says that theological differences "have left Christians believing that Jews have everything to learn from them and that they have little or nothing to learn from Jews . . . [that] . . . they had no ongoing need of Jews and Judaism."[6] Throughout this book we've repeatedly stated how much the church owes the Jewish community for its very existence. A restored church will continually rehearse its roots in the covenants fulfilled by a Jewish Jesus.

Raul Hilberg, one of the earliest scholars to analyze both the theological and anthropological implications of the Shoah, grasped how theological disputes were used to justify disallowing Jews *to live as Jews* among Gentiles, then disallowing Jews *to live among Gentiles*, and finally disallowing Jews *to live at all*.[7] The church needs to pick up on his analysis to undo the past marginalization of the Jewish people and express three ways Christians can love Jews.

First, Hilberg's first clause pertains to Jewish worship and culture. Christians can promote the freedom of Jewish worship and lifestyle as a liberty granted by the US Constitution's First Amendment Free Exercise clause—the same freedom granted to any American. Every Shabbat service concludes with a prayer for the United States of America. America was the first nation in history to fully allow Jews into its country granting them the same freedom of worship and lifestyle extended to any American. Both traditions subscribe to loving the other—whoever she may. If we even have to getting into loving one's enemies, Christians need to be reminded of Jesus' radical mandate which lets no one off the hook—friend or foe. After all, how long can an enemy remain such if we love them? Loving Jewish people is actualized in completely granting them freedom to be who they are and worship as they please.

Second, Hilberg's next clause addresses how non-Jews disallowed Jews the freedom to choose where they lived in a village or city. Of

---

6. Wilson, *Our Father Abraham*, 367.
7. Hilberg, *The Destruction of the European Jews*, 9.

course, this discussion cuts both ways. Did Jews *want* to live separately, or did the church along with other non-Jews *restrict* where Jewish people could live? That debate has no solution here. However, we do know that inhumane ghettoes evolved over time as staging grounds for shipping Jews to their deaths.

A restored church will become an advocate for fair housing for all marginalized people. A pro-Jewish realtor will show Jewish clients houses in any community and in any section of a community the same way he would for any buyer. History will show that wherever possible it was always the intent of Jewish people to assimilate into its resident culture. Jews fought for Germany in WWI and upon arrival in the United States took up active roles in medicine, law, business, and the arts just as they did in Europe. The church must advocate for the freedom of Jewish people to assimilate into society like anyone else which includes living anywhere they choose. If Jews choose to live in certain communities, that's their choice, not one that someone else made for them.

Third, Hilberg's final clause addresses the horror of the Final Solution, the deceitful result of disallowing Jewish worship, culture, and living space. The so-called Final Solution meant the systematic extermination of Jewish people only because they were Jewish. Throughout history the church has not only been a cause for anti-Semitism in a culture, but also a mere bystander when the wheels of injustice rolled out the genocide of millions of human beings only because of their ethnicity. Raul Hilberg exposed the underlying issues for the wholesale destruction of European Jews. Others pointed the way forward for why and how mutual love between Christians and Jews might take root in any society.

In sum, Raul Hilberg, one of the first voices to raise human conscience and awareness to the plight of Jewish persons, has set the stage for how all people, especially Christians, can dismantle the racism behind disallowing Jews to worship, reside, and freely live like any other human being created in God's image and for whom Jesus Christ died and rose from the dead.

Franz Rosenzweig (1886—1929)

"Franz Rosenzweig ranks as one of the most original Jewish thinkers of the modern period."[8] His unique life qualifies him as an excellent resource

---

8. "Franz Rosenzweig," *Stanford Encyclopedia of Philosophy.*

regarding how mutual love between Jews and Christians is possible. Born a Jew, he prepared to be baptized as a Christian and changed his mind after attending a Yom Kippur service during which he had a crucial spiritual experience—an encounter with God. No one else in history tasted by Christianity and Judaismm as he did. After analyzing both religious traditions, he returned to his Jewish roots. He died early at age 41 after living most of his life struggling against progressive paralysis. He wrote his tome, *The Star of Redemption*, on the back of postcards while a soldier in the Germany army during WWI—another ironical example of Jewish assimilation into a culture. Sadly, a culture which turned against him.

For Rosenzweig "the significant characteristic of a person is . . . [that] . . . The individual who must die must lay hold upon the eternal encounter with God, and not by analyzing the structures of existence."[9] He was far more concerned about the relational and spiritual aspects of life consistent with a reaffirmation of his Jewish faith which put him squarely in between his upbringing in Orthodox Judaism and the ethical idealism of liberal Judaism. Commenting on *The Star of Redemption*, Cass Fisher states, "The distant God is no less significant than the near one."[10] Fisher points out how it is only through God's distance that truly intellectual orientation toward God is no less spiritual than is an experiential nearness to God. Of course, Rosenzweig, as a Hebraic thinker, is not disturbed by the apparent contradiction; it is a *both-and* idea held in tension. This both-and resonates with Jesus' statements about the Kingdom of God which is also near, within you, and far into the future. When Christians and Jews gather together to discuss Rosenzweig, they'll discover how much they have in common regarding God's kingdom. Christians would especially be enriched theologically when studying Franz Rosenzweig.

He explains how Judaism and Christianity relate to one another. He pictures a Judaism which doesn't only proceed from the Law and a Christianity which does not only proceed from faith. He echoes David Stern's belief that non-Jewish Christ followers need to understand the uniqueness of God's relationship with the Jews. Both agree that Jewish people need no way back to God in at least the same way Gentiles do. The most prolific author of the New Testament, the Apostle Paul, was a Pharisee from the tribe of Benjamin who proclaimed one Messiah for Jews and non-Jews in Jesus Christ. Niebuhr stated that Rosenzweig's understanding

9. Ibid.

10. Fisher, "The 'And' in Franz Rosenzweig's Work," *Rosenzweig Yearbook 11*, von Herausgegeben.

about Judaism and Christianity was "more than the distinction between a religion of law and a religion of spirit. The commonality is obvious. Both religions worship the One God who is engaged in history. In a sense, both Judaism and Christianity are religions characterized by law and spirit expressed in obeying commands and faithful trust in God.

"*The Star of Redemption* is hailed as one of the most important books of the twentieth century."[11] Certainly Rosenzweig's book demands its own thorough investigation outside the parameters of this book. Here we simply echo his final words which link Judaism and Christianity reminiscent of the Moses' farewell to Israel urging them to choose life, the prophet Micah's familiar command to humbly walk with justice and mercy, and Jesus' manifesto of ministry:[12]

> Walk humbly with your God—the words are above the gate, the gate that leads out from the mysterious, wonderful illumination of the divine sanctuary where no man can remain alive. But whither do the wings of the gate open? You do not know? INTO LIFE.

Leo Baeck (1873—1956)

Another significant voice for the Jewish community is consecration camp - survivor, Rabbi Leo Baeck who conducted Shabbat services in Theresienstadt and escaped death because of a clerical error in the spelling of his name. He wrote three books: *The Essence of Judaism, This People Israel: The Meaning of Jewish Existence,* and *Judaism and Christianity.*

"Baeck's masterpiece, *The Essence of Judaism* (1905), established him as the leading liberal Jewish theologian."[13] Baeck's thoughts are especially useful in the Jewish-Christian dialogue in that he holds both mystery and commandment in tension, a sure example of elliptical Hebraic thought. That is, he's just as comfortable embracing the divine presence as he is urging an ethical imperative—both of which are a result of an encounter

---

11. Galli and Eliot R Wolfson, Series Editors, *Modern Jewish Philosophy and Religion,* from the back cover of *The Star of Redemption,* Franz Rosenzweig, 2005.

12. Micah 6: 8, "He has told you, O man, what is good! What does HASHEM require of you but to do justice, to love kindness, and to walk humbly with your God." Tanakh. Rosenzweig translates, "to love kindness" as "to be good with all your heart," 447. Recall our earlier discussion of Luke 4 and Isaiah 61 where Jesus launches his ministry prompted by the Spirit to reach out to the poor and the marginalized

13. Friedlander "Leo Baeck, German theologian," *Encyclopedia Britannica.*

with God which constructs a bridge between Judaism and Christianity. Overall, his insights offer a centripetal force bringing Jews and Christians closer to one another given their love for God as Creator.

Baeck's major contribution to the interfaith discussion is his refutation of Adolph Harnack's thought in his *The Essence of Christianity*. "Harnack denigrated the Pharisees and the Judaism they represented and committed lapses of scholarship singled out by the young Baeck."[14] Liberal German Protestantism during Harnack's time had no category for a Jewish Jesus and, fueled by 19th century German anti-Semitism, spoke of Christianity as unrelated to the Jewish religious and cultural tradition. Ironically, Baeck had a more biblical and Christian view of Jesus than Harnack, for the rabbi understood the Jewishness of Jesus and his resonance with the Pharisaic movement within Second Temple Judaism. Knowing this about Baeck, Christians must credit him for a more accurate view of Jesus than 19th century liberal Protestantism. Leo Baeck exposed the anti-Semitism of German Protestant Liberalism providing an alternative path toward mutual love between Jews and Christians.

Baeck's polemic essay, "Romantic Religion," captures the essence of his challenge to Christianity. "If we classify . . . piety . . . then we encounter two forms . . . classical and romantic . . . Judaism and Christianity . . . ."[15] He identifies romantic religion with feeling and sentimentality . . . "it is the world of the irregular, the extraordinary, and the miraculous . . . beyond all reality, the remote which transcends all things."[16] That is, Baeck denies the reality of every extraordinary [supernatural] encounter of Abraham, Isaac, Jacob and Moses with the divine. He characterizes Christianity as a moody religion devoid of any strong ethical impulse . . . "it would rather be outside the sphere of good and evil . . . ."[17] Here Christians receive an important insight from the other, even when it is closed-minded about the reality of the supernatural. It is hardly an endorsement of the Christian faith. Yet, Baeck benefits the Christian by proposing an objective voice, however misguided it may be. However, Christians must be open to the fact of an internal pious "moodiness." At very least Christians must take Baeck's challenge seriously as a trajectory for fruitful interfaith discussion which offers fear-dismantling knowledge creating space for love. Clearly, Baeck's views about the supernatural are anti-Christian while at the same

14. Ibid.
15. Baeck, *Judaism and Christianity*, 189.
16. Ibid., 190.
17. Ibid., 192.

time Christians have much to learn from his rabbinic teaching on internal sentimentality as a substitute for taking leaps of advocacy for others.

In *This People Israel: The Meaning of Jewish Existence* [published in Germany 1955 and in America 1964], Leo Baeck mollifies his critique of Christianity and references the Apostle Paul's teaching on hope. He identifies hope as one difference between man and animals. Baeck states, "Particularly in a religious world, since nearness and distance seek to unite, hope springs up everywhere,"[18] He credits the Apostle Paul for deriving his concept of hope from the Jewish people. "Paul, the great apostle who derived from this people, was right: where men *believe and love*, they hope."[19] [my italics]. Note how loving Jewish people theological and spiritually evolve from hope prompted by *belief and love*. Humanity's hope is rooted in Christianity's affirmation of Hebraic thought originating from the church's foremost missionary, the Apostle Paul, who did so as a Pharisaic member of Benjamin's tribe.

Baeck sees in the Jewish people a mission of witness. Based upon the fact that more history has been given to Israel than any other present nation. "This people understood that history and universe testify to oneness, and reveal totality and order."[20] Christianity simply picked up on the oneness of God and with Judaism sustained monotheism as its mission to the world beyond Judaism—a witness centered in the Incarnation as Immanuel, God with us. Despite the theological boundaries extant between the Jewish faith and Christianity, both traditions are inhabited by people in mission. Jews call it *tikkun olam*; Christians call it evangelism.

In sum, Leo Baeck helps Christians to love the Jewish people despite the doctrinal differences between the two traditions. Knowledge dismantles fear leading to love.

We now focus on a more familiar name both within and outside the Jewish community—Martin Buber.

Martin Buber (1878—1965)

In his prologue to *I and Thou*. Walter Kaufmann says this about Martin Buber: "He was not a man of formulas but one who tried to meet every

---

18. Baeck, *This People Israel: The Meaning of Jewish Existence*, 292.
19. Ibid., 402.
20. Ibid.

person, each situation, and each subject in its own way."[21] Buber's emphasis on the individual puts him squarely in the existentialist camp along with Rosenzweig, yet without submitting to a romanticism which flees reality and faces everything except the facts.

Anyone willing to make Martin Buber a conversation partner must grasp his programmatic thesis: "The world as experience belongs to the I-It. The basic word I-You establishes the world of relation."[22] His famous word pairs express the difference between a world of experience I-It and a world of relation I-You.

Martin Buber first mentions *God* in the context of the difference between the intimate German *Du* and the "God of the pulpits" *Thou*. He points out that the "God of the holy tone" is "not the God to whom one might cry out in gratitude, despair or agony, not the God to whom one complains or prays spontaneously . . . "[23] The I-You relation would apply to any person's relationship with God; that is, one not confined to experience as an I-It, where the It cannot experience the I. Buber would say that persons and God mutually experience one another as the I-You. It may very well be Buber's insight into the difference between personal relationship with God and "all pretensions to knowledge about God"[24] that appealed to Protestant theologians, who incorporated his paradigm into their own attempts to "rescue the religious dimension of life from the theologians."[25] That is, saving heart-felt relationship from neck-up head knowledge. Note how Buber's theological insights bind Jews and Christians together; for both own the concept of an I-You relationship with the Creator and Sustainer of life.

Buber, an existential theologian, spoke of God as " . . . him that . . . enters into a direct relationship to us human beings through creative, revelatory, and redemptive acts, and thus makes it possible for us to enter into a direct relationship with him." In the context of this profound observation, he talks about how "God is *also* a person . . . his person likeness from which Buber claims he can derive his own and all men's being persons . . . "[26] [author's italics]. Buber is one of the few theologians on either side of the liberal-conservative aisle who employs the *du*-form,

21. Buber, *I and Thou*, Walter Kaufmann, "Prologue," 16.
22. Ibid., 56.
23. Ibid., 14.
24. Ibid., 21.
25. Ibid.
26. Ibid., 181.

the I-You, when speaking of his relationship to Jesus. "From my youth onwards I have found in Jesus my great brother... I am more certain that a great place belongs to him in Israel's history of faith and that this place cannot be described by the usual categories."[27] Another Martin [Luther] wholeheartedly affirmed Jesus as his great brother. Jesus as one's brother is a profound insight rooted in Buber's Judaism and, thankfully, affirmed by Christianity's most famous theologian. The brotherhood Jesus for both Jews and Christians constitutes an excellent trajectory from which wholesome interfaith dialogue can begin.

Finally, Martin Buber concludes that "conversation with God... occurs... above the everyday... event upon event... The existence of mutuality between God and man cannot be proved any more than the existence of God. Anyone who dares nevertheless to speak of it bears witness and invokes the witness of those whom he addresses—present or future witness."[28] Certainly, Martin Buber provides a sturdy bridge over which Jews and Christians can cross finding genuine friendship and love for one another rooted in his theological insights regarding one's personal relationship with God.

We conclude this segment of loving Jewish people theologically by getting into Michael Wyschogrod's contribution to Jewish-Christian friendship.

Michael Wyschogrod (1928—2015)

"Michael Wyschogrod... [is]... perhaps the most original Jewish theologian of the past century."[29] He believes that anyone can love the Jewish people because God loves the Jewish people. He urges Christians to think that God had it right when he chose to love the Jews; and since God still does, so should we. "The biblical insistence that God's indwelling in the living Jewish people... requires us to believe that God is present in the physical people of Israel."[30] Of course, Wyschogrod is right because the Holy Spirit mysteriously indwelt a Jewish teenage woman resulting in the more mysteriously divine-human being in bodily form,[31]

27. Buber, *Two Types of Faith*, 81.
28. Ibid., 182.
29. Soloveichek, "God's First Love : The Theology of Michael Wyschogrod," *First Things* (2019).
30. Ibid.
31. Bischoff, *Mary Gave God a Body*, ix—xii.

the Jesus of faith, the historic Christ and the Messiah. There's a radical parallel here—the indwelling of God in the Jewish people anticipates the Christian doctrine of the Incarnation, the Word who became flesh. God became flesh in the womb of a Jewish young woman according to Christian belief. God as Immanuel, God with us, in the nation of Israel is a forerunner to the indwelling of the Holy Spirit in the life of a Christian. The incarnation of God in the Jewish people, the Christian doctrine of the Incarnation and the possible presence of the Holy Spirit in every human being is a study which merits its own discussion beyond the boundaries of this book. Such study constitutes another starting point for good discussion between Christians and Jews.

"Wyschogrod argues that Judaism's concerns . . . [include] . . . God's unique and preferential love for the flesh-and-blood descendants of Abraham . . . [and the] . . . election of the Jewish people . . . [which is] . . . the result of God's falling in love with Abraham and founding a family with him."[32] We concur with Wyschogrod's focus on the covenants which not only links the church with God's love for Abraham and all humanity, but also mandates love for those selected by God in particular through whom all humanity will be blessed. The aforementioned Genesis 12: 1—3 text is at the root of Wyschogrod's theology of the Jewish people and Judaism's huge contribution to the Christian faith.

At the risk of over-simplifying Wyschogrod's theology, his thoughts parallel the romantic falling in love of one person with another. God's special relationship with Israel can be explained in part by marriage. The ultimate vow in the form of a question in a wedding ceremony is: Will you be faithful as long as you both shall live? God loves Israel and has been faithful to her from the Abrahamic Covenant to the present day.

Jewish particularly implies love and blessing *for all humanity*. "God's love is directed toward who we are . . . there are those whom God loves especially, with whom he has fallen in love."[33] Can Christians love the people that God loves? Might that alone be a reason for doing so, despite "the crucial disagreement between Christians and Jews . . . over the Christian claim that Jesus is God?"[34] There is no implication that Christians need to abandon the basic tenets of their faith, any more than Jews need to compromise their differing beliefs about Jesus of Nazareth in order to love one another.

32. Soloveichik, "God's First Love: The Theology of Michael Wyschogrod."
33. Ibid.
34. Neuhaus, *Death on a Friday Afternoon*, 139.

We've entitled this segment *Loving Jewish People: Theologically* by citing major scholars revered within the Jewish community and respected in the wider theological community. Our goal has been to provide reasons to learn more about the roots of Christianity from Jewish scholars. Why study Judaism and its scholars? Because doing so dispels ignorance, discredits myth, and dismantles fear. But theological reasons don't have the final words in the interfaith dialogue which must lead to *loving Jewish people: spiritually*—the segment to which we now turn our attention.

What might it mean to love someone *spiritually*? When we say *spiritually*, we're speaking about practical ways to love Jewish people. Recall Leo Baeck's concern about internal piety replacing concrete acts and deeds of love. We might *know* all the theological reasons to love, yet fail to *show* love in our human relationships.

Loving Jewish People Spiritually

Rabbi David Hoffman asks, "What does it mean to relate to the Jewish people with love?"[35] While written to a Jewish audience, his thoughts apply as well to how Christians might love Jewish people spiritually. He differentiates between love and belonging. He observes that genuine love is an idea and value that has come upon some hard times recently—both from the right and on the left . . . on the right . . . critique is heard as betrayal of the people . . . On the left . . . its rejection of any privileging of Jewish experiences . . . has undermined the possibility of a full and loving embrace of the Jewish people."[36]

The Christian community stands to learn about love for itself and for our Jewish friends by adhering to Hoffman's rejection of a universalism which negates Jewish particularity and thus "reduces being Jewish to a mere marker of identity."[37] That is, he sees that belonging becomes thin without the accompanying responsibilities to others. Hoffman is concerned about losing love—a power which can "inspire and move us to try to become our best selves."[38] Even if Jews themselves dismiss their

---

35. Rabbi Hoffman, "To love or not to love the Jewish people?" *Times of Israel* (2021).
36. Ibid.
37. Ibid.
38. Ibid.

particularity, Hoffman reminds that in so doing, the dignity of being chosen by God is lost.

Returning to his earlier thought that critique is not betrayal, he personalizes his discussion of spiritually loving his people by stating that passionate love may involve holding them to a higher standard; that is, the Torah's high ethical demands. Writing to his own community, Hoffman states, "Our Jewish brothers and sisters need our total existential investment . . . need us to place its joys, needs and challenges at the center of our lives. It needs us to be one."[39]

Reread that last paragraph through a Christian lens. What would the Christian community eliminate from Rabbi Hoffman's analysis of *love*? Nothing. As we continue below to discuss loving Jewish people in an existential way, let's do so with high hope that both the Jewish and Christian communities need to be spiritually one despite our theological distinctives.

How will anyone ever know whether the church loves Jewish people *spiritually*? When it replaces anti-Jewishness with pro-Jewishness. That is, when it becomes an advocate and voice on behalf of and for the State of Israel and the Jewish people. During WWII Lutheran theologian-pastor Dietrich Bonhoeffer based his spiritual love for the Jewish people upon what he theologically called "vicarious representation." That is, Christ became the priest for all humanity during his life, death, and resurrection. A priestly representative becomes an advocate. A vicar advocates for the other. Bonhoeffer embodied this theology on behalf of Jews in Nazi Germany.

In plain language, "Christ voluntarily and vulnerably [stood] in our place before God . . . "[40] Bonhoeffer's concept originated from a Hebraic definition of love [*Ahavah*] derived from *giving*, the root of love. Bonhoeffer wasn't satisfied with a reduction of loving the other emotionally. His demonstration of loving Jewish people was behavioral, not based upon feelings. He saved several Jews and paid for it by being hung by piano wire in a Nazi death camp.

Father Kolbe became a vicarious representative when he died in the place of another inmate he never knew at Auschwitz.

Bonhoeffer and Kolbe would have certainly agreed with Mendal Kalmenson and Zahlman Abraham who state, "love is not all about you

---

39. Ibid.
40. Schilstra, "Dietrich Bonhoeffer: Stepping into the Place of the Other."

..., but about the other ... [it] ... calls us out of the confines of ourselves and into the wilderness of relationship ... [and] ... dethrones the ego ... "[41] The authors point out that love in marriage is based upon a legal document [*ketubah*] which defines marriage as the sacred relationship between one man and one woman spelling out "the material marital obligations between and husband and a wife ... written in Aramaic, which is the legal language of the Talmud ... "[42]

In his compelling article on Bonhoeffer's concept of vicarious suffering for the other, Will Fredstrom jettison's all abstractions of feelings. He favors loving Jewish people as an example of "God's freedom *for* humanity ... from the outside through the incarnation of the Son of God in the visible historical person, Jesus."[43] [author's italics]. Fredstrom points out the responsibility laid upon the church to vocally and behaviorally stand up for the persecuted Jews in Nazi Germany. " ... Christ is the vicarious representative for humanity, who on the cross creates the new humanity ... the church ... freed to be the vicarious representative for neighbors."[44]

Vera Kessler is a wife and mother of three children whose goal in life is to inspire Jewish woman to live their lives with meaning and a strong relationship to God. She interprets the Torah's command to love others as we *love ourselves* "Only when we believe in our own self -worth ... that we have something to contribute ... In order to want good for our fellow Jews, and value them as human beings ... "[45] As a mother, Kessler is qualified to discuss love not only within the Jewish community, but also for how Christians can love one another within the church. When either the Christian or Jew fully grasps what it means to be created in God's image with dignity which makes pride unnecessary, each is liberated totake risks of love for the other and for all others.

When does the church love Jewish people as they worship? When it attends a Shabbat service to discover the beauty of its choral singing, readings, prayers and sermons. When does a church repent of its silence when Jews are herded into some suburbs, but not others? When realtors willingly show Jews homes in *any* American neighborhood; when Jews

41. Kalmenson and Zahlman Abraham, "Love: Ahavah: I Give, Therefore I love."
42. Ibid.
43. Fredstrom, "Bonhoeffer's *Stellvertretung*: A Christ-Like Ecclesial Ethic for Serving 'Galilean' Neighbors."
44. Ibid.
45. Kessler, "Michal Horowitz: Loving Your Fellow Jews."

and non-Jews love one another as neighbors whether in urban, suburban or rural locations. When does the church atone for its voicelessness as both a perpetrator and bystander during the genocide of the Jews? When it joins public demonstrations in support of the State of Israel to exist and proclaims from its pulpits the right of Jewish people to live like any other ordinary human being. When the church speaks out about terrorism perpetuated toward Jews as today's Shoah. We have yet to see such a common voice by the church in America.

As I write this chapter, anti-Semitism is rampant on America's university campuses where Jewish students are experiencing hatred reminiscent of how Jews were treated in Germany and America during WWII. Some demons never die.

We wholeheartedly affirm the particularity of the Jewish people given God's sovereignty in the covenant He made with Abraham, Isaac and Jacob. Choosing to obscure the particularity of the Jews is tantamount to denying the Shoah. For the Jews were sent to gas chambers because of their particularity—*only for being Jews . . . the first people to represent God on earth.*

Shoah-survivor Elie Wiesel said, "The bystander: His presence is evasive, and commits him less than his absence might. He says nothing. He is there, but he acts as if he were not. Worse: he acts as if the rest of us were not."[46] Wiesel's profound insight is so basic that it's often overlooked. To love Jewish people spiritually is to acknowledge their real presence on earth as a people group in the same way *any* people group would be acknowledged. Jewish identity is all about God's selection of a people whom He decided to bless and through whom all families on earth are blessed.

Wouldn't you rather run the risk of standing up for Jewish people in our current anti-Semitic society since God's covenant with Abraham grants you life's blessing for doing so? Better yet, because it's the right thing to do for your neighbor?

Emil Fackenheim, Jewish scholar and professor, acknowledged a theology of the cross—the scandal of Jesus' martyrdom for humanity's salvation. It derives from Dietrich Bonhoeffer's compelling phrase: "participating in the sufferings of Christ for the world" included in letters he wrote from prison in the last year of his life. Fackenheim is right to suggest that Jesus would not have merely stood by when the trains took

---

46. Wiesel, "The Town Beyond the Wall," *Struggle for Understanding in Elie Wiesel's Literary Works*, 2019.

Jews to the created "town" of Treblinka, whose "population" decreased by the hour, but would have boarded the train with the Jews.

Loving Jewish people spiritually means acknowledging their insight into Christianity, specifically their discernment into how to apply non-Jewish theology to the Jewish experience of suffering and death. Emil Fackenheim references Bonhoeffer as one who would have asked this piercing question: "In 1945, why did Christian theology carry on 'almost seamlessly' where it had left off in 1933?"[47] He goes on to say that the Shoah was never considered a *Christian* catastrophe until over forty years later. Often it is the victim who liberates the oppressor. As a survivor of Sachsenhausen, Fackenheim has offered Christians the freedom to find redemption but only if they can agree with Bonhoeffer's statement: "The expulsion of the Jews from the West must entail the expulsion of Christ, for Christ was a Jew,"[48] followed by Bethge's application, " . . . if the expulsion of the Jews is the expulsion of Christ from the West, what is the meaning of their *annihilation*?"[49]

To love Jews is to love the State of Israel. Politics and policies cannot inhibit love for the right of any people to have its own nation. The church must speak out against any other nation, country or state who defines its own existence by obliterating the Jewish people from their homeland. Love for a state's political decisions and loving its people may at times need to be held in tension as apparent contradictions. But we've seen how Hebraic thought allows for such ironies. I can love the Jewish people despite what I may deem as wrong national policies. As an American, I need not stop loving my country because members of the "wrong" political party are in power with whose talking points I disagree.

In this chapter we've endeavored to offer both a theological and spiritual basis for *loving Jewish people*. Theologically, we've analyzed Scripture and referred to several Jewish and Christian scholars to support why love for the Jewish people is the best way to undo the past ill-treatment of Israel by the church. Spiritually, we've referenced both Jewish and Christian scholars who teach and model how initiate dialogue leading to concrete acts of love for one another.

In the Conclusion, we'll summarize the book as well as propose a parable whose nimshal is Christian-Jewish friendship and love.

---

47. Fackenheim, *To Mend the World*, xliv.
48. Ibid.
49. Ibid., *xlvii*.

Conclusion

IN *LOVING JEWISH PEOPLE*, we've proposed a four-part historical, theological, spiritual, and ethical foundation upon which Christians can befriend and love Jewish people.

Part One, "The Hebraic Kingdom of God," emphasized the importance of knowing how Jewish people think—to not only know about Judaism, but also to show how such knowledge evolved over centuries. Using its story, we discussed how Israel developed its world view. We defined the parable as a literary device employed in the Tanakh and the Oral Tradition to communicate and exemplify a Hebraic view of God's kingdom.

In Part Two, "The Christian Kingdom of God," we followed the same format as Part One for an analysis of Christianity's view of the kingdom of God. Centered on story of Jesus as Messiah, we spoke of how Christians came to know what they believe. Just as Israel as a nation is the focus of Hebraic Thought, the Jesus of faith as the Christ of history is the center of Christianity.

The Story of Israel anticipates the Story of Jesus and the Story of Jesus brings to completion the Story of Israel. Once again, we reiterate that inasmuch as this statement represents Christian thought, it is not the view of the Jewish community who would say that Judaism requires not fulfillment from Christianity, or any other religion.

We focused on how Jesus used parables, simile, and metaphor typically begun with the phrase, *the Kingdom of God is like . . .*

Part Three, "Distortion," discussed the origin, history and characteristics of both the synagogue and the church. We emphasized how church liturgy originates in the synagogue's readings, sermons and prayers. Further, we investigated how the church parted ways with the synagogue over the centuries resulting in the birth of global anti-Semitism leading to the Shoah.

Part Four, "Restitution," proposed a rediscovery of Christianity focusing upon a recovery of the gospel, a restoration of the church, and a reclamation of the Kingdom of God. Given such a rebound from its sad history, we challenged the church to repent of its anti-Judaism and racial injustice toward Jewish people by intentionally loving the people God, chose as an initial incarnation of himself on earth.

We now conclude the book with a new parable with a recognizable mashal whose nimshal affirms that to love God is to love the Jewish people.

A New Parable

Once there was a young man raised in a very strict religious home. As he grew up, he astounded the local religious leaders with his questions and knowledge. He felt a special spiritual connection with God as his *father* whom he wanted to please. His mother's husband, not his biological father, was a tradesman and was training his son to follow in his steps. The young man was more interested in spiritual and religious matters than in learning a trade. As time went on he sensed a calling to modify his religious upbringing by focusing less on rituals preferring a spirituality displayed by obedience to God's commands. He taught others the importance of having a personal relationship with God. He began reading and rereading the sacred literature of his faith and discovered a linkage with what the sages of old were saying and how he was thinking. He concluded that the current priests and teachers of his religion were missing the point. They maintained a strict outward observance of their religion without heartfelt care and love for others.

As an adult while attending a gathering within which he was raised, he was asked to read from a historical part of the sacred literature. It was a reading from a section of his religion's prophets talking about a Spirit who actually touched an individual energizing him to proclaim good news, heal the sick, visit those in prison, and liberate all who were oppressed. He claimed to be that individual. Everyone enjoyed the reading which they thought only pertained to them. The crowd was astounded and cheered him on; his mother wasn't surprised, for she sensed her son's calling to bring others closer to God.

After the crowd settled down he then proceeded to tell them that these blessings weren't only for them, but also for others outside their religion. Then the crowd's cheers changed to threats on his life. He committed himself totally to what he continued to call to the work of God on earth. He spoke of his mission to do his father's will, with no reference to his mother's husband who was a carpenter. The risks of going out on his own with untested spiritual beliefs was daunting. His claims and activity threatened the local religious leaders. He did, however, manage to gain support from a few followers.

He proceeded to encourage others to join him in his radical ideas. They went from village to village doing remarkable things, like healing those with paralysis and fevers; feeding large numbers of people and even raising the dead. He was honored as a miracle-worker. Word about him spread like wildfire around the land. People from everywhere wanted to meet him and benefit from his spiritual powers.

The local priests and teachers of his tradition challenged his methods of using puzzling stories to reach the uneducated in the faith. They were jealous of the response he was getting compared to the meager response they received. His work often put his parents in the awkward place of continuing in their religion and yet wanting to support their son. The local leaders didn't know what to do with him. They knew they couldn't challenge the evidence of his miraculous healings, nor convince the people that the young man didn't have a mysterious power from God. They also saw that many were beginning to follow him rather than them.

For about three years a rivalry between the inspired young man and religious leaders came to a head when he spoke metaphorically about destroying the sacred building in which they worshiped. As if that wasn't enough, he even claimed that he could rebuild their ancient place of worship in a matter of three days. No one believed that he could reconstruct their house of worship in so little time. They spread native rumors that he was offending God and their religion.

Finally, the local religious leaders conspired with the government of the land to put him to death. The government didn't know what to do with him either. They said it was the people's religious issue, not the government's, that he wasn't breaking any laws of the land, and that his activities pertained only to their religion.

CONCLUSION

During the last week of his life, the young man met secretly with his followers and celebrated one of their most sacred religious rituals. During this event he spoke about his pending death as a new promise. None of his followers knew what he meant; they feared more for their lives than hearing his words. Even their faith and trust in him waned as he become more and more a threat to peace in the state. Public opinion combined with mob rule created a mock trial which eventually led to the government caving in to having the young man publicly executed. He was sentenced to die, not for any crime against the state, but because of political pressure, even the religious leaders of his traditional community. He was buried by a secret follower in a private tomb guarded by state soldiers because he claimed to rise from the dead.

One day local women who followed and supported the young man's ministry went to apply spices to his body only to find that his body was not in the tomb. They experienced a jarring encounter with angels who told them that the young man had come back to life fulfilling his claim about resurrection. They told other followers who at first didn't believe them until they, too, went to see that the tomb was empty. The young man actually appeared to and spoke with hundreds of people. In fact, many of his original followers changed their fears and doubts about him and continued to be his followers, boldly proclaiming his message of God's mercy, grace and for all people.

When he left his followers by miraculously ascending off the ground into space, angels spoke of a mysterious return of the young man to earth sometime in the future. Later, an astoundingly public event occurred on an important traditional religious holiday which resulted in a community of all religions and nationalities celebrating the young man's teaching. A growing community met regularly to worship him as their divine spiritual hero. New spiritual communities of worship, teaching, and prayer following his example emerged throughout the known world.

Over time, troublesome conflicts and confusion occurred between the new communities and the traditional religion. Most of the conflict centered upon the claims the young man made about himself; especially about his relationship to his other father—God. Members of the original traditional religion were split over how to think of the radical new leader. Some followed his radical claims and teachings, others rejected him completely, and yet others continued to be confused as to how much the traditional religion should be practiced within the new faith. No apparent reconciliation seemed possible and grew to the point later in history

CONCLUSION

that hostility between the two religious communities led to demeaning attitudes on the part of the "new religion" against the historic traditional religion. It seemed that to define one's faith meant becoming antagonistic toward persons in the other religion. Two distinct religions, hostile toward one another, emerged resulting in religious discrimination promoted by the new religion toward the traditional religion. Eventually, all people seemed to hate the people of the traditional religion.

What began as religious disagreement became personal discrimination. Clearly, a far cry from the young man's teachings about loving one another. Centuries later, after one final cataclysmic event where millions of members of the traditional commuity were systematically exterminated, did the new communities seek to reconcile with members of the traditional faith. Dialogue between the two groups evolved leading to sporadic attempts at healing and reconciliation. Yet, as life went on, no substantive healing occurred and other religious groups continued to call for the death of people who followed the traditional religion.

One particular religion recalled the divine man's claim as the Messiah to return to earth to judge all human beings which would determine their destiny to eternal life or eternal death based upon a spiritual relationship with him. Members of the traditional religion continued to look forward to a special human being, called a Messiah, who would show up when global peace occurred. Most people without any affiliation to religion lived their lives without any expectation or hope that anyone would appear to solve the world's problems. As religious affiliation continued to wan around the world, a declining remnant remembered that God would bless anyone who loved the people the young man grew up with—even those who disagreed with his teachings and claims.

Both religious belief systems continued growing slowly or simply surviving within a culture hostile to God or religion in general. Few saw a need for improving the hostility between the two religions. Global hate continued becoming more and more like the attitudes which created space for the catastrophe of extermination to take on different methods. There was seemingly no stopping an embedded hatred for traditionalists who finally gained their own land and developed into a nation. That nation had some support from other countries as well as the ongoing hatred from centuries before.

Both religions prayed for and looked forward to that special person, human or divine who would come and resolve seemingly irreconcilable differences.

This parable can have no other nimshal than that love among members of the traditional religion and the new faith might offer hope that all adherents to any religious ideology may experience shalom in their relationships with one another.

Bibliography

Alter, Robert, *The First Five Books of Moses, The Prophets, The Writings,* New York: W.W. Norton, 2019.
Artson, Rabbi Bradley Shavit. "Circumcise Your Heart." Zeigler School of Rabbinic Studies, https://jewishjournal.com>author>rabbi_bradley.
Bacher, Wilhelm and Jacob Zallel Lauterbach. "Parable." *Jewish Encyclopedia,* https://jewishencyclopedia.com/articles/11898/parable.
Baeck, Leo, *Judaism and Christianity,* Philadelphia: Jewish Publication Society, 1958.
———, *The Essence of Judaism,* New York: Schocken Books, 1967.
———, *This People Israel: The Meaning of Jewish Existence,* Canada: Holt, Rinehart and Winston, 1964.
Baghos, Mario. "The Historical Context of the Nicene-Constantinopolitan Creed." https://sagote.edu.au/Baghos/The_Historical_Context_of_the_Nicene_Constantionpolitan_Creed.pdf.
Barker, Kenneth L., *New International Version Bible,* East Brunswick, NJ: International Bible Society, 1983.
Barnett, Victoria J., *Bystanders: Conscience and Complicity During the Holocaust,* Westport, Connecticut: Praeger Publishers, 2000.
Barrick, William D. "The Kingdom of God in the Old Testament." *The Master's Journal* (2012), 174.
Barton, Bruce and Larry Taylor, eds., *King James Version Bible,* Christian Arts, 2019.
Batalion, Judy, *The Light of Days,* New York: HarperCollins, 2020.
Bauer, Arndt, and Gingrich, *Greek-English Lexicon of the New Testament,* Chicago: University of Chicago Press, 1957.
Benner, Jeff A., *Ancient Hebrew Lexicon,* College Station, Texas: Virtualbookworm.com Publications, 2005.
Benthien, George W. "The Hebrew Language and Way of Thinking." https://gbenthien.net/docs/bebree.pdf.
Ben Zeev, Rabbi Schlomo' Niddah 17b – "So What's the Nimshal?" *Core Enumah*(2020)
Bird, Michael F. "Jewish Views About the Kingdom of God." *Patheos* (2019).
Bischoff, Paul O., *Evangelicalism Is Dead,* Eugene, OR: Wipf & Stock, 2020.
———, *Mary Gave God a Body,* Eugene, OR: Wipf & Stock, 2018.
———, *The Human Church,* Eugene, OR: Wipf & Stock, 2018.

BIBLIOGRAPHY

Bjoraker, William., *Engaging the Jewish World – The Biblical Era,* Monee, IL: Operation Ezekiel, 2022.

Bonhoeffer, Dietrich, *Discipleship,* Geffrey B. Kelly and John D. Godsey, eds., DBWE, Volume 4, Minneapolis: Fortress, 2003.

———, *Letter and Papers from Prison,* John W. de Gruchy, ed., DBWE, Volume 8, Minneapolis: Fortress, 2009.

———, *Life Together,* Geffrey B. Kelly, ed., DBWE, Volume 5, Minneapolis: Fortress, 1996.

Brett, Mark G. "The Nations of Abraham: Explaining Israel's Position in the Persian Empire." https://the torah.com/article/the-nations-of-abraham/explaining-israel's-position-in-the-persian-empire.

Bronstein, Rabbi Yisrael, *Jewish Parables: A Mashal for Every Occasion,* Rahway, NJ: Mesorah Publications, 2004.

Buber, Martin, *I and Thou,* New York: Charles Scribner's Sons, 1970.

———, *Two Types of Faith,* Syracuse: Syracuse University Press, 2003.

Cohen, Rev. A., *The Babylonian Talmud: Tractate Berakot,* Cambridge: Cambridge University Press, 1921.

Cohen, Shaye J.D., "The Ways that Parted Jews and Jewish-Christians in 150-100 CE," from

Jews and Christians in the First and Second Centuries, Joshua Schwartz and Peter Thomson, eds., Leiden: Brill, 2018.

Dauermann, *Christians and Jews Together,* Eugene, Oregon: Wipf & Stock, 2009.

Davidson, Rabbi Baruch S. When and Why We Started Reading the Haftarah." https://chabad.org?library>libtary>article_cdo>aid.

Denova, Rebecca, "The Separation of Christianity from Judaism," *World History Encyclopedia,* https://worldhistory.org/article/1785/the-separation-of-christianity-from-judaism/.

Divin, David. "The Amidah Prayer: A New Translation." *En-Gedi Resource Center* (2019).

Donaldson, Terrence L., "Supercession and the Early Church Definition," *JJMJS* (2016), 7.

Donin, Rabbi Hayim Halvey, *To Pray as a Jew,* New York : Basic Books, 1991.

Dorff, Rabbi Elliot N., *The Jewish Approach to Repairing the World,* Woodstock, VT: Jewish Lights, 2008.

Drews, Robert. "The Babylonian Captivity and Its Consequences." Chapter Four, *Judaism, Christianity, and Islam to the Beginnings of Modern Civilization,* Nashville: Vanderbilt University Press, 2025.

Dunn, James D. G., *The Partings of the Ways,* London: SCM, 2006.

Duvall, J. Scott, et. al., *The Story of Israel,* Downers Grove, IL: Intervarsity, 2004.

Eckhardt, A. Roy, *Elder and Younger Brothers: The Encounter of Jews and Christians,* New York: Schocken, 1973.

Eisen, Arnold, *Taking Hold of Torah,* Bloomington, Indiana: Indian University Press, 1997.

Fackenheim, Emil L. *The Jewish Return into History,* New York: Schocken, 1978.

———, *To Mend the World,* Bloomington, Indiana: Indian University Press, 1994.

Fields, Westen W. "Early and Medieval Jewish Interpretations of the Song of Songs." *Grace Theological Journal,* (1980), 221-231.

Fisher, Cass, "The 'And' in Franz Rosenzweig's Work," Rosenzweig Yearbook 11, ed., von Herausugegeben, https://lesejury.demedia.samples.
Fisher, Sarah. "Lechem: BREAD of Life," *Hebrew Word Lessons.* https://hebrewwordlessons.com/2019/02/24/lechem-bread-of-life/.
Flusser, David, *The Sage from Galilee,* Grand Rapids: Eerdmans, 2007.
Foster, Richard, ed., *New Revised Standard Version-Spiritual Formation Bible,* San Francisco: HarperCollins, 2005.
Fredstrom, Will. "Bonhoeffer's *Stellvertretung*: A Christ-Like Ecclesial Ethic for Serving 'Galilean' Neighbors." https://gcsynod.org/news/bonhoeffer's-stellvertretung-a-christ-like-ecclesial-ethic-for-serving-galilean-neighbors.
Freeman, Tzvi. "How Did the Torah Exist Before It Happened?" https://chabad.org. > library>article>cdo_aid.
Friedman, Rabbi Elisha. "An Analysis of the Role of the Oral Torah." *Shavuot* 5780: Self-Guided Torah Study Experience ou.org.
———, *Kuzari* (2:72).
Frishman, Elyse D., *Mishkan T'fillah,* New York: Central Conference of Rabbis, 2005.
Frymer-Kensky, ed., *Christianity in Jewish Terms,* Oxford: Westview, 2000.
Gonzalez, Ana Maria. "Reflections on the Good Samaritan." *Scripta Theologica* (2018).
Gordon-Bennett, Chaviva. "Discover Everything About Kiddush." https://.com/Kiddush-101-2076790.
Gowler, David G., *What They are Saying About the Parables,* Mahwah, NJ: Paulist, 2000.
———. "What can Renaissance and Howard Thurman tell us about the prodigal son." *National Catholic Reporter* (2023).
Guttman, Julius, *Philosophies of Judaism,* New York: Holt, Rinehart and Winston, 1964.
Henson, David, "God is the Prodigal Son," *Patheos* (2013).
Hepler, Reed. "Synagogue: Definition and Facts." https://study.com>learn>lesson>synagogue.facts.
Heschel, Abraham, *God in Search of Man,* New York: Farrar, Straus and Giroux, 1976.
———, *Man is Not Alone,* New York: Farrar, Straus and Giroux, 1955.
———, *The Prophets,* New York: HarperCollins, 1962.
———, *The Sabbath,* New York: Farrar, Straus and Giroux, 1951.
Hilberg, Raul, *Destruction of the European Jews,* New York: Holmes & Meier, 1985.
———, *Perpetrators, Victims, Bystanders,* New York: HarperCollins, 1992.
Hillel, "Shabbat 31a," *Talmud*.
Hockenos, Matthew D., *Then They Came For Me,* New York: Basic Books, 2018.
Hoffman, David. "To Love or Not to Love the Jewish People." *Times of Israel,*https://blogs.timesofisrael.com/to-love-or-not-to-love-the-jewish-people/
Hooker, Richard. "Ancient Jewish History: The Two Kingdoms." https://jewishvirtuallibrary.org/the-two-kingdoms-of-Israel.
Inrig, Gary, *The Parables: Understanding What Jesus Meant,* Grand Rapids: Our Daily Bread Publishing, 1991.
Jeremioas, Joachim, "The Sermon on the Mount," lecture given in London, 1961.
Johnson, Dru. "Why Does Hebraic Thought Matter?" *Center for Hebraic Thought*, https://hebraicthought.org/authors>dr_dru_johnson.
Johnson, Paul, *A History of the Jews,* New York: Harper & Row, 1987.
Kalmenson, Mendel and Zahlman Abraham. "Love: Ahavah; I Give, Therefore I Love." https://chabad.org/library/article_cdo/aid/5783136/jewish/Love-Ahavah.htm.

Keil-Delitzsch, *Commentary on the Old Testament, Vol VII, Isaiah,* James Martin, trans., Grand Rapids: Eerdmans, 1976.

Kessler, Vera. "Michael Horowitz: Loving Your Fellow Jews." *The Jewish Press* (2025).

Knight, Keven, ed., "The Epistle of Ignatius to the Philadelphians," *New Advent,* https://newadvent.org/fathers/0108.htm.

Knowles, Brian. "The Hebrew Mind vs. The Western Mind." https://godward.org/Hebrew-Roots.

Kohler, Kaufman and Samuel Krauss. "Baptism." https://jewishencyclopedia.com/articles>2456-baptism.

———. "Revelation," https://jewishencyclopedia.com/articles/12713-revelation.

———. Malkuta de-Adonai, "The Kingdom of God." *Jewish Encyclopedia,* 502.

Kohler and Blau, ""Shekinah (lit., "the dwelling"). *Jewish Encyclopedia,* https://jewishencyclopedia.com/articles/13537/-shekinah.

Lancaster, D. Thomas, "The Synagogue of Satan." *Messiah Magazine 29* (2024).

Levenson, Jon D., *Sinai and Zion,* San Francisco: HarperCollins, 1985.

Levine, Amy-Jill, *Short Stories of Jesus,* New York: HarperCollins, 2014.

———, "The Lord's Prayer and the Amidah: A Comparative Analysis," https://bible.org/2013/05scholars.

———, *The Misunderstood Jew: The Church and the Scandal of the Jewish Jesus,* New York: HarperCollins, 2006.

Leynor, Rabbi Jeffrey. "The Meaning of Baptism in the Jewish Culture." https://biblicalheritage/BHC_Handouts/Baptism_Handout.pdf.

Littell, Frank, *The Crucifixion of the Jews,* Macon, Georgia: Mercer University Press, 2017.

Lockman Foundation, *New American Standard Bible,* Grand Rapids: Zondervan, 2000.

Mauricio-Perez, Vladimir. "The Eucharist Throughout History." *Denver Catholic* (2019), 13.

McDermott, Gerald. "Is the Church God's New Israel." *Patheos* (2016), 7.

McGrath, Alistair, *Christian Theology: An Introduction,* Hoboken: New Jersey: Wiley-Blackwell, 2024.

McKnight, Scott, *The King Jesus Gospel,* Grand Rapids: Zondervan, 2016.

Medwed, Rabbi Dr. Karen. "Prayers and Practices of the Amidah." https://exploringjudaism.org.

Morris, Wm., ed., *American Heritage Dictionary,* Boston: Houghton-Mifflin, 1969.

Myers, Jeremy. "How do you heap coals on the heads of your enemies." https://redeeminggod.com/bible-theology-topics/burning coals/

Neuhaus, Richard John, *Death on a Friday Afternoon,* New York: Basic Books, 2001.

Niditch, Susan, *Oral World and Written Word,* Louisville: Westminster John Knox, 1996.

Olford, Stephen, *The Tabernacle: Camping with God,* Neptune, New Jersey: Loizeaux Brothers, 1975.

Overman, Christian. "Assumptions that Affect our Lives." https://markmedley.org/worldview-Greek-and-Hebrew-Thought.pdf.

Parkes, James, *The Conflict of the Church and Synagogue,* Philadelphia: Jewish Publication Society, 1961.

Parsons, John J. "Defining the Church." *Hebrew for Christians.* https://hebrew4christians.com.

Penner, Ken M., ed., *Lexham English Septuagint*, Bellingham, Washington: Lexham, 2019.
Peters, John Punnett, *The Religion of the Hebrews*, London: Wentworth, 2016.
Piper, John. "The Beatitudes and the Gospel of the Kingdom." https://strengthforthebattle.com/2013/02/24/matthew-51-12-the-beatitudes-and-the-gospel-of-the-kingdom/
Ratzinger, Joseph, "Reconciling Gospel and Torah," *Catholics for Israel* (2010).
Renner, Rick and Judy. "Who Were the Nicolaitans, and What Were Their Doctrine and Deeds?" https://renner.org/article/qho-were-the-nicolaitans-and-what-were-their-doctrine-and-deeds/Messiah.
Rich, Tracey R.. "Jewish Liturgy." *Judaism 101*, https;//jewfaq.org/liturgy.
Rijstenberg, Henk. "Thinking Hebraically." MATSATI.COM, (2011).
Roberts, Alexander and James Donaldson, eds., *The Complete English Translation from the First Volume of the Ante-Nicene Fathers, Against Heresies*, Irenaeus of Lyons, Lexington, Kentucky: Ex Fontibus, 2010.
Rosenzweig, Franz, *The Star of Redemption*, Madison: The University of Wisconsin Press, 2005.
Rozzini, Tony. "Irenaeus and Israel." https://jpost.com/Christ-on-Israel/Comment/Irenaeus and Israel/318416.
Rudolph, David. "One New Man, Hebrew Roots, Replacement Theology." https://collective.tku.edu/2021.
Rudolph, David, and J. Willitts, eds., *Introduction to Messianic Judaism*, Grand Rapids: Zondervan, 2013.
Ryan, Joel. "What is the Significance of Seventy-Times Seven in Forgiveness." https://christianity.com>wiki>sin>what-is-the-significance-of-seventy-times-seven-in-forgiveness.
Sacks, Jonathan, *Exodus: The Book of Redemption,* Jerusalem: Koren, 2010.
———, *Genesis: The Book of Beginnings,* Jerusalem: Koren, 2009.
Schaeffer, *Christianity Is Jewish*, Wheaton, Illinois: Tyndale, 1977.
Schilstra, Terence. "Dietrich Bonhoeffer: Stepping into the Place of the Other." https://missional.home.blog/2019/08/15/dietrich-bonhoeffer-stepping-into-the-place-of-the-other.
Schipper, Jeremy. "Breaking Down Parables: Introductory Issues." from *Parables and Conflict in the Hebrew Bible*, https://cambridge.org/breaking-down-parables-introductory-issues.
Schniedewind, William A., *How the Bible Became a Book*, Cambridge: Cambridge University Press, 2004.
Schoenberg, Shira. "Jewish Prayers: The Shema." https://the virtuallibrary.org/the-shema.
Scott, Brad. "Hebrew Mind vs Greek Mind: The Nature of Man." https://wildbranchministries. org>teach>hebrew-vs-greek-mind.
Shanks, Herschel, ed., *Christianity and Rabbinic Judaism,* Washington, DC: Biblical Archaeological Society, 2011.
———, *Partings: How Judaism and Christianity Became Two*, Washington, DC: Biblical Archaeological Society, 2013.
Silberberg. Naftali. "The Priestly Blessing." https://chabad.org>library>article_cdo>aid.
Silberman, Lou Hackett, "Synagogue," *Encyclopedia Britannica*, https://britannica.com/topic/synagogue.

Smith, J.A."The Ancient Synagogue, The Early Church, and Singing." *JSTOR* (1984), 1-16.
Snodgrass, Klyne, *Stories with Intent*, Grand Rapids: Eerdmans, 2008.
Soloveichek, Meir Y. "God's First Love: The Theology of Michael Wyschogrod." *First Things* (2009).
Soulen, Kendall R., *Irrevocable*, Minneapolis: Fortress, 2022.
Spangler Ann and Lois Tverberg, *Sitting at the Feet of Jesus*, Grand Rapids: Zondervan, 2018.
Steinberg, Milton, *Basic Judaism*, New York: Harcourt, Brace, and World, Inc., 1947.
Steinsaltz, Adin, *The Essential Talmud*, New York: Random House, 2006.
Stern, David H., *Parables in the Midrash: Narrative and Exegesis in Rabbinic Literature*,
———, *Restoring the Jewishness of the Gospel*, Clarksville, Maryland: Messianic Jewish, 2009.
Suchat, Chaya. "Eight Degrees of Giving." https://chabad.org/library/article_cdo/256321/jewish/Eight-Degrees-of-Giving.htm.
Telushkin, Rabbi Joseph, *Jewish Literacy*, New York: HarperCollins, 2001.
Thompson, Fr. Philip Silouan. "First-Century Christian Synagogue Liturgy." SILOUAN, https://silouanthompson.net/2007/09/first-century-christian-jewish-liturgy.
Thurston, Herbert. "Apostles' Creed." *Catholic Encyclopedia*, New York: Appleton Co., https://newadvent.org/cathen/01629.htm.
Tverberg, Lois, *Sitting at the Feet of Jesus*, Grand Rapids: Zondervan, 2009.
United States Holocaust Memorial Museum, "The Jewish Question," https://encyclopedia.ushmm.org/content/en/article/the-jewish-question.
Vijoen, Francois, "Why Jesus Spoke in Parables," *In Luce Verbi* (2009).
Vlach, Michael. "The Significance of the Five Quotations of Isaiah 6: 9-10 in the New Testament,." https://mikevlachblogspot.com/2017/17/the-significance-of-the-five-quotations-of-isaiah 6: 9-10-in-the-new-testament.html.
Weiss, Stewart, "What Do Jews Believe About the Afterlife," *The Jerusalem Post* (2019).
Wiesel, Elie, *Night*, New York: Bantam Books, 1982.
———, *The Struggle for Understanding: Elie Wiesel's Literary Works*, Albany: State University of New York Press, 2019.
Wilson, Marvin R., *Exploring Our Hebraic Heritage*, Grand Rapids: Eerdmans, 2022.
———, *Our Father Abraham*, Grand Rapids: Eerdmans, 2021.
Wisely, Luke. "Doctrine of Revelation and the Hebrew Bible." https://secundumscriptures.com/2021/10/20.
Wright, Mary Ellen. "Hebrew Letters and Meanings." *Hear God's Heart*, https://maryellenwrites.com.
Wright, Stephen I., *Jesus the Storyteller*, Louisville: Westminster John Knox, 2015.
Yoder, Perry B., ed., *Take This Word to Heart*, Eugene, Oregon: Wipf & Stock, 2005.
Young, Brad H, *Meet the Rabbis: Rabbinic Thought and the Teachings of Jesus*, Grand Rapids: Baker, 2007.
———, *Jesus and His Jewish Parables,* New York: Paulist, 1989.
———, *The Parables: Jewish Tradition and Christian Interpretation*, Grand Rapids: Baker, 2012.
Zalta, Edward N., and Uri Nodelman. "Franx Rosenzweig." *Stanford Encyclopedia of Philosophy*, https://plato.stanford.edu/entries/rosenzweig.
Zaslow, Rabbi David, *Reimagining Exodus: A Story of Freedom*, Brewster, Massachusetts: Paraclete, 2017.

———, *Jesus: First-Century Rabbi,* Brewster, Massachusetts: Paraclete, 2015.
———, *Reimaging Exodus*, Brewster, Mass.: Paraclete, 2017.
———, *Roots & Branches*, Ashland, Oregon: The Wisdom Exchange, 2011.
Zimmerman, Ruben. "How to Understand the Parables of Jesus: A Paradigm Shift in Parable Exegesis." *Acta Theologica* (2009), 158.

www.ingramcontent.com/pod-product-compliance
Lightning Source LLC
Chambersburg PA
CBHW051632230426
43669CB00013B/2276